MOUNTAINS OF NORTH AMERICA

MOUNTAINS OF NORTH AMERICA

Text written
and photographs selected
by Fred Beckey

BONANZA BOOKS

NEW YORK

The Sierra Club, founded in 1892 by John Muir, has devoted itself to the study and protection of the earth's scenic and ecological resources—mountains, wetlands, woodlands, wild shores and rivers, deserts and plains. The publishing program of the Sierra Club offers books to the public as a nonprofit educational service in the hope that they may enlarge the public's understanding of the Club's basic concerns. The point of view expressed in each book, however, does not necessarily represent that of the Club. The Sierra Club has some fifty chapters coast to coast, in Canada, Hawaii, and Alaska. For information about how you may participate in its programs to preserve wilderness and the quality of life, please address inquiries to Sierra Club, 530 Bush Street, San Francisco, CA 94108.

Permission to reprint material from the following copyrighted works is acknowledged:
Cosmos, by Carl Sagan. Copyright © 1980 by Carl Sagan. By permission of Random House, Inc.
Deborah: A Wilderness Narrative, by David Roberts. Copyright © 1970 by David Roberts. By permission of The Vanguard Press.
The Mountains of Canada, by Randy Morse. Copyright © 1978 by Randy Morse. By permission of Hurtig Publishers Ltd. and The Mountaineers.
Notes from the Century Before: A Journal from British Columbia, by Edward Hoagland. Copyright © 1969 by Edward Hoagland. By permission of Random House, Inc.

This 1984 edition is published by Bonanza Books, distributed by Crown Publishers, Inc., by arrangement with Sierra Club Books.

Manufactured in Japan

Library of Congress Cataloging in Publication Data
Beckey, Fred W., 1921–
    Mountains of North America.
    Bibliography: p.
    1. Mountains—North American.
2. Mountaineering—North America.   I. Title.
GB531.N67B43   1984   910'.0214'3   84-16885

ISBN: 0-517-461234

h g f e d c b a

CONTENTS

PREFACE

THIS BOOK is a descriptive, historic, and scenic odyssey among some of the most magnificent mountains on earth—the mountains of North America. It would be impossible to portray the mountains as a geographic entity because they occur in many separate ranges, spanning the continent from the West Coast to the Appalachians, from the volcanos of Mexico to the gigantic peaks of Alaska. Nor have I depicted the ranges and mountain systems in great detail. Rather, I have chosen to profile important individual peaks on a regional basis. By a clearly defined and limited focus on specific mountains, I hope to evoke the essence of a vast subject.

There are many more magnificent peaks on this continent—particularly in Alaska and Canada—than any one book can encompass. Probably few of the millions who cherish the mountain regions have seen all of the peaks represented here, let alone set foot on them. Scenic photography, travel literature, and media images tend to focus on certain mountains that can be seen from populated areas or tourist meccas. I have ignored some important mountains not to spite their popularity, but because my chief goal has been to choose peaks that are representative of their regions and ranges. Some of these peaks, like Mount Rainier, are the indisputable monarchs of their realms; in other cases, such as Mount Marcy, they barely surpass their neighbors in stature and are not nationally famous. The selections sometimes were based on my own experience with a certain mountain. Each of the chosen peaks has its distinctive character, which I have tried to evoke, and most have some noteworthy history associated with their discovery and exploration. Historic and contempo-

rary ascents are part of the story too; while this is not a mountaineering chronicle, climbing is often an important theme.

It should be noted that the spelling of many geographical features has changed over time, and styles still vary. I have made every effort to conform to official spellings of mountain ranges and peaks, but the reader will find inconsistencies with other sources. For instance, the Cascades were once called the Cascade Mountains but now are officially the Cascade Range. The Coast Mountains of British Columbia and Alaska are another source of perplexity; the official usage is Coast Mountains for the entire chain, and its various sections are called ranges. Usage has failed to establish a preference for either "range" or "mountains" to describe a large uplift. For convenience, the U.S. Board on Geographic Names and its Canadian counterpart have made the decision to drop the apostrophe from names with plural endings (for example, Clingmans Dome), even when the possessive is clearly implied.

Altitudes are eternally subject to correction. I have used the altitude given on government-published topographic maps of most recent issue. In some cases a long-accepted altitude may still be shown on small-scale regional maps and national park maps, but has been revised on new, larger-scale maps.

The 140 photographs in this book depict the splendor of our North American mountains as no words can. The contributing photographers are among the world's finest outdoor photographers, and with so many beautiful images to choose from, the editing process was both rewarding and frustrating. I am deeply grateful to all the contributors.

The research for this book began, in a sense, when I made my first mountain explorations, but the words on these pages are a distillation of the experiences of many besides myself. Much of the information in the text was gleaned from obscure and specialized papers and journals, and books long out of print. The selected bibliography included here indicates some of these sources, as well as suggestions for further reading. Libraries in many places on the continent have been a bountiful resource. In particular I wish to mention the libraries of the University of California (including the Bancroft Library), Stanford University, Brigham Young University, the Oregon Historical Society, the National Archives of the Canadian Rockies (Banff), the Appalachian Mountain Club, Mountain Travel, Inc., and the Museum of Northern Arizona. Research material also was made available to me at several of the national parks.

I owe a debt of gratitude to several librarians and others who assisted me in record searches and suggested specific background material for reading. Notable among these are Fran Belcher and Arlyn Powell of the Appalachian Mountain Club, and Barbara Lekisch of the Sierra Club's William H. Colby Library. A number of persons who specialize in environmental and earth sciences provided useful suggestions and valuable criticism of the text. In particular I wish to thank John Edmond of the Department of Earth and Planetary Sciences of the Massachusetts Institute of Technology, Paul Hammond of the Earth Sciences Department of Portland State University, Malcolm Clark of the U.S. Geological Survey, Menlo Park, California, and the staff of the Mount Washington Observatory.

The creation of a project of this magnitude would not have been accomplished without the guidance of Jon Beckmann and the astute editorial direction of Diana Landau, both of Sierra Club Books. I appreciate the cooperation and personal interest of others of the capable staff in the selection of photographs and the careful production of this book and its color images. Consulting editors Steve Roper and Joe Kelsey spent many painstaking hours in manuscript review and editing, resulting in a text considerably more accurate and more graceful than would otherwise have been possible.

Fred Beckey

CONTRIBUTING PHOTOGRAPHERS

William A. Bake
Fred Bavendam
Fred Beckey
David Black
Craig Blacklock
Peter L. Bloomer
William Boehm
Gary Braasch
George Bracksieck
Richard W. Clark
John Cleare
Ed Cooper
Jack Duggan
Janet Ann Fries
David C. Fritts

Jeff Gnass
Greg Gordon
Barry Hagen
John I. Hendrickson
Doug Herchmer
David Hiser
Alan Kearney
Joe Kelsey
Breck P. Kent
Rick Kline
Paul Knaut, Jr.
Stephen J. Krasemann
Russell Lamb
Wayne Lankinen
Brian Milne

Pat Morrow
Paul Muehl
David Muench
Barry Nash
John V. A. F. Neal
Rick Nolting
René Pauli
Richard and Ruth Pontius
James Randklev
Ray Richardson
Galen Rowell
Leonard Lee Rue III
Don Serl
Clyde H. Smith
Steve Solum

Bob and Ira Spring
Paul Starr
Lynn M. Stone
James Peter Stuart
Dick Stum
David Sumner
Jack Swenson
Ned Therrien
James P. Valentine
Rick Wilcox
Ron Willocks
Gordon Wiltsie
Art Wolfe

Introduction

Just as a universe is intimately and violently constructed with a subtle beauty of form, mountain shapes, born of fire and force, portray a similar magnificence.

Immanuel Kant

MY MOUNTAIN wanderings began several decades ago in the Cascades of northern Washington, where I was raised. On one of my first treks into this primeval wilderness I was drawn to Mount Triumph, an isolated peak in the heart of the range. Although it is not the highest peak in the region, the name seemed fitting as I viewed its pyramid silhouetted boldly against the sky.

Mount Triumph is only a moderately difficult climb by today's standards, but the ascent still took me the better part of a day. Standing at last on the summit, surveying the surrounding countryside with a sense of awe, I realized I had only a vague idea of the physical forces that had shaped the magnificent scenery spread before me. I did not know that Mount Triumph had triumphed over ice-age glaciers that poured south from Canada, its noble form sharpened by those glaciers. The terms geologists would use to describe my surroundings—hanging valley, lateral moraine, incised river—were strange to me.

As I returned from Mount Triumph, hiking through the great evergreen forests that appeared after the last ice sheets retreated, I savored the mountaineer's joy of success on a challenging peak, and in the course of seeking further adventures on other mountains of North America, I became increasingly curious about how these wonderfully diverse landscapes of rock, snow, and ice came to be.

Mountains, to many of us, are nature's most impressive creations. They change so little while the generations of mankind pass that we consider them symbols of permanence. The time scale of nature is inconceivably longer than that of humanity, so changes in the form of mountains and of continents are imperceptible to us. Yet the ceaseless interplay of earth-shaping forces has been building mountains— and tearing them down—throughout most of the planet's existence. In time, the peaks that now adorn the earth's surface will lie crumbled on the ocean floor or under new landforms, and other ranges will have been thrust up. The face of the land is forever being remade.

Mountains are not distributed randomly over the earth's surface but rather are found in distinct, typically narrow zones. A glance at a map of North America reveals a vast, flat interior flanked east and west by mountain chains. Near the Atlantic Coast are the gentle ranges of the Appalachians; far to the west lies the backbone of the continent, the Cordillera—a belt of higher, sharper mountains extending from Alaska for 5,000 miles through Mexico, then continuing through the Andes of South America. A closer look at the North American portion of the Cordillera shows it to be divided by basins and plateaus into two distinct chains: the broad Rocky Mountains, which are nearly a thousand miles inland, and, close by the Pacific Coast, a narrower series of ranges including the Sierra Nevada, the Cascades, and the St. Elias Mountains.

The oldest, most stable part of the continent is the low-lying interior, known to geologists as the

North American craton. The Appalachians, while not as ancient as the craton, are very old compared to most of the Cordillera. The different ages of the topography of these regions, deduced by geologists from the rocks themselves, are consistent with a revolutionary new theory of how the earth's surface has changed over time. This theory, known as plate tectonics, explains the wanderings of the continents as well as the processes and products of motions within the earth.

According to plate tectonics, not only are mountains created and destroyed, they stand on shifting continents. The outer portion of the earth is made up of a number of segments, or plates, upon which sit the land masses and oceans. Apparently heat flow deep in the earth, possibly combined with the earth's rotation around its axis, causes these plates to drift—to move apart, collide, or slide past one another. The Atlantic Ocean is widening as the African and Eurasian plates pull away from the North American plate; the Pacific plate is colliding with the western edge of the North American plate. Mountain building, or orogeny, occurs mostly along plate boundaries and is in part caused by the collision of plates.

An oceanic plate converging with a continental plate typically sinks under the continent, a process known as subduction. Sediments accumulate offshore in the trough formed by the oceanic plate's downturn, and as the plate descends, these sediments and submarine lavas are scraped onto the edge of the continent, increasing its land area. This added material is deformed over time by compression at the point of convergence, often resulting in mountain building. Sediments and lavas may be intricately folded and even altered in their composition, thus forming metamorphic rocks. Volcanic activity may also take place. Deeper, below the continent, the interaction of one plate sliding past another melts rock in the descending plate. The molten material, or magma, may create mountains in two ways. It may rise to the surface and erupt as volcanic material—as it has so often in the Cascades—or it may solidify below the surface into granite or similar types of igneous rock—as it did in the Sierra Nevada. This igneous rock may form the core of a range that is subsequently thrust up.

The mountains of the western portion of the Cordillera have been built chiefly as a result of the subduction of the Pacific plate under the North American plate. This plate convergence is still taking place in some form, and the Sierra Nevada, the Cascades, and the Alaskan ranges—all young mountains—apparently continue to rise. The subduction

also thrust the Canadian Rockies against the older continental platform, while the American Rockies are largely a vertical uplift of ancient crust. Between the Rockies and the coastal ranges, the crust is being deformed—stretched and shattered into many block ranges and basins.

Other great ranges, such as the Himalaya and the Alps, result from continent–continent collision. The creation of the Appalachians probably involved a collision between the North American and Eurasian–African plates when an ancient Atlantic Ocean closed, as well as subduction of ocean material at the continental edge. But this episode of mountain building occurred long ago, and the Appalachians, once lofty peaks, have been reduced over the millenia by the processes of erosion.

The plate tectonics theory and its corollaries are widely accepted today as a fundamental concept of earth science, but this acceptance is by no means universal, and many mysteries remain. This book cannot begin to sort out the vast array of factors that explain the existence and nature of North American mountains; however, in this introductory sketch and the chapters that follow, I have attempted to draw a reasonably accurate, if simplified, picture for the general reader.

AT THE TIME of my early ascent of Mount Triumph, the theory of plate tectonics had not even been articulated. If I could have consulted a geologist of today, I would have learned that the Cascade Range is a typical volcanic arc formed by the subduction of an oceanic plate beneath the Washington and Oregon coasts. Volcanos have been active in the Pacific Northwest for the past 20 million years, though the major volcanic cones such as Mounts Hood, St. Helens, and Rainier have formed from lava extruded mainly during the past 2 million years. In the environs of Mount Triumph, granitic rock and the similar metamorphic rock called gneiss were lifted toward the surface and exposed by erosion during the past 65 million years. These hard rocks, relatively resistant to erosion, tend to form the steepest peaks, the sharpest pinnacles. To the west, beyond what I later learned is the Straight Creek fault, a mixture of marine rocks from diverse Pacific environments had been plastered onto the edge of the land and incorporated into the continent.

On the first of many trips to California's Sierra Nevada, two features immediately impressed me. One was the distinct changes in plant life that I encountered while ascending from the foothills to the range's crest, passing through several climatic

Above: The Minarets, a jagged portion of the Ritter Range in California's Sierra Nevada, as seen from the forested meadowlands below Ediza Lake. By Ed Cooper.

Overleaf: Quaking aspens in brilliant autumn foliage decorate the lower slopes of Colorado's San Juan Mountains. By David Muench.

Page 10: Mount Winchell (left) and Mount Agassiz (center), two prominent peaks of the Palisades, a high alpine crest of the Sierra Nevada near Big Pine, California. By Gordon Wiltsie.

zones. The other was the Sierra's asymmetry—the contrast between the long, gradual western slope and the abrupt eastern escarpment. This asymmetry, I learned, is typical of fault-block ranges. Probably the Sierra block was uplifted, mostly during the past 10 million years, by faulting—movement along fractures in the earth's surface—on its east side. Faulting has raised Mount Whitney, North Palisade, and other high peaks 10,000 feet above nearby Owens Valley to the east and tilted the block to the west, thus explaining the long western flank. The rock that was uplifted is largely granite that formed from magma generated between 200 and 80 million years ago, as the Pacific plate slid below the North American plate. Numerous granitic monoliths, resistant to erosion, have survived as the domes for which the Sierra is famous.

Accustomed as I was to the moist Cascade Range, with its dense vegetation, its ferns and skunk cabbage, I was struck by the barrenness and aridity of the sagebrush-scented Basin and Range province, which I crossed on a pilgrimage to the Rocky Mountains. In the Basin and Range province, which begins east of the Sierra, evidence of faulting was abundant. Stretching of the crust in an east-west direction has created north-south faults, along which blocks have been alternately thrust up, as ranges, and down, as basins. Utah's Wasatch Range, on the eastern rim of the Basin and Range, is a particularly striking fault-block; its steep western front, Salt Lake City's backdrop, is one of North America's largest fault escarpments.

I crossed the Wasatch and climbed, endlessly it seemed, into the Rocky Mountain highlands of Colorado, following the Colorado River toward its source high in the mountains near Longs Peak. The Rockies were raised from an inland sea during a major mountain-building episode known as the Laramide Orogeny, which reached Colorado about 65 million years ago. The gradual upwarp of the newly born Rockies expelled the sea, which had extended from the Gulf of Mexico to the Arctic Ocean. Sediments deposited in this sea overlay ancient masses of granite and metamorphic rocks. These masses were not lifted uniformly; some blocks pushed higher than others and became the cores of mountain ranges. The overlying sedimentary rocks were folded, buckled, and in places stripped by erosion to expose the core rocks—Pikes Peak granite, for example.

On a later trip I visited the San Juan Mountains in southwestern Colorado. Here lava had erupted 20 million years ago, covering the older rocks, and magmas rich in gold and silver had been squeezed up

Above: Mount Gould, displaying a sheer limestone face, rises above Angel Wing and Grinnell Lake, Glacier National Park, Montana. The lake's turquoise color is derived from suspended particles of glacial silt. By Ed Cooper.

Facing page: An aerial view of the spine of Wyoming's Wind River Range in winter, showing steep rock walls, glacier-carved cirques, and high tablelands. By Galen Rowell.

from deep in the earth through fissures and along bedding planes—a geological occurrence that has had much effect on the San Juans' human history.

The spectacular Teton Range of Wyoming has been a magnet for mountaineers since the end of the last century, and its landscapes are as compelling as the climbing opportunities. The Tetons, another fault-block range of recent origin, tower over the down-faulted block of Jackson Hole. This basin's flat floor is formed of sediments carried from the mountains by the meandering Snake River and its tributaries. Standing on top of the Grand Teton, I felt that I might be at the center of the universe. To the southeast I could see all the way to the Wind River Mountains, some 100 miles distant. The Wind River granite, Precambrian in age—meaning it was created during the earth's first 4 billion years, before the existence of fossils long used by geologists to date

rock—was thrust up during the Laramide Orogeny.

During the ice ages of the past 2 million years, the great ice sheets that covered the northern and eastern part of the continent did not extend this far west. But local icecaps developed in the mountains, spreading glaciers into the valleys and leaving marks on the landscape that I learned to recognize. Ice-age glaciers are gone, and only smaller glaciers occupy high basins in the Tetons and Wind Rivers, but bouldery ridges called moraines and valleys with a U-shaped cross section are the legacy of larger glaciers.

My interest in mountains eventually took me to the other side of the continent. The train on which I traveled east passed through a series of parallel ridges whose folded sedimentary rocks could be seen clearly in railroad cuts. These ridges extend from Maine to Alabama. What we know of the story of the Appalachians begins when the eastern edge of the continent was a few hundred miles west of its present location. Streams carried debris to the continental shelf, where colliding plates created a long trough filled with marine sediments—a structure known in geologic language as a geosyncline. Hundreds of millions of years ago, long before the Laramide Orogeny in the West, North America collided with Europe and Africa. The geosyncline was crumpled and pushed up as a 1,600-mile-long mountain chain. The strata subsequently flexed like an accordion, and when erosion over the millenia reduced the once-lofty Appalachians, the more resistant layers formed the ridges I had noted, while the less resistant strata were eroded to form valleys.

The story of the Appalachians is further complicated by other effects of the continental collision. In the Blue Ridge province, sheets of rock sheared along fault lines and were thrust up to the west. In New England, the compressive forces caused the metamorphism of sedimentary rocks; the metamorphic rock of the Mount Washington massif is an example.

West of the Appalachian Mountains is the stable nucleus of North America—the craton. In the northern part of the craton, called the Canadian Shield, some of the earth's oldest bedrock is exposed: the ancient, worn-down Adirondack Mountains of New York, for example.

There are analogous mountain systems on either side of the craton. The Rocky Mountains of Canada (whose general form continues into the United States in Glacier National Park, Montana) began, like the Appalachians, on a continental shelf and were raised by colliding plates. While sediments that would become the Appalachians accumulated off the East Coast half a billion years ago, the sandstones and carbonate deposits that would form the limestones of the Canadian Rockies were collecting in a geosyncline off what was then the continent's west coast.

Driving west into the Rockies from Calgary, Alberta, I marveled at the abruptness with which the mountains rose from the plains, the peaks projecting as precipitous rock wedges. At about the time of the Laramide Orogeny, thousands of feet of sediments that had formed in the geosyncline were subjected to thrust faulting. Great blocks were thrust, along

Left: **Red fox at the entrance to its den, Alaska. By Brian Milne/Animals Animals.**

Facing Page: **Mist floats above a forested stream valley near Newfound Gap in the Great Smoky Mountains, North Carolina/Tennessee. By David Muench.**

faults, up and out over bedrock to the east, so that the displaced strata I saw exposed was actually older than the underlying beds.

Fossils embedded in the stratified walls of the Canadian Rockies have enabled geologists to determine the age of each layer. Yet chronology is only part of the geological story, and much is still unclear. The Canadian Rockies are bounded on the west by the linear Rocky Mountain Trench. This long fault zone, which separates the Rockies from the much younger Purcell and Selkirk ranges, is believed to mark the edge of the Precambrian continental platform, but its origin and true nature remain elusive.

West of the Purcells and Selkirks, which are two of the Interior Ranges of British Columbia, lie the impressive coast ranges of British Columbia and Alaska. Offshore, the Pacific plate moves northwest-

Above: A bighorn sheep in the Canadian Rockies. By Ed Cooper.

Facing page: Cirrus clouds fill the sky over Mount Rainier; paintbrush, pasque flowers, and lupine bloom in the meadow below. By John I. Hendrickson.

ward, and its subduction as it collides with Alaska is reflected in recent volcanic activity in the Aleutians and on the Alaskan mainland. The coast ranges are typical of young mountain chains on the edge of a continent, consisting of granitic cores, extensively metamorphosed rocks, volcanics, and a variety of rock types that have become attached to the continent's margin. The rapid uplift of these mountains has occurred mainly during the past 10 million years and has involved both block faulting and compression of the crust.

The Alaskan mountains, as a group the highest and most massive on the continent, hold some of the greatest mountaineering adventures as well as landscapes that recall the ice ages. The ample moisture here falls mostly as snow, which after compacting eventually becomes glacier ice. The coastal St. Elias Mountains contain North America's largest glacier system, but in most of the interior of Alaska elevations and precipitation are relatively low; here large glaciers have developed only in the Alaska Range, around such peaks as Mount McKinley. Even during the ice ages, a surprising portion of Alaska was free of glaciation, making possible the movement to North America of various large mammals.

As the land changes, so do its inhabitants. During the ice ages, mammals migrated from Asia to North America via land bridges that appeared and submerged periodically in what is now the Bering Strait; many species, such as the mastodon, are now extinct. Following the warming trend at the end of the ice ages, spruce, fir, and willow seeds arrived on the wind and found places to grow among boulders and on alluvial plains. A very fine glacial silt enabled forests and grasslands to evolve—and so to direct the migration of old-world mammals in a quest for benign habitats on their new continent.

Among these mammals was man. By the time humans arrived in North America, the ranges had long been aligned as they are today, though glaciers were still reshaping surface features in some areas. Even in prehistoric times, the location of mountains influenced the acquisition and settling of territory and determined routes of trade. Through their size alone, mountains greatly modify the character of terrestrial environments.

The most important asset provided by the mountains was water. Wind deflected upward cools; moisture condenses from cooled air and drops as rain or snow. Mountains, by forcing air to rise, obtain a disproportionate share of precipitation. Water itself, of course, is essential to man; moreover, trees made

possible by water provide shelter and warmth. Mountains also have provided minerals—obsidian for Indians, gold, silver, and copper for white settlers. Indians also pursued game in the mountains, particularly mountain goats and bighorn sheep. They apparently trapped eagles from blinds on Longs Peak and probably built a structure called the Enclosure not far below the summit of the Grand Teton.

Although the geography of the Cordillera allowed man to migrate near the end of the ice ages from the Arctic to the Great Plains and beyond, mountains have more often proved to be barriers to travel, as well as to the mingling of cultures. The Alaska Range limited the inland hunting forays of the Aleuts. The Adirondacks separated Algonquins and Iroquois, the Wind River and Big Horn mountains kept Shoshones and Cheyennes apart, while Miwoks were isolated from Paiutes by the Sierra Nevada. A single mountain—Shasta—segregated Modocs and Wintuns. The coastal Tlingits could cross the British Columbia mountains to trade with the interior Athapascans only by an arduous journey.

In addition to being both providers and barriers, mountains have long been something more to humans. Both as sources of inspiration and objects of fear, mountains have aroused a sense of the supernatural. Primitive peoples throughout the world have associated heights with power, made mountains scenes of exotic events, peopled them with spirits. Mountains were a realm between heaven and earth. The Greeks placed their gods on Mount Olympus; Moses received the Ten Commandments on Mount Sinai; Buddhists built temples in high places.

On this continent, the San Francisco Peaks appear in Hopi creation myths. Pico de Orizaba, the "mountain of the star," may have inspired the loftiest Indian art in the New World: the Great Temple of Tenochtitlan, crown of Aztec accomplishment, as well as the pyramids of Teotihuacan, are said to be imitative of mountain shapes. But Indians also associated mountains with many fearsome phenomena: windstorms, thunder and lightning, earthquakes. Fiery eruptions led them to personify volcanos, sometimes imputing to them evil motives. August Kautz, planning an attempt on Mount Rainier in 1857, wrote that "Indians were very superstitious and afraid of it." The Yakima Indian guide Sluiskin, in 1870, described the evil spirit that inhabited Rainier and dwelled in a "lake of fire" on its summit. John Muir related that "Mount Shasta, so far as I have seen, has never been the home of Indians, not even their hunting-ground to any great extent, above the lower slopes of the base. They are said to be afraid of fire-mountains and geyser-basins as being the dwelling-places of dangerously powerful and unmanageable gods."

Through the experience of countless generations, Indian tribes possessed an understanding of the North American wilderness and its creatures: they had developed a sense of balance with the forces of nature. The first European colonists, arriving in the seventeenth century, brought with them the concept of wilderness as a hostile environment and were uncomfortable in a landscape so unlike their homelands—though they did have better tools than the Indian did for altering this landscape. A typical early settler found the forest beyond his cleared settlement "a waste and howling wilderness."

The Appalachian chain, the first mountains encountered by the colonists, was regarded as an impediment to westward travel. The folded and faulted series of ridges and valleys not only hindered migration west, it isolated groups of settlers from one another, fostering the independence and insularity still found in this region today.

Yet the European settlers and their descendants did go west, and as they went, the mountains beyond the Great Plains loomed enigmatically, wrapped in an aura of mystery lacking in the well-explored countrysides of Europe. In addition, the mountains stood as symbols of freedom. The first white men to penetrate the heart of the mountain West were fur trappers and traders, men who were independent and individualistic, eccentric and antisocial. The first official explorers—as opposed to wanderers—were usually military expeditions, whose journals frequently belie the joy of wilderness life. Their accounts concern mainly the business of studying the terrain and locating trade routes, yet they sometimes were inspired to climb a mountain.

Shortly after President Jefferson purchased the Louisiana Territory from France, in 1803, an expedition led by Meriwether Lewis and William Clark set out to explore the United States' new acquisition, reaching the Pacific Ocean by way of the Missouri River, the Montana Rockies, and the Columbia River. In 1806, Lieutenant Zebulon Pike journeyed toward the headwaters of the Arkansas River. Pike was the first American to attempt an ascent of a big western mountain, and, though he failed to reach even the base of his peak, Edwin James of Stephen Long's expedition did ascend Pikes Peak in 1820.

South Pass, the Oregon Trail's gateway through the Rockies, was discovered in 1812, and in 1833, Captain Benjamin Bonneville, searching for a route through the nearby Wind River Mountains, climbed an unknown peak. In 1842, Lieutenant John C. Frémont, sent west to explore the territory and map the

Mount Hood's Eliot Glacier,
and, in the distance, from left
to right, Mount St. Helens
(before the 1980 eruption),
Mount Rainier, and Mount
Adams. By Bob and Ira Spring.

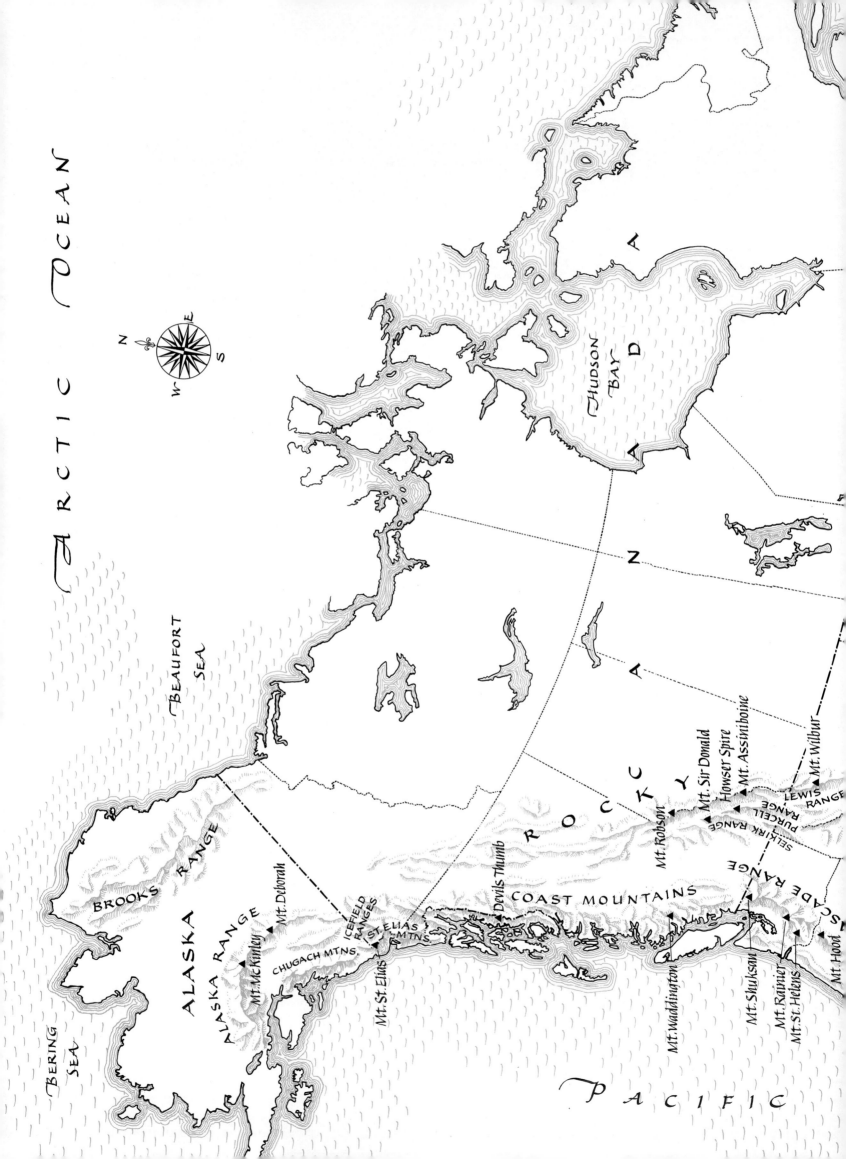

ATLANTIC OCEAN

CARIBBEAN SEA

GULF OF MEXICO

UNITED STATES

APPALACHIAN MOUNTAINS

Mt. Katahdin
WHITE MTNS.
Mt. Washington
Mt. Marcy
ADIRONDACK MTNS.

BLUE RIDGE MTNS.
Clingmans Dome
GREAT SMOKY MTNS.

Harney Peak
BLACK HILLS

Longs Peak
Pikes Peak

M O U N T A I N S

Gannett Peak
Fremont Peak
FRONT RANGE
SAWATCH RANGE
SANGRE DE CRISTO MTNS.

TETON RANGE
WIND RIVER RANGE
UINTA MTNS.
Maroon Bells
ELK MTNS.
Mt. Sneffels
SAN JUAN MTNS.

Mt. Moran
Grand Teton
WASATCH RANGE
Mt. Timpanogos
Ship Rock

San Francisco Peaks

Mt. Shasta

Mt. Ritter
North Palisade
Mt. Whitney

SIERRA NEVADA

COAST   RANGES

OCEAN

SIERRA MADRE ORIENTAL

Pico de Orizaba
Popocatepetl

SIERRA MADRE OCCIDENTAL

M E X I C O

MILES
KM

map by palacios

Oregon Trail, "went beyond the strict order of our instructions" and climbed what he believed to be the loftiest point in the Rockies, the Wind Rivers' Fremont Peak.

The ascents made by the first explorers were not difficult by modern standards, or even by contemporary standards in the Alps, but they did involve risks not encountered by present-day mountaineers: hostile Indians, becoming lost in unknown country a thousand miles from civilization, and possibly starvation. Pike wrote following another expedition that

> In the execution of this voyage I had no gentlemen to aid me, and I literally performed the duties (as far as my limited abilities permitted) of astronomer, surveyor, commanding officer, clerk, spy, guide, and hunter; frequently proceding the party for miles, in order to reconnoitre, and returning in the evening, hungry and fatigued, to sit down in the open air, by fire light, to copy the notes and plot the courses of the day.

Pike considered his soldier-comrades a "Dam'd set of Rascels." Yet even these bold adventurers were not immune to the aesthetics of the mountains. Frémont's journals abound with such phrases as "a view of the most romantic beauty met our eyes."

During the first half of the nineteenth century, the western mountains were accessible only to explorers on missions motivated by practical concerns. After settlements sprang up on the Pacific Coast, however, men could contemplate the shining ice cones of the Cascades from their doorsteps. By 1870, Mounts Hood, St. Helens, and Rainier had all been surmounted by adventurous locals, who managed to negotiate the crevasse-ridden glaciers without mishap.

Most climbing in the West during the second half of the nineteenth century, however, was done by members of federal and state survey teams. In 1863, the California Geological Survey, headed by Josiah Whitney, turned its attention to the Sierra Nevada. During the next several years surveyors William Brewer and Clarence King reached many of the highest summits. At the beginning of the decade, Mount Shasta was regarded as the highest point in the United States; by 1870, it was known that Mount Whit-

ney was. Two federal teams, the Hayden Survey and the Wheeler Survey, climbed numerous 14,000-foot peaks in Colorado during the 1870s. The more difficult Grand Teton was possibly climbed by Hayden surveyors Langford and Stevenson in 1872 and definitely was ascended by the Spalding—Owen party in 1898.

Climbing historian Chris Jones has commented that, "to the scientists and adventurers of the midnineteenth century, the climbing experience was often a one-time thing. With few exceptions these men were not dedicated mountaineers, and in general the climbs they made required little mountaineering skill." Englishman H.E.M. Stutfield remarked, in 1901: "It seems out West they have little appreciation of natural beauties, and, in spite of the general cuteness of the American mind, they have yet to learn the commercial value of scenery.... They look on all climbers, as so many people do at home, as lunatics." Stutfield notwithstanding, the expeditions and surveys of the nineteenth century drew a number of intelligent, sensitite, articulate men— Frémont, King, John Muir, John Wesley Powell, cartographer Charles Preuss, and artist William Henry Holmes, to name a few—and the literature and art produced by these men did much to make the American people aware of the extent and beauty of their mountains. And, if they did fail "to learn the commercial value of scenery," the work of explorers did lead to the creation of our system of national parks.

HENRY David Thoreau tried to explain how primitive man viewed the mountains: "The tops of mountains are among the unfinished parts of the globe, whither it is a slight insult to the gods to climb and pry into their secrets, and try their effect on our humanity. Only daring and insolent men, perchance, go there. Simple races, as savages, do not climb mountains—their tops are sacred and mysterious tracts." Not only primitive peoples felt that way; most of the inhabitants of civilized Europe felt the same until fairly recently. The literature of the Middle Ages depicts mountains as ugly and inhabited by dragons. "The Alps," wrote John Dennis as late as 1698, "are not only vast but are horrid, ghastly ruins."

But the curious men began to return from the Alps unharmed, and as fear gradually subsided, a mountain aesthetic began to take shape. In 1786, Mont Blanc, the Alps' highest peak, was climbed. By the early nineteenth century, climbing was an established leisure-class activity. The delight in wild nature was expressed in the paintings of John Ruskin

From high up on Mount McKinley a climber overlooks Mount Hunter, with typical daytime cumulous clouds obscuring the lower peaks of the Alaska Range. By Galen Rowell.

and others. Ruskin, also a critic, wrote that mountains are "the beginning and end of all natural scenery"; such sentiments also permeated the writings of Shelley, Byron, and Rousseau. The English especially were attracted to the Alps and made it financially attractive for local hunters to become mountain guides.

In North America, it was the mountains of Canada that first attracted British climbers and their sport of climbing for the sheer challenge and joy of it. Botanist David Douglas had ascended a mysterious "mountain of pure ice" in the Canadian Rockies in 1827, apparently solely for pleasure, and reported its elevation as 17,000 feet. But it was not until the end of the century that British sportsmen, led by Swiss guides imported by the Canadian Pacific Railroad, transplanted the techniques and aesthetics of the Alps to the alpine Canadian mountains.

In 1888, English clergymen Henry Swanzy and William Green visited the Selkirk Range of British Columbia and, though Mount Sir Donald, the obvious prize, eluded them, they made an impressive ascent of nearby Mount Bonney. In 1901, another British cleric, James Outram, with two guides, accomplished Canada's "most sensational mountaineering feat" up to that time, the ascent of Mount Assiniboine (often called the "Matterhorn of the Rockies"). The Reverend George Kinney made several assaults on the Rockies' highest summit, Mount Robson, setting the stage for the 1913 ascent led by intrepid Austrian guide Conrad Kain.

Meanwhile, the mountains of Alaska remained virtually unknown. An occasional navigator had explored glacial inlets and a few naturalists—including John Muir—had ventured onto coastal glaciers, but little was known that could not be seen from the sea. Mount McKinley had been seen from a distance, but its distinction as Alaska's highest peak, let alone North America's, was not realized; as late as 1897 it was still uncharted on maps.

The great ice pyramid seen from the sea by Vitus Bering and named Mount St. Elias was the first high Alaskan mountain to attract climbers. American and English parties failed to reach its 18,008-foot summit between 1886 and 1891, but in 1897 an Italian group led by Prince Luigi Amedeo of Savoy, Duke of the Abruzzi, made the first ascent. The photographs of Alaskan scenes made on that expedition by Vittorio Sella compare favorably with Ruskin's beloved paintings of the Alps.

St. Elias, only twenty miles from the coast, could be approached by glaciers that fall from its slopes to the sea, but the way to McKinley was less obvious. Not until 1902 did a United States Geolog-

Above: **A climber rappels the granite slabs of the Kain Route on Bugaboo Spire, Purcell Range, British Columbia. By Alan Kearney.**

Facing page: **Climber at about 17,000 feet on the southwest face of Mount St. Elias, Icefield Ranges, Alaska. In the distance lie Icy Bay and the Pacific Ocean. By Barry Nash.**

ical Survey party led by Alfred Brooks work out a practical route for reaching the interior giant. Attempts to climb McKinley were made in 1903, a false claim of an ascent was made in 1906, and the lower north summit was reached in 1910; not until 1913 was the main 20,320-foot summit attained.

Many summits were reached by tenacious surveyors assigned the complicated task of delineating the boundary between the Alaska panhandle and Canada, but only in 1925 did an expedition stand on Canada's highest summit, Mount Logan, which lies inland from St. Elias. In 1936, Mount Waddington, hidden in the Coast Mountains of British Columbia, was first climbed; the South Tower of Howser Spire in the Bugaboo group of the Purcell Range was climbed in 1941. I had the privilege of making the first ascent, in 1946, of Devils Thumb, on the Alaska–British Columbia border and, in 1954, of two Alaskan giants, Mounts Deborah and Hunter. The adventure continues for me, and for countless other mountaineers, whether they are finding unclimbed peaks in seldom visited ranges, pioneering new lines up often climbed peaks, or following the footsteps of others up North America's many beautiful, challenging routes.

MOUNTAINS are many things to many people. Some cherish mountains for scenic vistas, some gain inspiration; others find in the mountains both adventure and a kinship with nature difficult to find in modern civilization. Whether the attraction is a challenging lieback crack, a glittering snow face, a golden summit, a shimmering lake, an elusive mountain goat, or a scarlet penstemon, the possibilities are as endless as the changing light on a sawtooth crest. The mountains of North America continue to draw us to our varied pursuits. Humanity is discovering that a link with the mountains fills an essential need, that, as John Muir wrote in 1898, "going to the mountains is going home; that wilderness is necessity, and that mountain parks and reservations are useful not only as fountains of timber and irrigating rivers, but as fountains of life."

In this book I hope to present a scientific view of the mountains, an historical view, and my own intuitive view of the alpine experience. The essence of the experience, it seems to me, is the curiosity, the optimism, and the excitement with which we go forth to meet new sights, new challenges. There are always fresh wonders in nature, and the rewards include not only intense memories but the unique experience of communing with nature. If there is a message in this book, it is that the timeless beauty of the heights are close enough for us to discover personally.

Not all North American mountains can be portrayed here. Paring my selections to thirty-five was an agonizing task, and the exclusion of a mountain is not meant to deny its appeal. Yet I feel my choices reflect what is best about North American mountains and present the wide variety of forms found from the Atlantic Coast to the Pacific, from Mexico to Alaska. Some peaks, such as Mount St. Elias, are formed of sweeping ice slopes in a polar wilderness; others, like Mount Washington and Clingmans Dome, are wooded and accessible by automobile.

The photographs were chosen in an effort to show each mountain from as many facets, in as many different moods, as possible, and to depict the characteristic life forms of various mountain regions. But these views are a mere fraction of the whole; the possibilities for aesthetic pleasure in the mountains, fortunately, are endless.

Mount Katahdin

*"All the mountains are dangerous to those who
do not know them. But they are also filled with
delights. One of these is the sight of the rising
sun seen from the summit of Mt. Katahdin, the
first light to strike America each day."*

Henry David Thoreau
Maine Woods

RISING midway between the Maine coastline
and the St. Lawrence River, the isolated
bulk of Mount Katahdin is eastern America's most impressive peak. Totally dominating the surrounding landscape, the complex
mountain consists of several summits of nearly
equal elevation. The easternmost summit, Pamola,
is separated from the 5,267-foot main summit by a
spectacular stretch of ridge known as the Knife Edge.
Such rugged and varied topography makes Katahdin
an especially attractive mountain, even though its
height seems diminutive in comparison to the continent's western mountains.

The French explorer Samuel de Champlain was
perhaps the first white man to see the prominent
landmark. In 1605, while sailing along the coastal
waters, he noted that "large mountains are seen to
the west." Yet for the next two centuries no one
seems to have described the Katahdin region. To the
Puritans, of course, all land beyond their cleared
settlements was considered a worthless wasteland
that devils worshipped. The Bible equated wilderness with the last refuge for outcasts, and in taming
the wilderness the American pioneer was simply
doing God's work. But the clearing of the land was a
painstaking effort, and far-away Mount Katahdin
was guarded by thousands of square miles of thick
forest.

Early in the nineteenth century a pioneer
named Charles Turner visited the Katahdin region.
From the local Indians, Turner heard a grim tale: no
native who had attempted to ascend the peak had
lived to return—so, at least, went the legend. In an
account of his journey published in 1804, Turner
related a story told him by the natives: "They allege
that, many moons ago, seven Indians resolutely
ascended the mountain and that they were never
heard of afterwards, having undoubtedly been killed
by Pamola, a fierce avenging spirit of the mountain."
Perhaps reasoning that only natives vanished, Turner determined to attempt the peak. The Indians
cautioned him to retreat immediately if uncommon
sounds were heard, but he accomplished the climb
safely—it was the peak's first known ascent.

American and British surveyors climbed the
peak while charting the United States–Canadian
boundary around 1820, and the region became even
better known to the outside world. Nevertheless,
Mount Katahdin and its environs were still pristine
wilderness when the most famous of the early chroniclers of the peak arrived a few years later. Henry
David Thoreau, taking a respite from his solitary life
at Walden Pond, visited the area for the first time in
1846. His book, *Maine Woods*, is an eloquent record
of this journey and two subsequent ones; it remains
today as a fine paean to the forest primeval. Regarding the uncharted region as "a new world, far in the
dark of a continent," Thoreau undoubtedly formulated many of his ideas about the preservation of
wilderness while tramping through the north woods.

Although clambering to the top of Katahdin

was not high on the list of Thoreau's objectives, his visit to the summit proved to be an enjoyable if not heroic venture. In a chapter entitled "Ktaadn"—the former Indian name for the peak—the naturalist described his impressions of the heights:

> At length I entered within the skirts of a cloud which seemed forever drifting over the summit, and yet would never be gone, but was generated out of that pure air as fast as it flowed away. . . . Sometimes it seemed as if the summit would be cleared in a few moments, and smile in sunshine: but what was gained on one side was lost on another. It was like sitting in a chimney and waiting for the smoke to blow away. It was, in fact, a cloud-factory,—there were the cloud works. . . . It reminded me of the creations of the old epic and dramatic poets of Atlas, Vulcan, the Cyclops, and Prometheus.

Although entranced by his summit trip, Thoreau spent most of his time exploring the forested environs of the peak, and here he discovered a fascinating landscape: "It is a country full of evergreen trees, of mossy silver birches and watery maples, the ground dotted with insipid, small red berries, and strewn with damp and moss-grown rocks,—a country diversified with innumerable lakes and rapid streams."

In the 130 years since Thoreau so enthusiastically described the Katahdin landscape, numerous travelers have discovered that the region symbolizes the spirit of the rolling northern forestland which covers so much of eastern North America. Here, in the boreal forest, vast tracts of red spruce and balsam fir blanket the land, lakes and shallow ponds occupy the floors of ancient cirques, and deciduous trees erupt into a riot of flame each autumn. One of these trees, the paper birch, is quite well known, for its bark, which separates freely into thin sheets, has long been used in the construction of canoes.

The forest floor is a place of charm and variety, with mosses, ferns, and orchids growing everywhere. The twinflower, a lovely, creeping evergreen plant, will often be spotted growing on moss-covered fallen logs. The ground carpet also includes species such as Indian pipe, gold thread, wintergreen, wood sorrel, Canada mayflower, and creeping snowberry.

Upland bogs interrupt the forest on occasion,

Facing page: **Mount Katahdin from Taylor Pond, Baxter State Park; purple rhodora in bloom in late May. By Paul Knaut.**

Right: **Goldthread, Baxter State Park. This delicate flower is found in the mountainous woodlands of New England. By Fred Bavendam.**

and these features prove fascinating to the hiker who seeks them out. Relics of the last Ice Age, the bogs began their existence as shallow ponds occupying glacier-scooped pockets. Green algae gradually spread over the pond's surface; later, mosses and other water-loving plants blanketed the pond like a coverlet. The bogs slowly thickened until they became mats of spongy earth "floating" on the water. The conversion toward solid earth still goes on today as the bog accumulates humus, but the observant hiker will sometimes hear water gurgling beneath the seemingly solid ground.

The Katahdin bogs are best known for the ubiquitous sphagnum mosses which border the bog. Laced with dense, tangled stems of bushes, these mosses form soft, thick "rugs" which quiver when touched. Several species of the moss, each displaying a different shade of green or brown, inhabit the region.

The environment of a typical Katahdin bog proves ideal for unique communities of plants and animals that thrive in mutual dependence. Often nestled among the mats of sphagnum moss are plants such as the carnivorous pitcher plant and the sundew; both species compensate for their nitrogen-poor environment by trapping and eating insects. Another meat-eating plant, the bladderwort, has tiny bladders which can suck up aquatic organisms through a valve.

The wetlands of Katahdin also attract numerous species of birds. Marshes shelter shy rails and bitterns, while marsh wrens trill from the nearby cattails. During migration periods, great numbers of warblers flit among the vegetation. Loons glide across the ponds; their distinctive call, resembling maniacal laughter, often fills the air. Canada jays flitter through the rich forestland, competing for attention with ospreys, woodpeckers, great horned owls, spruce grouse, ruby-throated hummingbirds, and tanagers.

In addition to the varied avian population, numerous mammals also inhabit the Mount Katahdin region. Foremost among these is North America's largest hoofed beast, the moose. This enormous creature, weighing as much as 1,200 pounds, is the comic character of the north woods. Its long, spindly legs, short neck, and misshapen muzzle give the moose an air of awkwardness unmatched by any other North American mammal. Yet the moose thrives in an environment where most humans would perish. Thanks to the insulation provided by thick body hairs filled with air cells, the moose can survive nights where the temperature plunges to forty below zero. The beast can subsist solely on tree bark, although its preferred fare in the summertime is the water lilies and roots found in the ponds.

The Algonquin Indians called the moose *mongsoa*, meaning "the twig eater," but English settlers corrupted the word to its present form. The mammal's ancestors have been traced as far back as the Lower Eocene Period, and its relatives probably crossed the Bering Land Bridge from Siberia about 175,000 years ago. Adapting well to the new continent, herds of moose soon stretched across southern Canada and the northern tier of the United States. The largest herds today are found in Alaska and Canada; the moose populations have declined radically in the regions of extensive logging. When Maine's lawmakers voted to end moose hunting in 1935, the state's herd had dwindled to under 2,000, but today it is estimated that 20,000 of the mammals inhabit the northern portion of the state.

When Thoreau visited Katahdin in 1846, he noted moose tracks "covering every square rod of the

Above: A cow moose shakes off water in a pond. By Stephen J. Krasemann/DRK Photo.

Facing page: Looking down on Chimney Pond from near the summit of Mount Katahdin. A large valley glacier once covered this landscape; the pond and other basin lakes are a legacy of the ice ages. By Ed Cooper.

Aerial view of the summit of Katahdin, showing glacier-scoured cirques; the Knife Edge and Pamola are seen in the foreground. By David Hiser.

sides of the mountain." Everywhere he found twigs browsed, "clipt as smoothly as if by a knife. The bark of trees was stript up by them to the height of eight or nine feet, in long, narrow strips, an inch wide, still showing the distinct marks of their teeth. We expected nothing less than to meet a herd of them, and our Nimrod held his shooting-iron in readiness."

Hikers who climb Katahdin may not spot a moose en route, but they will be rewarded by spectacular views of a less elusive subject—the rock formations. The great, irregular-shaped peak, capped by an elevated tableland of Paleozoic granites, is incised by numerous deep glacial gorges which drop to the ponds nestled in the mixed forest. In the best known of these glacial cirques lies Chimney Pond, where boulders fallen from Pamola line one shore.

It is now estimated that the last glaciation to cover the mountain area took place between 15,000 and 9,000 years ago. The chain of basin ponds owe their existence to a moraine of Katahdin granite, which indicates that it was formed by valley glaciers that descended from the tableland. The combined effort of continental glaciers and old valley glaciers

eroded the cirques, but the most recent erosion—which gave the final rugged shape to the mountain—was caused by small valley glaciers which lingered in the cirques following the final melting of continental ice.

Ralph S. Tarr, a scientist who studied the effects of glaciation at the end of the nineteenth century, presented the first evidence that foreign rock fragments existed on the highest peak of Katahdin. The erratic boulders near the summits of many of the features in the region were marooned by the last continental glacier, although most moraines of similar material have been removed from the valleys by stream erosion.

In nearly every outcrop of Katahdin granite, dated at 360 million years, there are cracks called joints. Some of them result from the contraction of igneous rocks during cooling; others are caused by extreme weathering. Well-developed jointing promotes weathering, and this further weakens the rock. The curved and serrated ridge of vertically fractured rock which forms the Knife Edge is an erosional feature resulting from cirque and valley glaciation.

Vigorous frost action has tended to dislodge rock fragments beneath this narrow crest and enhance the form first sculpted by the ice.

I was curious to see Katahdin's rock at close range, but when I climbed the peak one October there was a sense of urgency to my progress, for a storm was forecast. The climate in New England is notorious for its uncertainty. Arctic and coastal winds prevent inland Maine from being warmed by the Gulf Stream, and the winter season often arrives early and suddenly. A cold and slippery hike took me through shaded boulders filmed with a dusting of snow from the previous storm. As I scrambled higher, toward the top of Pamola, I passed over a stretch of alpine tundra. Here, where the precipitation averages about forty inches annually, many species of grasses, shrubs, and heath plants have gained a distinct foothold in the poor and shallow soil of the Katahdin tablelands. Many of these plants are native to the Arctic zone, there growing near sea level. Geologic evidence indicates that with each advance of the ice sheets, Arctic plants and animals migrated southward. Some of the plants, living remnants of a glacial climate, survive in Katahdin's relative isolation.

Among the fractured rock outcrops, dwarfed and flattened trees formed dense mats called *krummholz*—German for "bent wood." The winds have so hammered these birches and firs that the climax forest here reaches only to a person's height. It was a landscape ravaged by the elements.

As I traversed the Knife Edge, surely the most spectacular mountain walk in New England, a veil of white scudded over the ridge ahead. Clouds swirled around in all directions as I clambered out of the cleft separating Pamola from the main summit. Ambling up along narrow ledges, occasionally hopping across boulders, I noticed the exposure for the first time. Anyone accustomed to the heights will find pleasure in such mild exposure, but hikers unfamiliar with steep terrain could have a few anxious moments.

The summit of Katahdin marks the northern terminus of the famed Appalachian Trail, a 2,000-mile path which begins in far-away Georgia. Many hikers have completed the entire journey, and the top of Katahdin is an appropriately spectacular end to such a marvelous adventure.

By evening the sun had fallen behind a blue-black line of clouds, and the wind whistling through the tops of the evergreens surrounding my camp at Chimney Pond smelled of rain. Sure enough, as I hiked back to the roadhead the next morning, sleet accompanied a gale-force wind.

The storm's intensity reminded me that hypothermia—which can end in death by "exposure"—has often struck cold and tired hikers on Katahdin. One especially tragic storm-related accident occurred in 1963. A woman who took a "short cut" down the flanks of Pamola became trapped on steep cliffs. A major storm arrived that night; both the woman and the ranger who attempted to rescue her died.

As a result of this accident—and several others—the authorities at Baxter State Park (in which Katahdin lies) established a new set of regulations for mountain activity. Hikers were prohibited from starting up Katahdin after certain morning hours, and some trails are closed at specific dates. Winter climbing, camping, and alpine skiing must have the approval of the park director. Various procedures to promote trip safety during the winter have resulted in equipment inspection, a minimum of four travelers per group, and the inflexibility of advance registration. Guy and Laura Waterman have written that "many climbers simply avoid Katahdin, rather than submit." There are many challenging rock routes, and the area is a first-class ice-climbing location in winter, but the many restrictions of freedom make many mountaineers echo what Paul Petzoldt said after one of his trips to the mountain: "It was like a prison camp to me."

The right of citizens to take risks, in situations ranging from the urban to the high mountain, has been the subject of much discussion and rhetoric. But this topic proves academic to most visitors to Mount Katahdin—those adventurers who in the summertime roam the bogs in search of an elusive orchid or wander through the boulders toward the classic traverse of the Knife Edge.

Mount Washington

*In the mountains of New Hampshire . . . the
bare peaks of granite, broken and desolate, cradle
the clouds; while the vallies and broad bases
of the mountains rest under the shadow of noble
and varied forests. . . .*

Thomas Cole
American Monthly, 1836

IT IS possible that the English explorer John Cabot glimpsed Mount Washington and the lofty White Mountains as he sailed along the Atlantic Coast in the waning years of the fifteenth century. But neither he nor his son, Sebastian, who visited the same stretch of coast in 1509, make any mention of the conspicuous mountain range. Credit for the discovery—by white men—of the major terrain feature goes to Giovanni da Verrazano. In a letter to the king of France, the Florentine navigator wrote that he was "keeping our course Northeast along the coast . . . with high mountains within the land." Subsequent voyagers used the peaks as a navigational aid, and cartographers, including Gerardus Mercator, soon depicted the range on their maps. A 1677 map of New England was the first to show a name for the uplift: the White Hills. This name, essentially unaltered for three centuries, referred not only to the snow which blankets the range for fully half the year, but also to the bald appearance of the whitish rocks visible during the summer months.

Located in northern New Hampshire, about sixty-five miles from the Atlantic coast, Mount Washington is the crown jewel of the Presidential Range—the climax of the White Mountains. The 6,288-foot mountain is a large massif whose flanks are sliced by several enormous ravines. Foremost among these is the Great Gulf, a complete glacial valley containing numerous cirques. Another remarkable gorge is Tuckerman Ravine, a curving gash on the peak's southeast side. On the eastern flank lies yet another major feature, Huntington Ravine. Each of these great cuts in the earth has its own character; all provide opportunities for adventure.

The curious visitor might wonder how the earth became shaped in such a dramatic manner. The White Mountains, ancient even by geological standards, delineate the former boundaries of plate convergence. While the European–African and American continents were joined—a time when the present Atlantic Ocean did not yet exist—a period of intense folding and faulting took place from about 375 to 350 million years ago in the region to become New England. During this mountain-building episode, known as the Acadian Orogeny, a segment of oceanic crust was added to the eastern margin of the North American plate. Compressive forces buckled horizontal beds of sedimentary rock into enormous folds. Intense heat and pressure metamorphosed these rocks into other forms. (What was once thick mud and sand on the continental margin was transformed in this manner into schists and quartzites that today can be seen on the summit of Mount Washington.)

The ancient White Mountains, which had been periodically raised by orogenies, were eventually reduced by erosion, leaving only their deep roots. When the continents began to drift apart some 250 million years ago, a rift formed between the land

Above: Two species of dwarf cinquefoil grow in the White Mountains region; one of them, Robbins' cinquefoil, is a rare and endangered species. By Fred Bavendam.

Page 38: Looking west from the Wildcat Ridge Trail toward Mount Washington; Tuckerman Ravine (left) and Huntington Ravine (right) can be seen in the shadow. By Ned Therrien.

masses; this was to become the present Atlantic Ocean. Magma was injected into weak zones of the crust at various times, rising and pushing up the older bedrock and forming intrusive rocks along a seventy-five-mile-wide belt. Inexorably, water run-off began chiseling deep cuts into the high, rolling surface of the land. During mountain uplift about 10 million years ago this water began to carve the impressive gorges seen today on Mount Washington.

A cooling climate about 2 million years ago initiated a process that was to alter radically the appearance of the Presidential Range. Glaciation, accompanied by a process known as mass-wasting—the downslope movement of rock and soil caused by freezing and thawing—shaped the mountain landscape to its present character. Valley glaciers formed and began smoothing the range's roughness. During this icy regime, these glaciers scraped the flanks and bottoms of the stream-carved valleys, rounding V-shapes to U-profiles, and creating vast bowls such as the Great Gulf. Glaciers flowed down both Tuckerman and Huntington ravines, and joining, continued nearly to Pinkham Notch.

The final shaping of the range was accomplished by the continental ice sheet, lobes of which moved inexorably south from Canada over hundreds of thousands of years. Mount Washington became an island in a vast sea of ice; finally, as the last holdout, it too vanished under 1,000 feet of ice. The ice mass came and went four times; the departure of the final ice sheet—known as the Wisconsin stage—left the Appalachian Highlands as far south as Pennsylvania littered with glacial debris. This same ice sheet was responsible for both the formation of well-known notches such as Pinkham, Franconia, and Crawford, which were plucked out from the bedrock by the pressure of the ice, and for two small ponds on the flanks of Mount Washington, the beautiful Lakes of the Clouds: these occupy the floor of a shallow basin scooped out of the bedrock by the ice.

After the last glaciers vanished from the Presidential Range—about 12,000 years ago—trees began to appear on the mountain slopes. Today, a deciduous hardwood forest prevails up to the 2,500-foot level. In this ecosystem, which receives about forty inches of precipitation per year, the predominant trees are yellow birch, American beech, and sugar maple.

Conifers such as red spruce and balsam fir begin to make an appearance above 2,500 feet, and by the 3,200-foot level the spruce-fir forest has replaced the deciduous species. Higher still, it becomes difficult for trees growing in the timberline zone to maintain their life processes because of thin soil, lack of moisture, lingering snow deposits, drying effects of the high winds, and summer frosts. Black spruce prove to be the uppermost trees, for this species can reproduce vegetatively; that is, without seeding. The spruce typically grows in dwarfed, intergrown *krummholz* mats, which spread horizontally among the boulders. By keeping this low profile, the highest trees and plants avoid the winds and take advantage of the sun's radiant energy, which heats up the ground surface.

Although the alpine environment of the Presidential Range is the largest in the eastern United States, only eight square miles of this above-timberline region exist. This fell-field area, the highest zone of plant life, is not the Arctic wasteland it appears to be from a distance. Alpine vegetation tends to grow most plentifully in moisture-retaining soils formed by small, stepped terraces, such as those on the Oakes Gulf side of Mount Washington's tableland. The vegetation on the benches of Bigelow Lawn, occupying the saddle between the cone of Washington and Boott Spur, includes lichens, mosses, and many species of dwarfed plants. Of the sixty-three Arctic species that have been identified in the Presidentials, one of the most commonly seen is the dwarf cinquefoil, which forms a dense rosette of tufted leaves and in summer displays bright yellow flowers. One species of this small plant is today endangered by the feet of hikers.

Above the zone of the highest plant life lies an austere region where the land is ravaged by the elements. An excellent example of this rock-strewn landscape can be found on the upper 1,500 feet of Mount Washington. This region is composed of a desolate heap of granite boulders covered with ice and frost-feathers much of the year. Attesting to the ferocity of the climate, a sea of enormous, angular boulders, known as a *felsenmeer*, have been thrust out of the bedrock by a phenomenon known as frost-heaving. This wild summit region of Washington is roughly similar to the lifeless zone at sea level on the Arctic Circle. (Ecologically, every 1,000 foot gain on Mount Washington is the same as traveling north for 250 miles.)

The climate that helped create the awesome desolation on upper Mount Washington would have pleased Typhon, the storm god of Greek mythology, for the weather on the heights is truly diabolical. The geographic location of the isolated peak appears to favor extremes in the weather: storm tracks from the Gulf of Mexico often converge near the White Mountains with the polar storm tracks traversing the Midwest. When this happens, moist, warm air clashes with dry, cold air, and the results are explosive.

When the tracks meet, the power of the wind is enhanced considerably. The orographic effect, a phenomenon whereby air is "squeezed" as it passes up and over mountains, also contributes to wind velocity here.

Indeed, when one thinks of Mount Washington's climate, the first thing that springs to mind is the wind's power. The *average* wind speed at the summit is 35 miles per hour, and winds have exceeded 100 miles per hour in every month of the year. The highest wind speed ever recorded, 231 miles per hour, occurred on the summit on April 12, 1934.

Mount Washington is not only a windy place; it is unusually cold and cloudy most of the year. The summit, shrouded in mist about 55 percent of the time, has an average annual temperature of 27° F. Even on summer afternoons, the most pleasant time to visit the summit, the average temperature is only 52° F. The combination of wind, cold, and precipitation can create a deadly chill factor at any time of the year; more lives have been lost on Mount Washington than on any other mountain in North America.

During the winter months Arctic conditions prevail; the temperature plummets below zero sixty-five days during an average winter. Snow plumes constantly radiate from the summit, and rime ice—a supercooled deposit of fog droplets which freeze upon contact with the surface—forms delicate banners that can build outward several feet into the wind.

Famed mountaineer Bradford Washburn verbalized the winter's fury after a March ascent in the 1920s:

> Ahead of us on the crest of the ridge we could see a terrific gale blowing the snow along before it. It was a magnificent sight—the white clouds of snow racing at stupendous speed, outlined in sharp contrast against the gorgeous blue of the sky. . . . We would lean over our whole weight against one of these [gusts] to keep from blowing over, then the wind would stop altogether for a second, making us stagger about ten feet to the right as we tried to regain our balance.

Winter climbing in Huntington Ravine began in 1928 on the initiative of British climber Noel Odell, who made the ascent of Central Gully with the Harvard Mountaineering Club. In 1930 a Yale party climbed the more formidable Pinnacle Gully. Since that time ice climbing has flourished in this locale, and the severity of the weather can make a climb a test of judgment and fitness.

In November, 1980 John O'Brien and I waited

Rime ice coats the buildings and transmission towers on the summit of Mount Washington during a rare clear day in midwinter. By Greg Gordon, Mount Washington Observatory.

two weeks for a prime day to make the summit ascent via Huntington Ravine, and our patience paid off. My diary records our progress after leaving the road for the trail at Pinkham Notch:

> The rooty, rocky trail is frozen with ice. The ice axe is welcome as a cane. On the slabs alongside the Central Gully John and I augment the cane with twelve-point crampons. They are a blessing. So is the weather. Would you believe it— just a light breeze! As we climb out of the frozen slabs we pull balaclavas down over our chins, but the wind is still toying. The frost feathers on the cone's slope are amazing! They cover rock and hollow and are hard enough to walk on without boots breaking through. We keep on crampons for a better grip.

I had heard that the summit cone in wintry sunlight was beautiful, but its splendor must be seen to be believed.

The climatic extremes of the White Mountains undoubtedly impressed the Abnaki branch of the Algonquin Indians. Living below the peaks, they considered the summits the abode of superior beings who often reveal their presence by causing appalling tempests and deafening noises. Ascents of mountains were therefore regarded not only as perilous but sacreligious. Although several Indian legends relate dramatic events associated with the heights, the natives apparently felt little desire to stand atop them.

The first adventurer known to have ascended Mount Washington—or, as it was called in colonial times, Christall Hill—was Darby Field, an Irishman who in 1642 reached the summit with two Indians. Field returned from his eighteen-day trip excited about his discovery of "shining stones"—probably quartz crystals. Reporting on Field's trip, Governor John Winthrop of Massachusetts wrote: "The top of all was plain about 60 feet square. On the north side there was such a precipice, as they could hardly discern the bottom."

The names "White Mountains" and "Mount Washington" first appeared in print during the 1780s; they were probably the brainchild of the Reverend Jeremy Belknap. In 1784 he climbed the peak via rugged Tuckerman Ravine. An apt description of the terrain was given by a member of the party: "This ascent is like steep stairs, the rocks of different forms, wedged in by one another in various attitudes of bigness. . . ."

By the mid-1800s the White Mountains had become a famous resort area, attracting many cultured persons. The Notch House, an inn west of Mount Washington, claimed among its guests Henry David Thoreau, and three of America's most noted preachers and patriots of that era: Thomas Starr King, Henry Ward Beecher, and Phillips Brooks. Starr King was one of the most brilliant orators of the famous Boston pulpits, and, more than any other writer, made the mountains popular as a summer resort. His poetry, containing much vigor and spiritual insight, waxed rhapsodic about the White Mountains. Beecher established a summer parish in the range, and hundreds of the faithful filled a large tent to hear the great man preach.

Other famous men visited the White Mountains during this period. Landscape painter Thomas Cole, a leader of the respected Hudson Valley School, undoubtedly found much to his liking. Two world-famous geologists, Sir Charles Lyell and Louis Agassiz, spent time in the range; the latter noted unmistakable evidence of the former glaciers. Writers also flocked to the hills: Anthony Trollope, Henry Wadsworth Longfellow, Ralph Waldo Emerson. William Cullen Bryant hiked up the newly built path to the top of Mount Washington, later recording his impressions: "The depth of the valleys, the steepness of the mountain-sides, the variety of aspect shown by their summits, the deep gulfs of forest below, seamed with the open courses of rivers, the vast extent of the mountain region seen north and south of us, gleaming with many lakes, filled me with surprise and astonishment."

The building of a carriage road to the summit, completed in 1861, was an amazing engineering feat for its time. America's first toll road, it rose 4,600 feet in eight miles at a grade of twelve percent. The first passenger vehicle to reach the summit was a stagecoach drawn by eight horses. Travelers who rode in carriages paid a nickel per mile; hikers paid two cents per mile. The road early became an arena for stunts, including a walking wager by a fat lady, and carriage races and foot races were popular. Later, auto races were scheduled regularly.

While hiking the mountain in 1852, Sylvester Marsh, a wealthy inventor of the species *Genius yankee,* became lost in a storm. Thinking there must be an easier method of reaching the summit, he soon formulated a bold idea for a cog railway system. Railroad experts regarded Marsh's plan as impractical, "a railway to the moon." But the man who had made his fortune in meat-packing machinery was no idle dreamer. Forming the Mount Washington Steam Railway Company, Marsh designed an engine and a unique cog system; within ten years he had completed a three-mile line which climbed 3,700 vertical feet. The first train to the summit, in July, 1869, accomplished the steep pull in seventy minutes.

Marsh's enterprise attracted immediate attention; among the luminaries who made the trip during the first season was President Ulysses Grant. In 1875, 7,000 tourists enjoyed the spectacular ride.

The founding of the Appalachian Mountain Club in 1876 marked a new epoch in the exploration and study of the White Mountains. The range's first hut was built by the club in 1888; since then, they have erected eight other trailside hostelries, spaced one day's hiking apart. With this chain of huts—the only such one in the United States—and its 400 miles of maintained trails, the club has striven to make the mountains accessible.

The huts have attracted hundreds of thousands of hikers, and there are countless episodes and traditions involving the hut system and trails. One amusing incident, related by Charles Newhall in 1906, concerned a club member who invited two New York friends to accompany him to the mountains. One of the men went to Abercrombie and Fitch to be completely outfitted, including a suit of "duck's back" material and a pair of six-foot-long snowshoes. Later, on the steep mountain slopes, the hapless city slicker slid backward on his outsized snowshoes faster than he could climb.

Supplies had to be carried to the huts by human labor; the packers usually consisted of college youths. One stalwart lad in the 1920s made ten trips from the Lakes of the Clouds to the summit of Mount Washington in one day, descending each time with 100 pounds. Covering a total of 30 miles up and down, he earned 23 dollars for this feat.

A writer in 1922 became nostalgic when thinking of his past experiences. "These huts," he recalled, "with their little stories of rough bunks, burnt porridge, green New Yorkers . . . will always be a part of my fondest memories."

The fact that the White Mountains lie within weekend driving distance of one-quarter of the nation's population suggests that stringent measures need to be taken to preserve the region. As user damage to this highland increases (200,000 persons now use the various huts each summer), even the Appalachian Mountain Club has been criticized for "marketing" the backcountry. The organization has examined its role in hut- and trail-building, as well as reconsidering their guidebook publishing program. But the club claims it merely manages, not produces, the great hiker impact. No one can deny that the huts have lured many thousands of people into the range. But many of these hikers care deeply about the wilderness, and their growing reverence for nature offers hope that the mountain lands will retain their vitality and beauty forever.

Favorable winter conditions have made ice climbing in New England popular among mountaineers. By Rick Wilcox.

Mount Marcy

Above, the eagle flew, the osprey screamed,
The raven croaked, owls hooted, the woodpecker
Loud hammered, and the heron rose in the swamp.
As water poured through hollows of the hills
To feed this wealth of lakes and rivulets,
So Nature shed all beauty lavishly
From her redundant horn.

Ralph Waldo Emerson
The Adirondacs

UPPER New York State is blessed with an extensive, relatively wild mountainous area called the Adirondacks. I had never visited these famous mountains, so it was in an anticipatory mood that I began my hike to the region's highest summit, Mount Marcy. On this ascent I had the good fortune to be accompanied by Tony Goodwin, a local outdoorsman who had done the trek many times. During the course of the day, Goodwin explained in lucid fashion the geological and human history of this beautiful island of wildness.

The Adirondacks, I soon learned, form the southern apex of the Canadian Shield, the ancient mass of rock which forms the nucleus of the North American continent. As part of the Shield, the Adirondacks were raised and depressed at various times. More than a billion years ago eastern North America and the beginnings of the Adirondacks lay under water. In time, an accretion of deposits were crumpled and uplifted by great continental forces, the final result being a lofty, lifeless ancestral range perhaps five miles high. This range, which then bordered the continent, floated on the denser rocks of the earth's mantle, much like an iceberg floats on water. Intense metamorphism occurred in the root zone about a billion years ago, and the extreme heat caused some of the rock to melt, thus producing the granitic magma which subsequently intruded older overlying sediment beds.

In time the ancient mountains were reduced to a peneplain by erosion. Gradually the crust sagged and a sea invaded the region east and southeast of the Adirondacks, which remained as a peninsula attached to the Canadian Shield. More than 400 million years ago the collision between the North American and European continental plates initiated a new cycle of mountain building; its violent forces of deformation and folding formed today's pattern of subranges and valleys.

The rounded mountains, I soon learned, are transected by numerous deep valleys which trend southwest to northeast. These valleys follow faults which are perhaps 400 million years old, although the excavation by ice of the weaker rocks in various zones is far more recent. During the past few million years, the Adirondacks were covered more than once with sheets of ice, and the topography underwent radical changes. The ice rounded the mountains, plucked notches out of weak fault zones, and carved great U-shaped valleys. The deglaciation process, started only 20,000 years ago, was extremely complex. Valley glaciers remained on the highest Adirondack peaks while the ice sheets blocked many of the lower valleys. As the ice melted, enormous lakes of impounded meltwater formed; remnants of these can be seen today.

Following the ice ages, forests became established

Aerial view of Mount Marcy in winter. By Clyde H. Smith.

in the valleys. Today, the Adirondacks are a virtual museum of eastern trees. The lower mountain slopes are blanketed with deciduous species such as maple, birch, ash, oak, and black cherry. The most aristocratic tree of this lower region is the American beech, a handsome species growing to a height of 100 feet. Distinguished by its smooth, gray bark and exquisite foliage, the beech prefers moist soils where its shallow root system can thrive.

The yellow birch is another interesting hardwood; this species provides the healing cover on slopes ravaged by fire or logging. The fast-growing trees soon provide a canopy below which conifers can establish a foothold.

I had purposely planned my trip to coincide with the arrival of the famous autumn display of colors. And here, on the slopes of Mount Marcy, I was not disappointed. Bright splashes of red, yellow, and orange surrounded us as we began our ascent; the sugar maples proved especially spectacular. No two trees displayed the same coloration; some had just begun to turn, while others had already shed a few leaves. In six weeks or so every tree would be bare. The reason for the coloration is simple: when the weather turns cold, the tree is "programmed" to seal the opening where the leaf joins its stem. This action stops the movement of chlorophyll, allowing other pigments to take over.

Higher on the mountain, Goodwin and I passed through pure stands of balsam fir, the most dominant tree of the upper regions. Near the summit, the trail winds among thick, stunted specimens of red spruce, then ascends the final bare-rock slope. Clouds and a frigid wind induced us to leave the summit promptly, and we descended quickly, via a different route, to Lake Tear of the Clouds.

While we were admiring this lovely pond, Goodwin informed me we were standing on a historic spot. Here, on the afternoon of September 13, 1901, Vice President Theodore Roosevelt was met by a messenger who told him that President William McKinley, shot a week earlier, was dying. Roosevelt hurried back to civilization and that night made a reckless fifty-mile journey by buckboard to the nearest railhead.

Below the lake we hiked alongside a brook which churned thunderously through a deep gorge. Soon we were traversing the precipitous north side of Avalanche Lake, whose shoreline is ringed by wet cliffs which plunge directly into the water. Here we had to negotiate rickety log bridges, climb wooden ladders, and cross engineering oddities nicknamed "Hitch-Up Matildas."

These suspended log bridges, bolted to the rock face, commemorate an incident involving Matilda Fielding, an early enthusiast of the Adirondack wilderness. The trail was a rudimentary one in 1868, and at one spot along the shore Fielding climbed onto her guide's shoulders to stay dry while he waded a short section. But the water proved deeper than expected, and as the guide sank lower and lower, Fielding's garments and posterior came dangerously close to the lake's surface. Watching from nearby, convulsed with laughter, Fielding's husband and niece shouted, "Hitch up, Matilda, hitch up!" The bridges were soon built to avoid such incidents.

In gathering darkness we tramped through Avalanche Pass, the watershed boundary between the Hudson and St. Lawrence rivers. As nightfall approached, and we stumbled among the tree roots, we heard the resonant booming of a great horned owl, the most abundant nocturnal bird of the Adirondacks. It was a signal to me that the muddy hike would soon be over, and that within a few hours we could be enjoying a meal cooked on the old iron stove in Goodwin's rustic forest house.

In the days following my hike up New York's highest mountain, I explored more Adirondack terrain, learning much about the exploration of the early pioneers, the wildlife, and the environmental problems which plague the region.

Indians, of course, were the first to explore these ridges and valleys. Some time after French navigator Jacques Cartier ascended the St. Lawrence River in 1535, the various tribes of the Iroquois Confederacy withdrew into the Adirondacks and in time became fierce and powerful foes of their former allies, the Algonquins. In 1609, when Samuel de Champlain explored the huge lake later to bear his name, he was accompanied by an Algonquin war party. Champlain's thoughtless attack on a group of Mohawks—members of the Confederacy—turned the Iroquois against the French and initiated a conflict that lasted more than two centuries.

In this conflict, the power of the Iroquois increased until they were the dominant Indian nation east of the Mississippi. The fight for control of the Lake Champlain waterway, just east of the Adirondacks, intensified as the British disputed French claims on the region; by 1690 the colonial ambitions of the two powers had turned the valley into a hotly contested war zone. Domination of Lake Champlain was once the key to the political fate of North America. A vital passage during the French and Indian Wars, the lake also served as an avenue for the British invasions of 1776 and 1777. Control of the lake was again important during the War of 1812, when the British planned to move south through the valley.

Above: Dwarfed red spruce amid the summit rocks of Mount Marcy. By Ed Cooper.

Facing page: October snow and fall foliage in the Adirondack Mountains; from left to right are Gothics, Armstrong Mountain, and Wolfjaw Mountain. The view is from Noonmark Mountain. By Clyde H. Smith.

The last phase of the conflict between the Crown and the rebel colonies was settled decisively in 1814 by the American fleet.

While the Lake Champlain Valley quickly became better known to settlers as a result of its strategic importance, the interior of the Adirondacks remained isolated and uncharted. The name "Adirondack"—honoring an Indian tribe that had once hunted in the hills—was first applied to this mountainous region in 1838 by Ebenezer Emmons, the chief geologist of the New York Topographic Survey. Emmons located the range's highest peak by triangulation, naming it after William Learned Marcy, then governor of the state. (The Iroquois had called the peak "Tahawus," or "cloud splitter.")

The first recorded ascent of Mount Marcy took place in 1837, when a survey party led by Verplanck Colvin reached the top. Colvin was the foremost authority on the Adirondacks for many decades; his vivid speeches and writings influenced the state legislature, who in 1892 created the Adirondack Forest Preserve, a 2.3-million-acre tract of land.

The exposure of a number of leading painters and writers of the day to Adirondack scenery—and its expression in their work—helped to popularize the idea of preservation. Chief among those who perceived the need to befriend nature was Ralph Waldo Emerson; he eloquently expressed the idea that man should learn to live in harmony with nature instead of exploiting it.

The first of the famous "Philosopher's Camps" was held on the shores of a small pond near Saranac Lake in the summer of 1858. Included among the illustrious group of intellectuals were Emerson, James Russell Lowell, and Louis Aggasiz. Mark Twain later introduced summer camps in the lake country, and Robert Louis Stevenson, who came to recover his health, wrote many of his essays in the vicinity. Henry Ward Beecher, the colorful preacher, and writers such as Henry Wadsworth Longfellow and Herman Melville spent Adirondack summers in country manors. It was an era when millions of Currier and Ives prints featured timeless Adirondack scenes of "roughing it."

Like Emerson, the Reverend William Henry Harrison Murray was enchanted by the Adirondack landscapes; he wrote that the wilderness brought God close to the human heart in ways the plow and field or city street could never accomplish. Murray incorporated his mountain adventures into his sermons, portraying the Adirondacks as a paradise that promised clean air and good health. His book, extolling the healthful quality of the area, drew thousands of city dwellers to the forested slopes and valleys.

After Dr. Edward Trudeau opened his world-famous sanatorium for tuberculosis at Saranac Lake in 1884, cartoons in *Harper's New Monthly Magazine* showed the sickly receiving the "wilderness cure" in the Adirondacks.

To the public, the scenery, clear air, and abundant wildlife were compelling reasons to visit the region. By the summer of 1900 some 250,000 visitors flocked to the private camps and hotels of the Adirondacks. Visitors during this period included the Astors, Vanderbilts, Whitneys, and Harrimans—the richest members of American society. Another prominent visitor, Theodore Roosevelt, was fascinated by the birdlife of the Adirondacks.

During these years of popularity, the resorts employed "backwoods" guides who took the guests fishing, hunting, and hiking. The best of these guides proved to be humorous and eccentric individuals who could, given the right provocation, treat their wealthy clients with a firmness that bordered on insubordination. Nevertheless, such guides were sought out by the same clients the following summer, an interesting commentary on human nature.

Striding along an Adirondack trail one day, reflecting on the fascinating cast of characters who had once roamed the region, I turned a corner and came upon a small pond full of dead and dying trees. A well-constructed barrier of logs at the outlet showed me immediately that beavers had been at work. Weighing as much as sixty pounds, these remarkable creatures build efficient dams in running water, creating ponds to establish a watery empire ideal for gathering their favorite foods, aquatic plants and the bark from deciduous trees. When the mammals have consumed all the edibles in the vicinity, they abandon the pond. The dam soon disintegrates, releasing

Above: **The eerie cry of the common loon can be heard throughout the Adirondack region. By Wayne Lankinen.**

Top: **Whitetail fawn at rest. By Leonard Lee Rue/Alpha Photo.**

its impounded water; eventually the site becomes a stream-cut meadow. This, in time, invites encroachment of the forest. As the new growth of willow, birch, and poplar appear, the combination of running water and a fresh supply of food will attract a new family of beavers to begin the cycle anew.

Temporal beaver ponds are noteworthy for their number and unexpected locations, but the true scenic delights of the Adirondacks are the more than 2,000 lakes. Some, like Lake Champlain on the region's eastern margin, are enormous; Champlain is the site of former naval battles. One of the smallest, the previously mentioned Lake Tear of the Clouds, forms the source of the Hudson River. The most famous is probably Lake Placid, the site of two Winter Olympic Games.

These lovely lakes, symbols of the Adirondack region, are today threatened by a major ecological disaster: acid rain. This unplanned offspring of industrialized society occurs when oxides of sulfur and nitrogen, released by the incomplete combustion of fossil fuels, remain in the atmosphere long enough to interact with water particles, thus creating sulfuric and nitric acids. These caustic substances can linger in the atmosphere as long as six days and can be borne thousands of miles by the wind. Eventually, when conditions are right, the acid falls to earth with rain or snow which may be up to ten times as acidic as normal precipitation.

Large areas of the northern hemisphere are being blanketed with acid rain, which threatens aquatic ecosystems, forests, and plants. In the United States the major affected region is the Northeast; the Adirondacks and other mountainous areas are particularly susceptible, a fact discovered only a few years ago.

In the mid-1960s researchers from Cornell University who were investigating puzzling changes in Adirondack fish populations found wilderness lakes had turned alarmingly acidic. By 1975 the scientists had listed 91 high-mountain lakes that were too acidic to support fish; four years later the number had increased to 170. The researchers learned that when a lake's buffering capacity becomes minimal, it goes acidic rapidly. Evolutionary habitats that took thousands of years to create vanish quickly. Well-buffered soils, which are thick and highly alkaline, can neutralize the acid as it enters the ecosystem. However, most Adirondack soil is thin, barely covering the granitic bedrock; here, the acid quickly runs off and enters the waterways.

In New England it is estimated that seventy percent of the acid in rainfall consists of sulfuric acid from power plants, much of it originating in far-away places. For instance, because Ohio's coal has a high sulfur content, regulatory agencies forced the utilities to construct extra-tall stacks. But these pipelines to the atmosphere merely exported the oxides to New England on the prevailing winds. Similarly, a smelter in Sudbury, Ontario, vents huge amounts of sulfuric oxide into the air, where the winds transport it eastward.

Some 25 million tons of sulfuric oxide are released into the atmosphere each year in the United States alone. Such pollution is expected to increase as more and more utilities convert their power plants to burn coal instead of oil. The industry must obviously install more scrubbers to filter out the oxides. But the effort to clean the air has been politically controversial, hindered by employment problems and strong labor unions. America's fuel consumption also contributes to the deterioration of fragile ecosystems. A critical question for the 1980s is: Who will stop the rain?

Clingmans Dome

For those who have seen the Alps or the Rockies, the Appalachians are not likely, as mountains, to stir the heart. They are, rather, a forest upon a high-rolling floor, and in all the continent, in all the world, I believe, there is no such hardwood or deciduous forest as this. All the beauty of the Appalachians is forest beauty. . . . Everywhere the murmur of leaves, the trickling or the rushing of water. . . .

The Journal of André Michaux, 1787

THE Appalachian Mountains, stretching 1,600 miles from the St. Lawrence River to central Alabama, consist of dozens of major ranges. Some of the most interesting of these, from a scenic and historical perspective, lie in the western half of North Carolina. Here, the Blue Ridge province of the Appalachian Highlands becomes a wide, complex mass of ridges and valleys. The easternmost portion of the Highlands, known as the Blue Ridge Mountains, consists of a highly dissected uplift that forms a steep escarpment overlooking the Piedmont Plateau. The western margin of the province includes several short ranges, the principal one of which is the Unaka Range; the better known Great Smoky Mountains are a unit of this range. Transverse ridges also cut across the landscape; one of these, the Black Mountains, contains eastern America's highest peak, 6,684-foot Mount Mitchell.

What we know of the formation of the Appalachians began in the early Paleozoic Era, about 600 million years ago. At that time a great oceanic trough (a geosynclinal basin) extended from the St. Lawrence depression to the Gulf Coastal Plain. Sinking of the geosyncline, concurrently with deposition in the trough, resulted in the accumulation of sedimentary beds to a thickness of 30,000 to 40,000 feet. As the westward-moving ancient Atlantic Ocean crust passed beneath the North American continent, friction and pressure caused the sedimentary rocks to crumple and fold, in time altering them to metamorphic forms. Deformation was most intense in the deepest part of the geosyncline, now the core of the present Appalachians.

Over a period from about 450 to 250 million years ago the ocean floor was swallowed, causing the North American and Eurasian–African continents to collide; this led to the building of a vast and lofty Appalachian Mountain system. During this great uplift, called the Appalachian Revolution, the thick flat-lying sediments were compressed into open folds that trended from northeast to southwest. As the core rose, strata on flanks of the uplift became tilted: some folds overturned and broke into giant sheets which thrust westward, each one sliding over the next like playing cards. Sometimes older basement fragments were thrust up over younger strata. Precambrian sedimentary rocks of the Ocoee Series —so old they contain no fossil traces of plant or animal life—pushed northwest along the Great Smoky fault over rocks half their age of the Valley and Ridge province. The mountain-building process was completed about 180 million years ago, and from that time until the present, the Appalachians have been subject only to the forces of erosion.

Within a relatively small section of North Carolina and Tennessee lie 125 peaks that exceed 5,000 feet. Local relief, at times, is great: one peak, Mount LeConte, rises one vertical mile, in a single bold

sweep, from the East Tennessee Valley. Yet the individual peaks are not especially spectacular, for they are mere remnants of the former, greater range. For instance, Clingmans Dome, the subject of this chapter, has been chosen not for its intrinsic beauty or significance, but more because it symbolizes the Great Smoky Mountains, surely the finest example of the southern Appalachians.

Mountains, of course, need not be dramatically shaped in order to be interesting. One striking feature of this region inspired the naming of both the Blue Ridge and the Great Smoky Mountains: the subtle blue haze that constantly hovers over the ridges. This tenuous mist softens all outlines and causes objects only a few miles away to appear very distant. Remote ridges become intangible and mysterious because of the curious atmospheric effects. Perhaps the most fascinating aspect of the Smokies, however, is their vegetation, whose diversity is unequaled in the world's temperate regions.

Three principal reasons explain the near-tropical luxuriance and variety of vegetation: the favorable climate, the well-developed soil cover—resulting from 60 million years of accumulation—and the fact that the mountains escaped the scouring effects of glaciers. The forests of the Smokies boast 130 native tree species—far more than in all of Europe. On the range's slopes grow the last great hardwood forests of North America. During an ascending mountain hike, one may encounter such species as elm, gum, sycamore, and persimmon; higher, one enters a region containing beech, birch, basswood, magnolia, flowering redbed, holly, buckeye, hickory, box elder, ash, butternut, maple, and poplar.

In ideal habitats, some of these deciduous trees attain record proportions. Sweet gums, members of the witch hazel family, rise to 150 feet in height. The yellow poplar, or tulip tree, found elsewhere only in the forests of China, sometimes reaches a diameter of eleven feet; its straight trunk can soar as high as eighty feet before the lowest branch is reached. These trees, relics of warmth-loving species that were pushed south during the ice ages, now mingle with the endemic species of the southern latitudes to create a unique mélange.

Facing page: One of the countless waterfalls of the Great Smoky Mountains. By David Muench.

Page 52: Autumn foliage at Cade's Cove, Great Smoky Mountains National Park. By Clyde H. Smith.

The region receives the heaviest rainfall east of the Mississippi River, and this lavish watering of the deep, fertile soil forms an ideal environment for plant life. In summertime the upper reaches of the Smokies are one vast floral garden. Masses of white and pink rhododendron, flame azalea, and laurel emblazon the slopes and treeless areas. Wildflowers, reaching their climax in late spring, occur in profusion; one will find plants such as iris, orchid, columbine, paintbrush, phlox, monkshood, Indian pipe, phacelia, and wood sorrel. By autumn the flowers have wilted and faded, but the deciduous canopy of trees radiate every shade of yellow and red.

It is estimated that some 200 species of plants are endemic to the region; that is, they occur nowhere else. Some of these plants have close relatives in Asia; it appears that the Bering Land Bridge was the conduit responsible for a migration which took place some 65 to 40 million years ago. The most noteworthy endemic plant in the Smokies is the Catawba rhododendron, which in summer displays large, dense, lavender flower clusters. This species grows thickly, often in close association with the white-flowered Lapland rosebay rhododendron. Other endemics include the trailing phlox, white-fringed phacelia, silver bell, and a ragwort.

The origin of bare areas called "grass balds" is unclear, for they do not reflect timberline conditions. These scenic patches, usually only a few acres in extent, are probably floral relics of an earlier, harsher climate. Indian traditions suggest the balds have existed for at least 200 years. Considerably different from the grass balds are other open areas on ridgecrests above 4,000 feet in elevation. Known locally as "laurel slicks," botanists call them "heath balds." From a distance these areas appear to be a smooth, grassy carpet; upon closer inspection, one discovers an almsot impenetrable tangle of head-high rhododendron, mountain myrtle, azalea, and other members of the heath family that originated after the removal of forest cover by fire, landslide, or lumbering. Botanists have yet to provide a complete explanation for these openings. One theory is that in the wake of the last glacial epoch, the warming period nearly eliminated spruce and fir from the lower summits. When the climate cooled again, the conifers did not recover because of the absence of a local seeding source for reforestation.

It was William Bartram who first described the rich botanical Eden of western North Carolina. In the mid-1770s the Quaker naturalist came seeking plants for his father's famous garden in Pennsylvania. During his travels, Bartram discovered and named the remarkable flame azalea; he was also the

Above: Flame azalea decorates a grassy bald in Ashe County, North Carolina. By James P. Valentine.

Facing page: Hikers on the Appalachian Trail in the Roan Mountain Scenic Area stride along the divide separating North Carolina from Tennessee. By William A. Bake.

Pages 56-57: Sunset over the ridges of the Great Smoky Mountains, viewed from Clingmans Dome. By David Muench.

first to describe the white buckeye and the mountain magnolia. *Travels,* his account of these adventures, was long considered a definitive description of the eastern wilderness.

Soon after Bartram's pioneering journey, the French botanist André Michaux, on a mission to collect trees and flowers of the New World for Louis XVI, wrote glowingly of the wondrous azaleas and rhododendrons. His enthusiasm peaked on Grandfather Mountain, for here he sang "La Marseillaise," convinced he had climbed North America's highest point.

The two botanists were the first scientists to describe the southern Appalachians, but other explorers had previously traversed them. During his epic trek to the Mississippi, Hernando de Soto named the mountains after a Gulf Coast tribe called the Apalachee; he crossed the Blue Ridge in 1540. Some 210 years later, Dr. Thomas Walker discovered and named Cumberland Gap, a natural break in the mountains some seventy-five miles north of the Smokies. This corridor became famous as the chief pathway between Virginia and the great Appalachian Valley.

During the 1760s, Daniel Boone ranged across the Blue Ridge and Unaka mountains on long hunting expeditions into eastern Tennessee. After Cherokees attacked him while blazing a route through Cumberland Gap, Boone in 1775 led an armed band of colonists through this corridor, at the same time building his famed Wilderness Road. With the way opened for settlers, Boone began to colonize Kentucky in open defiance of the British. Three days after the Battle of Lexington, the flag of the new colony of Transylvania waved over the fort at Boonesborough. The isolated rebels did not learn of the Declaration of Independence until the following year.

White settlers, mostly of Scottish or Irish descent, arrived in Tennessee at the time of the Revolutionary War and established farmsteads in the Appalachian Valley. Settlements in isolated mountain localities followed, and the inhabitants developed strong ties with the land. These Appalachian frontiersmen were the first Americans to cut loose entirely from the seaboard and fall back on their own resources. They were also the first to establish governments in defiance of king and aristocracy.

Following the Revolutionary War, various Indian tribes still controlled the mountain passes, and for years afterward skirmishes took place throughout the southern Appalachians. Treaties were signed but rarely observed. The Cherokees were loyal to the United States during the War of 1812, but after the election of Andrew Jackson in 1828, the Indians were deprived of property and legal rights. The states of Georgia and North Carolina began to evict the Cherokees from their ancient homelands; later, the Indians were forced into a great exodus—when troops under General Winfield Scott rounded up the Indians and marched them westward into Oklahoma.

Although military activity had opened routes into the Highlands, much of the mountainous terrain remained unsurveyed. Two men, Professor Elisha Mitchell and United States Senator Thomas Clingman, took various observations, but eventually came to disagree about which of the region's peaks was the highest. Mitchell left on a solitary trek in June, 1857, to establish a new line of observations. He failed to return from this trip; his body was discovered at the base of a cliff some time later. The peak he championed now bears the name Mount Mitchell. The following year Clingman made the first measurements of the highest peak of the Smokies, and one of his men cut a path to the summit of what became Clingmans Dome.

Throughout the nineteenth century, time virtually stood still for the inhabitants of the region. Isolated settlements in the remote backcountry of the southern Appalachians remained relatively independent of the rest of the nation. The "mountaineers" of Appalachia were distinguished by their unique manner of speaking and by their unchanging customs. In his book *Our Southern Highlanders*, published in 1913, sociologist Horace Kephart considered the inhabitants "creatures of the environment enmeshed in a labyrinth that has deflected and repelled the march of our nation for three hundred years."

A monograph published in 1901 told of women living in mountain cabins who had never been to a village only four miles away. In many hamlets a man was his own farmer, blacksmith, carpenter, gunsmith, and cobbler. One individual was described as a magistrate, veterinarian, storekeeper, and dentist; one wonders about his competency in some of these diverse occupations.

Isolation, a mixture of cultures, and a desire for independence caused many inhabitants of Appalachia to disregard the law. The most notorious of the illegal practices was moonshining. Immigrants from Scotland who preferred distilled spirits produced from their own barley saw no reason to pay heavy taxes on this libation.

Scant attention was paid to moonshining until 1876, when the federal government, concerned over being defrauded of its revenues, discovered that some 3,000 illicit stills were thought to be operating in Appalachia. Public sentiment, however, was unanimously in the moonshiner's favor. One of Kephart's informants undoubtedly spoke for many highlanders when he plaintively stated: "We-uns hain't no call to be ashamed of ourselves, nor of ary thing we do. . . . We stay 'way up hyer in these coves, and mind our own business." Not surprisingly, revenue officers were resisted; some were slain.

Moonshining may still be practiced, but as I drove the winding rural roads of western North Carolina in 1980, it was evident that few of the traditional ways of the highlander are preserved today. A scattering of isolated farm plots, tucked into the vales between the foothills, gave me a brief glimpse into the past. And I occasionally heard people talking in dialects. But the newer influences—proximity of cities, television, automobiles, and tourists—have inevitably altered the style of the region. This fact was brought home to me one day as I wandered through a country store. A customer asked the storekeeper if he could have a poke in which to put some bulk beans. The bewildered shopkeeper, new to the region, didn't know that a poke—as in the expression "pig in a poke"—was a sack.

As I wound through the foothills toward Clingmans Dome, I saw that the great hardwood forests of the southern Appalachians have become heavily slashed by the logging industry. Because of the early

insularity of the Highlands, no voice as eloquent as Henry David Thoreau's emerged to challenge the ravishing of this forest. However, the writings and speeches of Horace Kephart eventually influenced legislators and led to the creation of Great Smoky Mountains National Park. This reserve of nearly 800 square miles was set aside in 1926 at a time when a growing population, shortsighted and swelling with self-interest, was becoming the greatest enemy of the national park idea. The British diplomat James Bryce once remarked that the setting aside of inviolable national parks was America's unique contribution to the democratic idea.

Reflecting on Bryce's concept, I drove upward through the thick deciduous forest. It was a cold November morning, and most of the trees had already shed their bright leaves. On one shadowy hillside I noticed a spectacular display of ice; winter would not be long in coming.

Where the park highway reaches Newfound Gap on the main divide of the Great Smokies, I intersected the Appalachian Trail. A few weeks earlier I had encountered the same trail on Mount Katahdin, the northern terminus of the 2,035-mile-long path. Here, near Clingmans Dome, the highest point reached by the trail, I was relatively close to its southern end. Some 4 million people annually hike a portion of the world's most famous footpath; approximately 1,000 serious walkers set out each spring to walk its entirety. A consortium of sixty-three hiking organizations spend much money and time in maintaining the footway and several hundred shelters en route. Parts of the trail are jeopardized by urban sprawl, private ownership, and timber clearing, but a cooperative effort has been made by the National Park Service, state governments, and hiking clubs to protect the path from further encroachment. Benton MacKaye, the forester who proposed the creation of this footpath in 1921, was a visionary when he spoke of the need for a corridor of wilderness where city dwellers could go to enjoy nature.

I left my car at a parking lot one-half mile below Clingmans Dome and began the short stroll to the top. A brisk wind ruffled the treetops; at a lower level chickadees and titmice flitted through the branches.

The top of Clingmans Dome, at 6,643 feet, is covered with a thick stand of conifers. To make sure the tourists obtain an impressive panorama, the National Park Service has built a controversial observation tower. Although this concrete structure seems ludicrously out of place amid the primeval forest, I had to admit that the view it allowed was a spectacular one indeed.

I gazed out over hundreds of square miles of forested mountain forms. In every direction dark, gentle ridges overlapped one another; there seemed to be no end to them. The Smokies, I realized once again, may lack spectacular individual peaks, but this historic range does possess a timeless quality which can only be termed spiritual.

CHAPTER FIVE

Pico de Orizaba and Popocatepetl

There is a hill eyght leagues from Chollola, *called* Popocatepec, *which is to say, a hill of smoke, for manye tymes it casteth out smoke and fier.* Cortez *sente thither tenne Spanyardes, with manye* Indians, *to carry their vituall, and to guide them in the way. The ascending was very troublesome, and full of craggie rockes. They approached so nigh the toppe, that they heard such a terrible noyse which proceeded from thence, that they durst not goe unto it, for the ground dyd tremble and shake, and great quantitie of Ashes whyche disturbed the way. . . .*

The Pleasant History of the Conquest of the
Weast India (London, 1578), quoted in *American
Alpine Journal*, 1947.

THE lowland approaches to most North American mountain ranges are fairly predictable. One drives along a wide, smooth highway to a small town nestled at the foot of the range. Here one can stock up on supplies and grab a last-minute hamburger. Then a dirt road winds deep into the foothills to a parking lot where, without a second thought, one abandons the car for days or weeks. Few people will be encountered in the mountains, little trash will be visible, and huts are infrequent.

Our trip to climb the Mexican volcanos did not conform to the above scenario, but we did not really want it to. Reed Tindall, Mike Warburton, and I were eager, in fact, to explore the varied aspects of a different culture. Although climbing the huge peaks was our chief goal, we suspected that many of the adventures awaiting us would take place far from the glaciers and craters.

Our adventure began at the border station at Nogales, Arizona, where two Mexican customs officials, inspecting our station wagon, became somewhat perplexed by our ice axes and other climbing paraphernalia. Remembering that Leon Trotsky had been assassinated in Mexico City by a man wielding an ice axe, we quickly assured the inspectors that we were simply crazy North American mountain climbers. After checking our travel documents, the two men stood silently by our car, as if waiting for us to make the next move. After an uncomfortable few minutes, one man asked quietly, "Anything for tips?" Amazed by this forthright query, we fished a few bills from our pockets and were soon competing with hordes of pedestrians and dusty cars for access onto the main road leading south from town.

Driving during the daylight hours was a delightful experience except for the constant stream of trucks and buses which noisily emitted such copious quantities of diesel fumes that we imagined there had to be a local acid-rain problem.

After darkness set in, however, our delight turned to apprehension. Pedestrians in dark clothing walked casually along busy, shoulderless highways; we flashed by them with only inches to spare. Stalled cars were abandoned on the road, invariably, it seemed, on curves. Truck drivers, by some strange logic seeking to save money, barreled along narrow, pot-holed roads without benefit of headlights. It did not take us long to reconsider our driving schedule: dawn-to-dusk travel proved far less demanding than the noon-to-midnight shift.

The traffic became perplexing once again as we arrived on the outskirts of Mexico City. Planning to meet a Mexican climber who lived in the city, we

Popocatepetl, the second-highest of the Mexican volcanos, rises behind a row of Hartweg pines. By David Hiser.

first had to telephone him to find out where he lived. But the traffic surged along relentlessly and no telephone booths were visible. Tension mounted as we were swept into the great city by the flood of cars and buses. Our inability to understand road signs added to the sense of frustration.

Finally, Mike caught sight of a familiar sign: a Denny's restaurant. Surely it would have a telephone. Using our best urban instincts, we wheeled left—with a green light—across the main highway and into the sanctuary of the parking lot. But right on our heels was a policeman, blowing his whistle and shouting "Infracción!" This was a word we had little trouble understanding. Our turn, the man claimed, was illegal. With horror we envisioned most of our greenbacks clutched in his greedy fist. We persuaded the officer to accompany us into the restaurant, hoping someone would speak English. The restaurant manager not only spoke English; he also understood the fraudulent nature of the infraction. After a brief conversation the officer departed, not to be seen again. We celebrated by ordering a large meal.

On locating our friend, we made plans for the next few days. Since Mexico City lies at 7,800 feet, we decided it would be a good place to spend a few days acclimating in preparation for our first climb. We visited the famous pyramids north of town, marveling at the thirty-square-mile site which, 1,500 years ago, may have supported a population of 85,000.

Coming back from the pyramids, we witnessed thousands of pilgrims flocking toward Mexico's holiest Catholic shrine, the Basilica of Our Lady of Guadalupe. Parking nearby, we joined the throngs. It was December 12, the day of Guadalupe, and we had inadvertently stumbled into the midst of the Western Hemisphere's largest pilgrimage. For several hours we observed the colorful crowd, some of whom wore intricately embroidered Aztec costumes. This marvelous cultural event seemed a fitting prelude to our own pilgrimage to Mexico's fabled volcanos.

The time had come to cease being tourists and get back to being mountaineers. Driving eastward from Mexico City, we were soon free of the strangling traffic jams. Our goal, Pico de Orizaba, lay only 125 miles distant, and it was not long before we saw the 18,700-foot peak glimmering through the haze. Massive though the peak looked, it seemed odd that the solitary volcanic cone is North America's third-highest peak; only Mounts McKinley and Logan rise higher.

In Aztec legend Orizaba contains the spirit of Quetzalcoatl, the feathered serpent whose body, im-

molated on the peak by divine fire, became Venus. The native name for the peak is Citlaltepetl, or Mountain of the Star.

We had been warned not to trust our station wagon on the rough road which led to the Piedra Grande hut, the beginning of the climb. So in the quaint village of Tlachichuca we hired a guide named Joaquin Canchola Limon to take us onward and upward in his four-wheel-drive vehicle. Within a mile we were glad we had switched cars, for the road, climbing steeply through fields of maize and groves of pines, was deeply rutted. Far above us, Orizaba's glaciers radiated an unearthly light. Passing timberline, we wound through boulderfields, eventually arriving at the hut, a small metal shack at 13,800 feet.

Several other climbers greeted us, but luckily we found space in the twelve-bunk hut. Limon, claiming our sleeping bags would not be safe while we were on the climb, insisted on remaining at the hut until our return.

The next morning we were off before first light. A crude path led up through rocky volcanic terrain toward the glaciers, some two hours from the shelter. Soon we strapped crampons to our boots and began ascending the uniform, thirty-degree snowslopes. Short icy patches alternated with long stretches of breakable crust, but we encountered absolutely no technical climbing.

While climbing these tedious slopes, we speculated on the whereabouts of the Aztec wind god, Ehecatl, and their cruel war god, Huitzilopochtli, who in mythology ruled the land. To be sure, it was a windy morning. But otherwise we encountered no hostile obstacles such as were reported in an account in the 1867 *Alpine Journal*:

Boulders undermined by the thaw of ice came spinning after each other at fabulous rates of speed. Shafts of ice 30 ft. long, loosened by the falling boulders and snow slides, slipped from their moorings. . . . Huge masses of earth, and boulders, and scoria, loosened by the melting snow, came thundering and hissing from above, fairly flying past our heads on to the next projecting ledge. . . . A heavy boulder came whizzing by on its downward course; some one called out, "S—— has fallen!" The rock struck him on the shoulder, breaking it, and hurled him 100 ft. down the steep gully. The guide reached him soon after. . . .

Orizaba is a relatively easy mountain to climb, except for one thing: its height. Above about 16,000 feet, depending on the individual, unacclimated climbers tend to become weak and sick, even experiencing hallucinations at times. Mike began feeling the altitude as we progressed, but Reed and I felt especially strong. Fortunately, none of us displayed the symptoms which plagued some participants of the aforementioned 1867 group: "Blood began to pass from nose and ears, and faces were swollen so that old friends knew each other only by the dress. A few continued the journey a thousand feet higher, lay down, slept on the snow or black dust, gasped for breath and awoke."

As we steadily gained height on the crispy glacier, large crevasses, sometimes invisible because of a thin covering of fresh snow, cut across our path. We were able to circumvent these deep slashes with only minor detours. The sense of isolation became acute and, in a way, existence seemed dreamlike, with thoughts lost in a maze of uncertainty. Finally, we reached the Aguja de Hielo, the Ice Needle. This steep slope of rock and ice leads to the upper west ridge, which overlooks the deep funnel of the crater. Mists embraced the crater as we circled upward around its rim to the highest point of the volcano.

Six hours after leaving the hut, we stood gazing eastward at the Gulf of Mexico, some seventy miles distant. We wondered if Lieutenant William Reynolds, an engineer in General Winfield Scott's army, had been fortunate enough to spot the gulf during the first ascent of Pico de Orizaba in 1848. To commemorate this historic climb—it was to be the highest North American summit reached in the nineteenth century—Reynolds and his companions planted a staff, complete with an American flag, on the rim of the crater.

By this time Mike was displaying classic symptoms of altitude sickness. With slurred speech he querulously complained about Reed's and my belaying skills. We humored him, knowing he was not in any real danger. And, sure enough, by the time we reached the hut again, Mike had regained his usual good cheer and was the first to embrace Limon, the faithful guard of our equipment.

Limon graciously invited us to stay in his house, and we were quick to accept. After we had consumed a delicious dinner, I glanced out the window and discovered that the abode of the serpent spirit was bathed in great billowing clouds.

Orizaba may be the loftiest of the Great Mexican volcanos, but it is certainly not the most famous. That honor belongs to the second-highest peak, 17,887-foot Popocatepetl. This symmetrical cone—and its companion peak, Ixtaccihuatl—can be seen easily from the capital on those few days a year when the smog vanishes.

According to Aztec legend, Ixtaccihuatl was a prosperous and beautiful young woman; her lover, Popocatepetl, was a famous and brilliant warrior. While the young man was far away during a war, a jealous rival spread false news of Popocatepetl's death in order to win the lady's heart. Ixtaccihuatl was so overcome by this news that she fell into a deathlike swoon. Popocatepetl returned from the war, carried his sleeping lover high up the mountain, and covered her with a white shroud. Ixtaccihuatl still sleeps today; her curvaceous profile is outlined by a mantle of snow. Beside her, patiently seated in expectation of her awakening, is Popocatepetl.

When the Spanish vanguard arrived in central Mexico in 1519, Popocatepetl was in eruption. Hernán Cortés sent Diego de Ordás, nine Spaniards, and several Indians to undertake the ascent of the huge volcano. Historians still do not agree about the degree of success of this party. In his letter to Charles I, King of Spain, Cortés related the details of this expedition:

Eight leagues from this city of Cholula there are two marvelously high mountains whose summits still at the end of August are covered with snow so that nothing can be seen on them. From the higher of the two both by day and by night a great volume of smoke comes forth and rises up into the clouds as straight as a staff, with such force that although a very violent wind continuously blows over the mountain range, yet it cannot change the direction of the column. Since I have ever been desirous of sending your Majesty a very particular account of everything that I met with in this land, I was eager to know the secret of this which seemed to me not a little marvelous, and accordingly I sent ten men such as were well fitted for the expedition with certain natives to guide them to find out the secret of the smoke, where and how it arose. These men set out and made every effort to climb to the summit but without success on account of the thickness of the snow, the repeated windstorms in which ashes from the volcano were blown in their faces, and also the great severity of the temperature, but they reached very near the top, so near in fact that being there when the smoke began to rush out, they reported it did so with such noise and violence that the whole mountain seemed like to fall down; thereupon they descended, bringing a quantity of snow and icicles for us to see, which seemed a novelty indeed, it being so hot everywhere in these parts. . . .

**Pico de Orizaba, the
third-highest mountain in
North America, is seen here
from near Tlachichuca Pueblo.
By Clyde H. Smith.**

During the time of this valiant effort, the volcano was spewing ashes so far that fields of corn sixty miles away were set aflame. It seems miraculous that none of the men were killed.

Three years later Cortés needed gunpowder and offered a reward for sulfur brought from the summit. A soldier named Francisco Montaño and four other men set out for the peak amid great acclaim: one version of the event mentions that thousands of sightseers were excited about this assault on the heights. Indian porters loaded ropes, bags, and blankets onto their backs, securing their burdens by means of tump lines across their foreheads. When night came, the party dug a cavity in the snow for shelter from the cold. As they moved about in an effort to keep warm, one of the Spaniards fell into a crevasse; luckily, he managed to catch himself on a huge icicle and climb back to his comrades.

Cortés wrote his king in May, 1522, telling of Montaño's troubles: "The Indians gave us to understand that it was a very evil place and that they would die if they ascended. . . . At the time of their ascent the smoke was being ejected with such a rumble that they neither dared nor could arrive at the mouth of the crater." But the men were determined to return with a supply of sulfur, for their reputation for bravery was at stake. With a rope tied around his waist, Montaño descended into the crater. As the oppressive fumes endangered his consciousness, he

must have wondered if the slender support would hold; if not, he would tumble into the hell-fire beneath. After gathering seven bags of the precious substance, Montaño was relieved by one of his companions. As a result of these efforts, a total of about 300 pounds of sulfur was obtained. This adventure, unique in the history of mountaineering, marks the first known mountain climb ever done in the Western Hemisphere.

Unable to resist climbing such a noteworthy peak, Reed, Mike, and I left Limon's house in Tlachichuca and sped west about 100 miles, eventually arriving at Tlamacas, a hotel and hut complex near the saddle separating Popocatepetl from Ixtaccihuatl. This beautiful locale, situated in a sparse forest at 12,800 feet, is the normal starting place for the ascent of Popo.

In the pre-dawn darkness we followed a path which wandered up the sandy cliffs below the glacier-clad upper peak. By dawn the wind was howling so fiercely that we considered turning back. But while we were putting on crampons at the highest hut, at 16,000 feet, the gale abated. Soon we were trudging up an easy snowslope which ended on the sloping crater rim. From here, in 1922, one party saw "a huge curling mass of smoke shooting skywards" from the seething and hissing crater. But we found the mountain warrior quiet, fanned coolly by the wind god.

CHAPTER SIX

Harney Peak

As might be imagined from the peculiarities of the surface, there can scarcely be a country where the scenery is more varied. From the top of some lofty peak the explorer gazes in wonder at the infinite variety at his feet. Great mountains, frowning crags, gloomy abysses, dense forests, and intricate jungles alternate with lovely parks, smooth lawns, and gentle slopes. Each portion of the Hills has its own especial peculiarities of scenery.

Richard Irving Dodge
The Black Hills, 1875

DENSE FORESTS of ponderosa pine so blanket an isolated group of mountains in the southwest corner of South Dakota that when seen from a distance, they appear to be black. The Sioux Indians, to whom these hills have always been sacred land, referred to the region as *Pa Saps*, or "black heads." Many years later, settlers bestowed the present name, the Black Hills. This relatively small cluster of hills, capped by 7,242-foot Harney Peak, has long been regarded by westward-bound travelers as the beginning of the mountainous West.

Upon close inspection it is not the pines which strike the eye so much as the rock formations. Delicate granite spires, mixed with massive blocks of stone, interrupt the skyline in every direction. The hiker who takes the time to explore the backcountry of the Black Hills might round a sheer rock pinnacle to find, only a few feet from its base, a lovely meadow cut by a sparkling brook. It is a land of contrasts.

It is hardly surprising that the Sioux thrived in this mountain fastness, with its abundance of game and water. Here, amid a mixed forest consisting mainly of pines, aspens, and birches, the Sioux established their camps. One especially straight-trunked tree, when felled and trimmed, served admirably as the center pole for a teepee; white men later gave a name to this species: lodgepole pine.

In spite of the mountainous terrain, where one might expect the winters to be particularly harsh, the Sioux were able to live comfortably all year in the Black Hills. Arctic air, pouring southward in the wintertime, fills the surrounding plains to an elevation of about 2,500 feet. But, in a classic example of temperature inversion, the Black Hills remain relatively warm.

The Sioux arrived in the Black Hills only after the mid-eighteenth century, and then via a most circuitous route. Crossing the Bering Land Bridge some 40,000 years ago, early men moved southeast, stalking the huge grass-eaters that preceded them: bison, musk oxen, moose, and mammoths. But, over a period of thousands of years, increasing aridity doomed many of these animals. Some of the native peoples who had arrived in eastern North America then began migrating slowly westward, pursuing smaller game and engaging in agriculture. This migration, hastened by the influx of settlers in the East and conflict with the powerful Algonquins, led one branch of the Sioux tribe into the Black Hills, where they successfully ousted the Cheyenne, a less warlike tribe.

The Sioux did not long enjoy their mountain paradise. With the westward expansion of white settlers came the threat of territorial conflict. The proud Sioux proved to be the most resolute of all the Great

Above: The jagged forms of the Cathedral Spires, near Harney Peak in the Black Hills. By Craig Blacklock.

Facing page: Bison mother nursing calf at Custer State Park, South Dakota. By Janet Ann Fries.

Plains tribes in their resistance to incursions on their land. Alternating hostilities and agreements between the Sioux and the United States government led to the signing, in 1851, of a pact between them: the Treaty of Fort Laramie. Sadly, this agreement was extremely short-lived.

The Sioux Wars, which were to last more than twenty years until the final pathetic battle at Wounded Knee, were triggered by the massacre of a thirty-man military party in August, 1854. The following spring General William S. Harney led a large punitive expedition to avenge this act. This was the first stage of what was to become a virtual military occupation of Indian territory. The destruction of the Sioux Nation was inevitable.

Accompanying Harney in 1855 was an army engineer named Gouverneur Kemble Warren, who carefully surveyed the expedition's route. Two years later Warren was ordered to take a survey party into the Black Hills. As it was a scientific expedition, this group was not prepared for a skirmish with the Indians, so at the first sign of trouble they retreated. The army's response was predictable. A force under Captain William Raynolds entered the Black Hills in July, 1859 with a dual purpose: to learn the strength of the indigenous tribes and to ascertain the mineral wealth of the region. However, this expedition returned with little new knowledge of the Black Hills.

Lieutenant Warren went on to create several excellent maps of the Dakotas and the surrounding territory. His overall map of the West, completed in the late 1850s, marked the culmination of decades of effort to chart the general outlines of western topography. The official reports issued by government surveys form a marvelous encyclopedia of the early western experience. Some of these reports were lavishly illustrated. Certain artists, perhaps overwhelmed by the variety of the landscape, exaggerated wildly; others, most notably F. W. von Egloffstein and John Mix Stanley, faithfully depicted the scene. In one of Stanley's most evocative illustrations, a vast herd of bison stretches for miles across a gentle Dakotan landscape; this drawing gives a striking sense of the scale of the frontier.

It is fortunate that Stanley portrayed such a remarkable scene for posterity, for the person who visits the Great Plains today will see no such spectacle. The bison, incorrectly called buffalo by the early settlers, once roamed as far east as New York and as far south as Mexico. Half a millenium ago, up to 60 million of the beasts ranged the prairies and forests of North America. By the end of the Sioux Wars, barely 1,000 animals survived. Bison were often slaughtered for their valuable hides, but an even more rep-

rehensible reason for the animal's demise was the army's policy of exterminating the beasts in order to deprive the Indians of their food supply. Like the decimation of the Indians themselves, the virtual extirpation of the bison remains a blot upon the nation's conscience.

The Sioux, naturally incensed by the slaughter of the bison, were further aggravated by the encroachment of white settlers. A focus of their resentment was the government's attempt to construct a wagon trail through the Bighorn Mountains, some 175 miles west of the Black Hills. This track, known as the Bozeman Trail, was to cut across the tribe's

favorite hunting grounds. One tragic result of this controversy took place near Wyoming's Fort Phil Kearney in 1866. In an incident known as the Fetterman Massacre, all eighty-one members of an army supply troop were slain by a band of Sioux led by Crazy Horse. Another Fort Laramie treaty, this one signed in 1868, proved as tenuous as the first. Continual skirmishes along the Bozeman Trail finally convinced the government to abandon the trail and guarantee the Indians possession of all of South Dakota west of the Missouri River.

The Sioux remained relatively peaceful for the next few years, but trouble was soon again brewing. In 1874 the army sent Lieutenant Colonel George Armstrong Custer into the Black Hills to establish a military post. This expedition, composed of more than 1,000 men, was one of the largest ever launched on the frontier in peacetime. Five newspapers sent correspondents to cover the story, and geologists, zoologists, and botanists went along to study the

environment. The Indians correctly felt the expedition's true purpose was to obtain information of military importance.

Rumors that gold was to be found in the Black Hills had persisted for some time. This supposition was proved accurate when Custer's expedition discovered the precious metal near what is present-day Custer, a town on the southern fringe of the mountains. The United States in the 1870s was ripe for another major gold rush—everyone knew of the riches that had been found so recently in California. Not surprisingly, then, the promotional outpourings of the press fell upon receptive ears. *Harper's Weekly* ran an illustrated story and urged the government to purchase the Black Hills from the Indians. By 1876 some 4,000 fortune hunters roamed the mountains, and the town of Custer flourished. It is estimated that miners extracted at least $3 million worth of gold from the gulches surrounding Deadwood, a town a few miles north of Custer.

In theory, the Black Hills were part of the Sioux Reservation, but the gold-struck miners paid scant attention to this fact. Federal troops made some effort to enforce the treaties and keep prospectors out, but their strength—and perhaps their will—to control the situation was inadequate. Hostilities escalated and, following various massacres, the miners formed a militia and offered rewards to anyone bringing in an Indian's head.

By 1876 Custer had earned a reputation as the army's most famous Indian fighter and was chosen to put an end to the depredations of the Sioux. The overconfident commander, however, greatly underestimated the tenacity of his opponents. In late June, Custer and his entire contingent of more than 200 soldiers were killed at the Battle of the Little Bighorn.

Later in 1876 the army managed to divert Crazy Horse and his band from their sanctuary in the Black Hills. They were compelled to accept a treaty that gave the mountain stronghold to the white man, clearing the way for more towns and mining camps. Soon the Black Hills could no longer be called uncharted. By the end of the nineteenth century, with the Indians subdued and the gold fever long since abated, wondrous rock formations of the Black Hills were beginning to entice tourists.

The heart of these remarkable formations, those encircling Harney Peak, have been given the general name Needles. The myriad pinnacles owe their form and beauty to the weathering of a once-solid mass of granite. This weathering process began along sets of vertical fractures, eventually creating long, freestanding ribs of rock. Later fracturing of the pink, coarse-grained granite caused huge blocks to fall out, resulting in the formation of pinnacles.

The spires naturally attracted the region's first explorers. Professor Aris B. Donaldson, a writer who accompanied Custer's 1874 expedition, called the area "a landscape design of the Infinite Architect." Members of this expedition sought to reach the highest point, Harney Peak. Wandering through an intricate network of portals and cool, shadowy cliffs, the men clambered upward. Donaldson described one portion of the ascent in terms understandable to present-day rock climbers: ". . . wedging ourselves into the clefts, and pushing ourselves up after the fashion of chimney sweeps, clinging to projecting points and straddling over ridges."

The party scrambled past needle-shaped columns to the base of the final tower of bare granite. But the peak's highest point, only seventy-five feet above their location, proved inaccessible, and the group, including Custer, was forced to retreat. The true summit of Harney Peak was reached the following year by surveyors, who used long poles and ropes to surmount the final cliff.

Although many travelers of today admire Harney Peak and the Needles when driving along the scenic Needles Highway, this cluster of rocky spikes is of secondary interest. It is Mount Rushmore, the "Shrine of Democracy," which draws hundreds of thousands of visitors to the Black Hills each year. In 1925 Congress commissioned the well-known sculptor Gutzon Borglum to supervise the building of a monument at the Black Hills site. When completed in 1941, the project was regarded as one of the most artful engineering feats of all time. High on a granite cliff, the faces of four American presidents—Washington, Jefferson, Theodore Roosevelt, and Lincoln—gaze outward toward the prairie.

While most visitors to the Black Hills cluster around the base of Mount Rushmore, another group, far smaller in number, infiltrates the granite labyrinth of the Needles to pursue a more esoteric activity. Lured by hundreds of airy summits, the rock climber can choose ascents of every difficulty.

Although the first technical climbs in the Needles were made in the mid-1930s—by noted mountaineer Fritz Wiessner—it was not until the late 1940s that a determined assault was made on the pinnacles. A climbing couple named Herb and Jan Conn, having fled the maelstrom of life in Washington, D.C., moved to the town of Custer and opened a small leather shop. Soon they became enthralled with the idea of standing atop as many pinnacles as possible. The Conns were later to recall that in 1947 they felt "like two cats in an unattended fish market." During the next fifteen years they accomplished about 215 first ascents, some extraordinarily difficult for the era.

I first visited the Needles in 1952, making a few first ascents of formations the Conns had overlooked. Many years later I returned to see if the climbing was as enjoyable as I had remembered.

For our first climb, Paul Muehl and I chose a classic with the unfortunate name of Spire One. Originally named Praying Madonna by Wiessner, it was re-named by the Conns, who made the first ascent. (Only a few pinnacles bear numbers; most of the spires have been christened with far more imaginative names, such as Wicked Picket, Eyetooth, Gruesome Twosome, and Lightning Rod.)

Spire One consists of a 160-foot-high pile of neatly stacked blocks, each one smaller than the one it rests upon. The route is typical of most climbs in the Needles in that it involves face climbing up variously sized knobs of quartz and feldspar. What makes Spire One so interesting is the route's complexity. Paul and I spiraled up and around the entire shaft, arriving on the summit only after completing one and a quarter turns.

From the tiny summit of this superb climb I gazed across the dark, pine-covered ramparts of the Black Hills, attempting to decipher the intricacies of the Needles. It proved to be an impossible task. For all practical purposes the complex rock formations, interrupted on occasion by wooded glens, are endless. Surely they must contain former Indian hideouts that have never been seen again. Watching the continual flow of traffic along the Needles Highway, I could not help wondering if these hurried travelers truly appreciated the splendor of this storied locale.

Above: Climber rappelling from the Needle's Eye, Custer State Park. By Paul Muehl.

Facing page: An abandoned gold mining cabin at the edge of the wilderness area below Elk Horn Mountain and Harney Peak. By Craig Blacklock.

Pikes Peak

Arose hungry, dry, and extremely sore, from the inequality of the rocks, on which we had lain all night, but were amply compensated for toil by the sublimity of the prospects below. . . . Commenced our march up the mountain, and in about one hour arrived at the summit of this chain: here we found the snow middle deep; no sign of beast or bird inhabiting the region. The thermometer which stood at 9° above 0 at the foot of the mountain, here fell to 4° below 0 [22° Fahrenheit]. The summit of Grand Peak, which was entirely bare of vegetation and covered with snow, now appeared at the distance of 15 or 16 miles from us, and as high again as what we had ascended, and would have taken a whole day's march to have arrived at its base, when I believe no human being could have ascended to its pinnacle.

Lieutenant Zebulon Montgomery Pike
An Account of Expeditions to the Sources of the Mississippi, and Through the Western Parts of Louisiana, 1806

THE Colorado Rockies consist of numerous separate ranges, a fact not noticeable to a person approaching from the eastern plains. The Front Range, west of Denver, and the Pikes Peak massif, one of its components lying west of Colorado Springs, rise out of the prairie in such a dominant fashion that they seem to be part of a cohesive edifice of nature. Yet this impression of simplicity is illusive, for behind this well-known façade lies one of the most complex mountainous regions in the United States.

The Colorado Rockies are formed of a series of sloping uplifts, in most of which Precambrian rocks are exposed in the cores. Younger formations steeply abut these uplifts; prominent examples of these "tilted-on-end" formations are the Boulder Flatirons and the Garden of the Gods.

The earliest rocks, the deep core of schist and gneiss, were formed in Precambrian time. Then a billion years of erosion took place, wearing down the ancient mountains. Shallow seas entered the area, and the ocean floor became a repository for the thick layers of sand and mud that were later to become sandstone and shale. For a great span of time the Rockies lay barren under waters that rose and fell with the pulse of the sun and moon. About 700 million years ago another generation of mountains heaved upward to push the seas aside. Eventually, great blocks formed ridges and valleys of a barren, lifeless land—the ancestral Rockies of some 325 million years ago. Erosion again stripped the sediments from the mountains; the sea again covered the land.

During Triassic time, North America was the home of the earliest dinosaurs, and the reptile *Ichthyosaurus* was thriving in the seas covering what are now the western states. Mammals appeared. The Front Range was first folded about 200 million years ago—about the same time as the Appalachian folding ended. During Cretaceous time, the culmination of dinosaur evolution, a mediterranean sea connected the Gulf of Mexico with the Arctic Ocean, covering all the Rockies now in Colorado and New Mexico.

By the end of Cretaceous time, some 65 million years ago, the Laramide Orogeny had begun, and crustal movements had expelled the sea from the area of the Rockies for the final time. The central

Above: **Lodgepole pines growing in Pikes Peak granite in the Lost Creek Wilderness Area of the Front Range. By David Sumner.**

Facing page: **Mountain lion crossing a stream in the southern Colorado Rockies. By Ron Willocks.**

Page 72: **Pikes Peak from the Garden of the Gods after a fresh snowfall. By David Muench.**

part of the great basin extending to Alaska was gradually being folded into high mountains. Great forces, developing in the crust of the earth, began to move huge masses of the continent. As the land rose for millions of years, it did so unevenly, leading to the creation of great river valleys.

The Rockies of today began with the Laramide Revolution; the folding and faulting lasted until about 40 million years ago. This dramatic episode was followed by lesser uplifts and broad arching of mountains in Miocene time. The Colorado plateau to the west yielded finally to the strain and broke into a mosaic of blocks. In Pliocene time another uplift occurred; a warp lifted the Rockies and Great Plains 5,000 feet to their present heights. At this time the elevated Miocene surfaces were trenched by streams. High peaks became surrounded by gently sloping plains that later were deeply cut by glacial ice into their present shapes.

The science of geology was in its infancy when the first white men laid eyes on Pikes Peak. Early American explorers were naturally more interested in the general lay of the land than in the age of the rocks. So it was with great interest that Lieutenant Zebulon Montgomery Pike, traveling up the Arkansas River in November, 1806, caught a glimpse of a high peak far to the west—a peak "which appeared like a small blue cloud." The peak was of special interest to Pike, for it was the first significant one he had seen since he left St. Louis with orders to chart a possible invasion route into the western territories held by the Spanish.

From what is now the city of Pueblo, Colorado, Pike measured the towering peak, concluding that it was 18,581 feet high. So confident was he of this figure that he did not even bother to round it off. "The peak," Pike wrote later, "was so remarkable as to be known to all the savage nations for hundreds of miles around, and to be spoken of with admiration by the Spaniards of New Mexico." Because of the peak's prominence, Pike decided to attempt to reach its summit.

On November 26, Pike and three soldiers set out for the mountain, which they had named Grand Peak. Expecting to return that same day, the party left all provisions at base camp. Pike later described that day's effort: "We commenced ascending, found it very difficult, being obliged to climb up rocks, sometimes almost perpendicular; and after marching all day, we encamped in a cave, without blankets, victuals, or water. . . ." Like others unfamiliar with mountainous terrain, Pike had underestimated the task of climbing a large, complex mountain.

On the following day the four adventurers finally reached the summit of a minor peak to see, many miles distant, the huge hulk of Grand Peak. Realizing it would be impossible to reach it, the expedition returned to base camp. No one will ever know exactly which prominence Pike reached, but it was probably a peak of about 9,000 feet located east or southeast of Pikes Peak. In any case, to Zebulon Pike goes the honor of making the first serious attempt of a Rocky Mountain peak.

Pike and his troops spent the next several months wandering through or around many of the central Colorado mountain chains. He charted the courses of numerous rivers, and members of his party may have been the first white men to reach the source of the Colorado River. Winter is not the time to explore the Colorado mountains, and the men suffered intensely. One soldier complained that "it was more than human nature could bear, to march three days without sustenance, through snows three feet deep, and carry burdens only fit for horses."

Pike's expedition later entered Spanish territory, and he and several men were prisoners for a short time before being released at the boundary of the Louisiana Territory. Donald Jackson points out in *The Journals of Zebulon Montgomery Pike* that "the geopolitical aspects of the [1806-07] expedition take on a new meaning as we sense the atmosphere of confusion, self interest, and bad faith in which Spain and the United States approached the problems created by the Louisiana Purchase."

These border controversies continued for years. In 1820 Major Stephen H. Long, an army engineer, was among those ordered west by the War Department. Among other duties, Long hoped to discover a new pass through the Rockies that would allow easier access to the Pacific than the route followed by Lewis and Clark.

Long and his men approached the northern portion of the Front Range, finding there a huge peak dominating the prairie; it would later be named in Long's honor. However, the men soon realized that this peak could not be the one that Pike had made famous fourteen years earlier. Moving south, the expedition approached the correct peak. On July 13 a small party led by botanist Edwin James started for the summit. In his book *Guide to the Colorado Mountains*, Robert Ormes describes the ascent:

> Dr. James' companions were a soldier and a civilian employee of the Long Expedition. The climb was successful in spite of the fact that the climbers broke most modern mountaineering

A head frame, relic of gold-mining days on Cripple Creek. By David Muench.

rules: the soldier, instead of "going light," carried a gun (in case of hostile Indians); they carried no emergency rations; they left their warm clothes in camp; the party did not stay together—the civilian got tired and took a nap below timberline, causing Dr. James to lose time and patience hollering for him. But the worst thing they did was to fail to put out their fire the morning after they bivouacked on the ascent. When they came off the mountain they found their cached supplies burned and a good part of the forest with them. Colorado's first careless campers!

A few days after this historic ascent—the first high peak ever climbed in the United States—Major Long named the mountain "James Peak." But later explorers continued to refer to it as the one Pike had discovered, and eventually the current name was placed on the influential Frémont-Preuss maps of 1845 and 1848.

Much of the early attention paid to Pikes Peak centered on gold: the rush of 1858 brought hundreds of prairie schooners emblazoned with the well-known slogan, "Pikes Peak or Bust." This gold rush was fraught with much hardship, danger, and disappointment, but it brought handsome rewards to successful miners. On occasion, hoaxes were perpetrated: salted claims led people to invest in worthless stocks. Most of Colorado's gold was found north of Pikes Peak, in the region west of Denver, but in 1891 gold was discovered on the slopes of the peak by a cowboy who sold his claim cheaply and drank up his profit. The claim on Cripple Creek later yielded some $400 million.

In the late nineteenth century, a carriage road was built to the summit; it was soon followed by a cog railway. This, the world's highest standard-gauge line, attacks grades of up to twenty-five percent. The railway, in operation for over nine decades, is one of the state's best-known tourist attractions. Equally famous are the various races—automobile, ski, and foot—that annually wind up or down the great peak.

Adventurers who prefer a quieter and more natural way to reach the summit may choose from any of several trails which wind upward through the coniferous forest to the alpine zone. Most popular of these is the Barr Trail, which begins in Manitou Springs, a town nestled under the eastern flank of the peak. This twelve-mile trail involves an elevation gain of more than 7,500 feet, and one must be in top condition to enjoy it.

I was quite fit when I visited the Pikes Peak region, but I was also pressed for time. I decided, therefore, to hike part way up the peak, then join the road and hitchhike the remaining distance.

The hike proved to be as wonderful as the hitchhike was amusing. A man and wife in a spacious car stopped, apparently considering me respectable. But it was not long before the man became terrified of the downslope road exposure. His wife took the wheel and displayed a rather uncoordinated style of driving while simultaneously craning her neck to talk to me in the back seat. We all sighed with relief as she pulled into a turnout to look at the view. Her first words upon getting out of the car were, "My, look at all that uninhabited land!" Mine were: "I'd be very glad to drive for you." But she insisted on continuing, and soon we were weaving incompetently up the fog-enshrouded highway. At last, panicked, she pulled over onto the shoulder and announced her intention of turning back.

Luckily for me, another car had stopped on the same shoulder. Its passengers also had lost their nerve, but they eagerly accepted my offer to maneuver their car to the top. We were all extremely surprised to reach the summit in a mere 100 yards.

The summit of Pikes Peak, at 14,110 feet, is not a place of solitude and quiet. Several buildings mar the rocky landscape; inside the principal one I saw people wearing "I Made It—Pikes Peak" T-shirts, carrying bumper stickers announcing the same sentiment, having their pictures taken, and voraciously consuming coffee and doughnuts. A saleswoman informed me that blue china, made in England, sells very well.

My new motoring friends, anxious to keep me in sight (I had agreed to drive their car down the mountain), pointed out the plaque honoring Katherine Lee Bates. In 1893 this English professor was so inspired by Pikes Peak that she later composed "America the Beautiful." She was undoubtedly spiritually moved by the grand vista of the endless prairie to the east and the welter of summits on the other three sides of the mountain. If one can successfully ignore the commercialization of the summit, the view is no less inspiring today.

Longs Peak

As we were about to leave the summit Major Powell took off his hat and made a little talk. He said, in substance, that we had now accomplished an undertaking in the material or physical field which had hitherto been deemed impossible, but that there were mountains more formidable in other fields of effort which were before us. . . .

L. W. Keplinger
The Trail, June, 1919

I N LATE June, 1820, a scientific expedition led by Major Stephen Harriman Long approached the Rocky Mountains after a tedious westward journey across the Great Plains. Edwin James, the twenty-three-year-old botanist of the group, later described the first view of the enormous chain of mountains: "For some time we were unable to decide whether what we saw were mountains, or banks of cumulous clouds skirting the horizon, and glittering in the reflected rays of the sun. . . . We soon remarked a particular part of the range divided into three conic summits, each apparently of nearly equal altitude. This we concluded to be the point designated by Pike as the highest peak."

But, as noted in the preceding chapter, it was not Pikes Peak the group was looking at, but rather a slightly higher peak 100 miles farther north. James and three other men set out to climb the towering peak but misjudged the distance so completely that they never even reached its base. (The history of mountaineering is replete with such blunders: Pike had made the same error on his peak earlier, and John Frémont was to discover that the Wind River peak

named for him was much farther away than he had anticipated.)

Although French trappers had called the mountain *Les Deux Oreilles* ("the two ears"), Long showed it on his maps simply as "Highest Peak." An 1829 map, however, designated the mountain as "Long's Peak," and so it remained until 1921, when the apostrophe was officially dropped by the U.S. Board on Geographic Names.

The mountain now known as Longs Peak is one of the highest points of the Front Range, a thirty-mile-wide uplift extending nearly two hundred miles from Canon City, Colorado north to Wyoming. The western mountain flank slopes steeply away from the crest of the range, but the eastern slope is characterized by broad, dissected benches that descend in steps to the plains. From the eastern edge of the Front Range summits, a ramp surface cut into the bedrock descends fifteen or twenty miles. Such ramps were formed in Tertiary time when arid conditions existed.

The igneous and metamorphic rocks of the Front Range are an extension of the ancient basement rocks of the plains. This crystalline core is essentially Precambrian granite, schist, and gneiss. The core of the range is nearly everywhere bordered by steeply tilted, outward-dipping Paleozoic rocks. Perhaps the finest examples of this are the Boulder Flatirons, a spectacular series of hogbacks at the edge of the plains; these tilted pinnacles mark the upturn and emergence at the mountain front of Mesozoic strata that overlie ancient basement rocks.

Longs Peak itself owes its striking pyramidal shape to the glaciers that long ago carved an ordinary-looking mountain into a form distinguished by

Above: Sharpshinned hawk on nest with its prey, a yellow-rumped warbler, in Rocky Mountain National Park. By Ron Willocks.

Page 78: Golden fleabane and mule's ears in a meadow beneath the east face of Longs Peak, Rocky Mountain National Park. By David Sumner.

great rock walls and narrow ridges. The 14,255-foot peak totally overshadows its neighbors, only one of which even approaches the 14,000-foot level. In his book *Longs Peak: Its Story and a Climbing Guide,* Paul Nesbit describes the mountain's significance:

> While its location has helped to make it famous, that is by no means all. The peak itself has character. It is rugged and severe. It is flanked by distinctive cliffs on all sides instead of by gentle slopes up which roads may be built. Longs Peak dominates. It is a challenge to those with red blood. It is of good repute among skilled climbers. It is never twice alike. The lighting effects, the clouds which hover near it, the storms which play about it, the seasons, and the viewpoint are frequently changing. It is like having a continuous outdoor show for one's amusement; an art gallery for one's appreciation.

Because of its prominence and distinctive shape, Longs Peak was one of the first high peaks ever climbed in the Colorado Rockies. A serious attempt in 1864 by William Byers and a companion ended on the summit of nearby Mount Meeker; the two men considered the rugged terrain leading over to Longs Peak to be impossible. Byers, however, returned four years later and was a member of the first-ascent party. This 1868 climb was led by a figure soon to become nationally famous for his adventures in the Grand Canyon, John Wesley Powell.

Of all the various characters who explored the American West, Powell is one of the most important and intriguing. His contributions to the study of the vast region have been excellently chronicled by Wallace Stegner in *Beyond the Hundredth Meridian.* As a major in the Civil War, Powell had lost an arm, but this was not to deter him from a life of adventure.

By 1867 Powell was a professor of geology at a small Illinois university. Raising funds from his college and several others, Powell headed west on a scientific expedition. Much work was accomplished that summer, and one major peak was ascended: Pikes Peak. During the following winter Powell obtained the necessary financial backing to descend either the Green or the Grand (Colorado) rivers. But in 1868 Powell felt the need of yet another season to explore the plateau and canyon country of western Colorado before embarking upon his river explorations. Therefore, August, 1868, found Powell and his party encamped near present-day Berthoud Pass, collecting animals, plants, and geologic specimens.

Powell was keenly interested in the summit vista from Longs Peak, for he felt that from this high place he could trace the river systems that eventually led to the Colorado River. From Grand Lake the mounted party set out toward the peak; by afternoon they had reached timberline on a crested rock ridge at about 11,000 feet. An attempt on the peak the following day failed miserably, and the men set up a new camp in what is now Wild Basin.

On the evening of August 22, one of the men, L. W. Keplinger, made a daring solo dash for the summit, hoping to discover a passable route. He ascended the southern ramparts of the peak and passed through an erosional feature now called the Notch. He made his way to the upper rock slopes, overlooking the sheer east face. Here, however, he had second thoughts about continuing. He wrote later that "a lonesome feeling" had overcome him; he also considered it unfair to reach the top without the rest of his group. Down he went, but darkness soon overtook him. Guided by beacon fires Powell had built, Keplinger reached camp at ten o'clock.

August 23 was a beautiful day, and the party had little trouble following Keplinger's route. It was only ten in the morning when the seven men reached the flat summit rocks. Byers described the ascent for the *Rocky Mountain News:*

> Our course was over a great rockslide and then up a steep gorge, down which the broken stone had come. In many places it required the assistance of hands, as well as feet, to get along, and the ascent at best was very laborious. There was no extraordinary obstacle until within seven or eight hundred feet of the summit. Above that point the mountain presents the appearance, in every direction, of being a great block of granite, perfectly smooth and unbroken. Close examination, however, removed this delusion in some degree, and we were most agreeably surprised to find a passable way, though it required a great caution, coolness, and infinite labor to make headway; life often depending upon a grasp of the fingers in a crevice that would hardly admit them.

Someone in Powell's party had had the foresight to carry a bottle of wine for a celebration in case of victory, so this was broken out as the men constructed a summit cairn. One of the climbers, a solemn Quaker lad, later wrote to a friend that "2 of us withstanding all entreaties did not drink on Longs peak, whatever the papers may say to the contrary." After Powell made the speech quoted at the beginning of this chapter, the men departed for their base camp and further non-mountaineering adventures.

The Powell group had discovered one of the easiest ways up Longs Peak. But mountaineers are seldom content merely to attain a summit, and it was only a few years before other, more difficult, routes were made. One of the most remarkable of these early accomplishments was actually a descent, not an ascent. In 1871 the Reverend Elkanah J. Lamb climbed the peak, then decided to return via a prominent gully on the huge east face of Longs. This slot, up to fifty degrees in steepness, led down to Broadway, a ledge system that slices completely across the east face. Lamb somehow managed to work his way down the gully—now called the Notch Couloir—and across Broadway. Below here, however, he had to descend a steep snow tongue which dropped 800 feet onto the glacier reposing at the base of the wall. According to his account, Lamb barely escaped with his life on this section, later named Lamb's Slide.

Lamb had followed that path of least resistance down the great eastern escarpment, wisely choosing ledges and gullies instead of cliffs. In 1922, however, a Princeton mathematics professor named James Alexander decided to attempt to find a way up the cliffs to the north of Lamb's Slide. Although he was a rather inexperienced mountaineer, Alexander made a noteworthy solo ascent to the summit. One admirer wrote later that the professor had been "required to cut seventy-six steps in the ice and from then on completed his climb by clinging to the small projections of the rock in constant peril...."

After Alexander repeated the route several days later with park ranger Jack Moomaw, the latter wrote: "While climbing out of the Notch Chimney, the professor kept losing his hand-holds. I was just behind him on good footing, and braced myself but I did not try to boost him because I felt that it might hurt his pride...."

Although Alexander and Moomaw carried a rope on their climb, they did not use it, a remarkable feat considering that modern-day climbers not only use a rope but pitons as well on the route called Alexander's Chimney. One reason the two climbers didn't break out their rope was that they didn't know how to use it properly. American climbers of the era were not at all familiar with rope work and pitoncraft; only European alpinists understood these techniques.

It is not surprising, therefore, that the first truly technical route on the east face of Longs Peak was made by climbers trained in Europe. Two brothers, Joe and Paul Stettner, had emigrated from Germany in the mid-1920s, settling in Chicago. In the summer of 1927 the pair drove west on their motorcycles with a few pitons and carabiners, hoping to try a new route on the challenging face.

Spotting a system of cracks several hundred feet to the right of Alexander's Chimney, the brothers roped up and began working their way up the steep, complex wall. Partway up they arrived at an alcove at the base of an intimidating cliff; this proved to be the crux of the climb. Pounding pitons into a nearby crack, the leader managed to free climb the pitch now known as the Piton Ladder. (Many modern climbers, unable or unwilling to free climb this section, hang on to the pitons as an aid.) Stettners' Ledges, as the route was named, remained for two decades the most difficult climb done in Colorado. The Stettner brothers owed part of their success to their equipment, but they also had a rare combination of exploratory instinct and psychological readiness for risk-taking.

Mountaineers established many other routes on portions of the east face in the years after the Stettners' ascent, but all climbers carefully avoided the Diamond, the awesome central facet of the east face. This striking feature, named for its distinctive shape, rises 900 feet above Broadway in one sheer sweep. By the 1950s climbers finally felt ready for this challenge, but they were denied permission by the National Park Service on the grounds that the climb was too dangerous and that rangers should not have to risk their lives in a possible rescue. This prohibition, which lasted throughout the 1950s, reflected bureaucratic ignorance and arrogance; it is curious indeed that in the "land of the free" government agencies have sometimes decided what risks adventurers can take.

The government edict against "stunt and daring trick climbing"—a phrase which infuriated competent rock climbers—was finally lifted in the summer of 1960. The first climbers on the scene that summer were Dave Rearick and Bob Kamps, two Californians trained on the huge granite cliffs of Yosemite Valley. On August 1 the pair began climbing a continuous crack system that rose directly to the apex of the Diamond. After climbing a few rope lengths the pair became aware that water was beginning to drop onto them. "I looked up apprehensively," Rearick wrote later. "They came, not from the clouds which were already gathering over the peak again, but from a waterfall which was plunging free from our chimney far above. . . . This proved that some 400 feet of the route ahead would be slightly overhanging."

Because of threatening weather, the pair descended to Broadway, leaving their ropes fixed in place on the wall. Returning to their high point the following morning, the men continued upward to a sloping ledge located twenty feet *behind* the falling water. Above, the rock was poor and the wall over-

hanging. Scores of pitons were driven for direct aid, and by dark the two Californians had gained only a few hundred additional feet.

Rearick described the night's bivouac: "We put on all our clothes, ate some food, and tied in for the night. I sat in a cross-legged position all night, while Bob was able to recline partially. The night was clear and we watched the shadows from the moon creep stealthily along. . . . We both manged to doze for a few hours. Since the temperature stayed above freezing, the waterfall continued all night, occasionally splashing us."

On August 3, Rearick and Kamps climbed the last few hundred feet to the top, finding that their waterfall emanated from blocks of ice lodged in the chimneys. This 1960 route, later named D-1, was a serious undertaking, considering its altitude and the degree of commitment called for.

Other routes were soon established on the Diamond; there are presently fourteen. Most of these ascents involve a mixture of free and aid climbing and take climbers two days. Although much of the climbing is strenuous and difficult, perhaps equally intimidating to a climber is the unpredictable weather. Storms move in from the west so rapidly that the transition from sunny weather to a violent hailstorm takes only an hour or two, a rather depressing prospect to a climber perched on a small ledge high on the Diamond.

Climbers, of course, are not the only ones to feel the full force of these storms. Many hikers have been caught in a sudden summer lightning storm close to the summit. During the summer these squalls rarely linger, and the prudent hiker has little to worry about. But in the winter months storms can reach arctic severity. A climber named A. Lynn Richey ascended the peak on New Year's Day, 1929, and witnessed first hand a storm's fury:

The wind seemed to be rising, and looking over toward the west we could see that it would not be long before a gale would strike us. . . . On some of the boulders were little growths of snow that I can liken to nothing but some unnatural fungus or sponge formation. The most delicate whorls, blades, cavities and convulsions, all arrayed together. . . . These lovely creations are formed by the action of the wind.

Climbers work their way up the sheer golden granite of the Diamond, east face of Longs Peak. By Ed Cooper.

. . . The gale struck us soon after we left the bottom of the lower cable. The first puff came with the voice of a thousand demons, and ready for it though we were, with our bodies flat against the rock, faces down and anchored fast with our hands and feet in the crevices, it nearly tore us from the cliff. The crystallized snow sifted through the tiniest seam in our clothes, down our necks, up our sleeves, and lashed our faces with the sting of a whip.

The cable that Richey mentions once formed part of a hiking trail and climbing route up the northern flank of Longs Peak. Constructed in 1925 by the National Park Service, this trail had steel cables to aid hikers up a 200-foot section of steep slabs. The Cable Route proved to be a far more direct way of reaching the summit than the 1868 first-ascent route or its variation, the Keyhole Route. Thus, by the 1960s, some 100 persons scrambled up the Cable Route on each summer day. The cables were dismantled in 1973 in order to restore the mountain to its pristine condition. The Keyhole Route, used by most of the pre-1925 hikers, has once again become the standard route.

My only experience with Longs Peak began on a mid-October day not long ago when Mark Losleben and I pitched camp among the whitebark pines at 11,400 feet. The next morning we climbed the old Cable Route, finding some of the cracks filled with ice from early autumn storms. We reached the four-acre summit around noon after a pleasant climb. A cool, brisk wind and high stratus to the west heralded the onset of wintry weather.

On the descent, it was interesting to see the Keyhole Route in reverse. Numerous hikers were clambering up the Home Stretch, the smooth, sloping rock of the upper portion. We traversed the narrow ledge appropriately called the Narrows, where both the exposure and iced rock has led to fatal falls. Below here, the long gully known as the Trough led down to the traverse across to the Keyhole. It was evident that this route can prove treacherous at times, but we both felt that the removal of the cables was justifiable. This challenging mountain should be kept in its natural state as much as possible.

Maroon Bells

The gorges or cañons cut by Castle and Maroon Creeks and their branches, are probably without a parallel for ruggedness, depth, and picturesque beauty in any portion of the West. The great variety and color of the rocks, the remarkable and unique forms of the peaks, and the extreme ruggedness, all conspire to impress the beholder with wonder.

Ferdinand V. Hayden
Annual Report of the U.S. Geological and Geographical Survey of the Territories, 1874

THE Elk Mountains of west-central Colorado form one of the most spectacular uplifts in the state. The principal peaks of this high spur of the Sawatch Range are Maroon, Capitol, Castle, and Snowmass; the most striking of all these 14,000-foot peaks is Maroon Peak, a towering, double-summited formation popularly known as the Maroon Bells.

Although a few of the peaks of the Elk Mountains are granitic—Capitol Peak and Snowmass Mountain, for example—the Maroon Bells are composed of a reddish sedimentary rock dating back to the Carboniferous Period, some 300 million years ago. Ledges of this rock slant across entire faces of the Maroon Bells at an angle of fifteen degrees, giving the mountain a distinctive and pleasing shape.

The Ute Indians probably passed close by the Maroon Bells, for it lay only a few miles away from their trade route linking the Arkansas and Gunnison rivers. Lieutenant John C. Frémont was the first white man known to have skirted the Sawatch Range. In 1845 he descended the Eagle River—only a few dozen miles from the range—following his crossing of the Continental Divide. Other military expeditions visited the environs of the range in the ensuing years, and a few hardy prospectors penetrated into the high valleys. But it was the government's survey groups who, between 1867 and 1879, were the first to chart the range with precision and climb some of the major summits.

Two of the four major survey groups of this era were conducted under the auspices of the War Department and were led, respectively, by Clarence King and Captain George M. Wheeler. The other two surveys, undertaken by the Department of the Interior, were organized and led, respectively, by Ferdinand V. Hayden and John Wesley Powell. The voluminous reports issued by these four surveys laid the basis for knowledge of the geology, topography, and natural history of the West. But since these reports (with the exception of Powell's) were dry and technical, and their distribution limited, many of the surveyors' achievements were little known to the American public. Nevertheless, the maps produced after vast labors helped emigrants settle, and the Hayden Survey of 1871 specifically led to the creation of Yellowstone National Park.

Wheeler explored and mapped the mountainous regions of Colorado in 1873, climbing some three dozen peaks as part of his survey. Forty-one volumes of scientific findings resulted from this important survey. It was the Hayden surveys, however, which were responsible for charting the remote Elk Mountains.

The overall Hayden Survey was broken into divisions and these were dispersed to various regions. Usually there were six or more groups; a quar-

The Maroon Bells reflected in Maroon Lake, Elk Mountains, Colorado. By Ed Cooper.

termaster party made rounds through the Rockies to supply the field groups. Each of these field parties contained a topographer, his assistant, a geologist, a cook, several packers, and occasionally a botanist or a zoologist. Hayden, a superb organizer, was fortunate in obtaining some of the finest topographers of the era, including Henry Gannett, James Gardner, Allen D. Wilson, and William Henry Holmes.

A typical day in the Elk Mountains involved at least twelve hours of strenuous labor. The party would select a prominent peak, then figure out a way to reach its summit. Sometimes this proved impossible. The Maroon Bells, for instance, were considered an excellent place for triangulation, but the men had to be satisfied with a lower point, for the summit appeared inaccessible. Castle Peak, at 14,265 feet, was the region's highest summit, but the surveyors were disappointed after their long climb. "We reached the top of the mountain," Gannett recalled many years later, "just in time to be enveloped in a storm, and the few glimpses of the surrounding country which we obtained through gaps in the clouds were very unsatisfactory."

When everything went well, as it did on the August, 1873 ascent of Snowmass Mountain, the men obtained an enormous amount of information in a matter of hours. On the summit the men set up a theodolite and a mercury barometer. The topographer made a careful drainage sketch while his assistant worked on a profile of the land. Uncompromising honesty in interpreting the contours of the land and its portrayal on paper was essential, and the expert in this type of drawing proved to be Holmes, whose magnificent sketches have become artistic classics.

The ascents of the 14,000-foot peaks of the Elk Mountains were not easy, but the men seemed to enjoy their work nevertheless. William Henry Rideing, an English writer who tagged along on the climb of Snowmass Mountain, later contributed an article to a book called *Picturesque America.* In it he describes the rugged terrain of Snowmass and a moment of levity:

In the distance we have seen two mountains which are temporarily called Snow Mass and Black Pyramid. The first of these we are now ascending. It is a terribly hard road to travel. The slopes consist of masses of immense granite fragments, the rock-bed from which they came appearing only occasionally. When we reach the crest, we find it also broken and cleft in masses and pillars. Professor [William Dwight] Whitney ingeniously reckons that an indus-

trious man, with a crow-bar, could, by a week's industrious exertion, reduce the height of the mountain one or two hundred feet. Some of the members of the expedition amuse themselves by the experiment, toppling over great fragments, which thunder down the slopes and furrow the wide snow-fields below.

Prospectors arrived after the departure of the survey groups, and soon men were systematically combing the mountain slopes of western Colorado in search in mineral wealth. In the summer of 1879 silver and lead deposits were discovered in the region immediately northeast of the Maroon Bells. It is probable that these first prospectors—men who had been mining around the town of Leadville—had observed on the newly created geological maps that the Paleozoic rocks which contain silver nearly encircle the Sawatch uplift.

The chief mining camp in this new location was called Ute City because it was Indian land on which prospectors trespassed. Lured by dreams of riches, many men arrived in the area and established claims. In February, 1880, a man named B. Clark Wheeler arrived in Ute City after a seventeen-day snowshoe trek from Leadville. He surveyed the mining camp and changed its name to Aspen because of the extensive groves of quaking aspen that blanketed the mountain slopes.

The initial drawback to the development of Aspen was its inaccessibility; the nearest railroad lay some forty miles away, across rugged terrain. The first ores were transported from Aspen to Leadville on the backs of burros. Such primitive means of transportation did not last too long, for the railroad was extended to Aspen in 1887. But six years later Aspen was dealt a great blow when the federal government repealed the silver purchase acts, which had given miners such impetus to seek out the precious metal. The mining camps were ruined and the district's economy collapsed.

Following World War II, however, Aspen again became a boom town; snow replaced silver as the region's most valuable resource, and Aspen is presently among the world's best-known ski areas.

As mentioned, members of the Hayden Survey did not reach the top of the Maroon Bells; its summit, Gannett wrote, was "nearly, if not quite, inaccessible." No one knows exactly who was the first person to stand atop the peak, but there is evidence to suggest that the first ascent could have been as early as the 1880s or 1890s. The first recorded ascent, however, was made by Colorado mountaineer Percy Hagerman in 1908. Climbing alone, the thirty-nine-

year-old businessman worked his way up the steep rock of the mountain's southwest flank. Although Hagerman's route was not technically difficult, the sedimentary rock proved loose and crumbly, and his ascent was far from routine.

Other mountaineers established routes on the peak in the decades following Hagerman's climb. The now-standard route ascends the Buckskin Pass Trail to the rock-filled gulch that trends east under the mountain's north face. After reaching the top of North Maroon—the massif's northerly subsummit—the climber must drop several hundred feet into the notch separating the two summits. From here a jagged but relatively easy ridge leads upward to the top of the 14,156-foot mass.

Four routes have been accomplished on the peak's steep east face. When Jim Goodwin and I made the first ascent of this face in 1943, during our Mountain Troop days, we enjoyed a sense of freedom that I have rarely felt since. The strata proved excellent for handholds and footholds, and we progressed rapidly, unencumbered by equipment. Perhaps we were inspired by the exquisite flowering meadows on the approach; perhaps it was our good condition; but somehow we managed to climb a direct line to the summit with as few detours as possible, a feat I later thought should have frightened me more than it did at the time.

On this climb, as I gazed across the wide expanse of loose rock and steep snow, I reflected that the combination of difficult routefinding, loose rock, and icy couloirs could prove dangerous to inexperienced or tired climbers. Even on the standard route, finding the best way up can prove so tricky that climbers can easily stray onto more difficult rock. In addition, mountaineers often find themselves high on the peak very late in the day, having misjudged the bulk and high altitude of the complex massif. It is not surprising, then, that climbers have occasionally come to grief while ascending the Maroon Bells. So many deaths have occurred, in fact, that the mountain has acquired a grim nickname—the "Deadly Bells." At least eleven persons have been killed on the Maroon Bells since 1965; seven died as a result of falls down icy slopes; the others either slipped on steep rock or were struck by rocks knocked off by higher climbers.

I returned to the Maroon Bells area nearly forty years after my climb of the east face. The city of Aspen, a sleepy village when I had first visited it, hummed with activity. West of town, however, the terrain remained as beautiful as I had remembered. I drove toward the base of the Bells through fine stands of the tree from which the town is named. Indians had called the aspen "noisy leaf" because its long stems hold the nearly round leaves so lightly that they catch the slightest zephyrs. At the end of the road, as I stared upward once again at the towering Maroon Bells, the leaves on the trees around me trembled, shimmering like sunlit gold coins.

Since I had already climbed the Maroon Bells, I decided on this trip to try for Capitol Peak, a nearby mountain with an excellent reputation. This 14,130-foot mass is the hardest of the Elk Mountains to reach and to climb; knife-edged ridges block easy access to the summit. Colorado mountaineer Carl

Above: Two young great horned owls, just learning how to fly, perch on a fallen log in a field of blooming arrowleaf balsam-root in Colorado's Roaring Fork Valley. By Richard W. Clark.

Facing page: Engelmann spruce ring a beaver pond in the Elk Mountains. Crested Butte is seen in the background; Gothic Mountain rises on the right. By David Sumner.

Blaurock described the peak in a 1926 issue of *Trail and Timberline:* "No matter from what side one approaches, he sees a gigantic hulk towering with vertical walls over deep chasms, confined by narrow 'saw-toothed' ridges, radiating out from the central mass in all the cardinal directions. An experienced mountaineer realizes at once that here stands a challenge to his prowess and craftsmanship."

Phil Eastley and I left Aspen early one morning and tramped up the long trail leading south up Capitol Creek. Choosing the standard route up the northeast arête, we found ourselves, in the early afternoon, on the famous knife-edged summit ridge. A storm was brewing and several parties ahead of us turned back because of the danger from lightning. Our hair tingled from the effects of the static electricity, and the skies looked black to the west. Nevertheless, we decided to continue for a while longer. Fortunately, the nucleus of the storm passed us by, and we scrambled up the ridge toward the top.

We found it unnecessary to progress on our hands and knees as the first-ascent party did. The ridge was definitely exposed, but a climber accustomed to this can virtually walk across the tilted edge, occasionally using the hands for balance.

The register book on the summit of Capitol showed nearly 200 entries during the preceding six weeks, a testimony to the peak's popularity. Taking a final look at the massive Maroon Bells, only a few miles away, we began descending the ridge; it was a long way back and much of the hike would be in the dark.

Above: **Members of the Colorado Outward Bound School descend the Knife Edge on Capitol Peak. By David Hiser.**

Mount Sneffels

*Mt. Snaefell is admirably placed for a view-point.
. . . To the east, the Uncompahgre group, with its
marvelous castellated ridges, the main peak
overtopping all,—a grand pyramid in form. . . .
Yet we needed not look far to see the most
beautiful sights. Near to our station were peaks
unscaled and unnamed,—peaks with towers,
and peaks with spires; mountains with graceful
and beautiful forms. Down at our feet, on the
north side of the peak, were several large lakelets,
and we could see the upper edges of the great
snowfield on the north side of Snaefell. . . .*

Frederick H. Chapin
Appalachia, December, 1880

THE San Juan Mountains occupy an area in the southwestern corner of Colorado more than one hundred miles from east to west and seventy miles from north to south. The San Juans, which are not a mountain range in the sense of being a continuous chain of peaks but are rather an aggregation of many clusters of peaks, are separated from the main body of the Rocky Mountains by plateaus and broad valleys. The largest mountain group in Colorado, the San Juans include thirteen summits with elevations above 14,000 feet. The highest is 14,309-foot Uncompahgre Peak, a pyramid truncated by a wide, triangular summit flat, but the showpiece of the San Juans is a 14,150-foot peak of classic alpine form named Mount Sneffels.

Uncompahgre, Sneffels, and most of the peaks lie west of the Continental Divide, their slopes drained by three large tributaries of the Colorado River: the Gunnison, Dolores, and San Juan rivers.

However, the Divide, which crosses most of Colorado at a longitude well to the east, bends sharply west in a horseshoe outline to accommodate the eastward-flowing Rio Grande, which has its headwaters near the heart of the San Juans.

The San Juans have been one of the great metal-producing areas of the nation ever since the 1870s, when the original inhabitants, the Ute Indians, were pushed west in stages and finally forced, in 1881, into the Uinta Basin in Utah. One of the main towns of the San Juans, Ouray, is named for the Ute's chief during this involuntary migration (it was originally called Uncompahgre City). The names of other towns—for example, Silverton and Telluride—are legacies of the first white settlers and their quest for the ores of silver and gold, as well as less valuable metals.

I passed through Ouray on my way to Sneffels on a Fourth of July weekend, and the steep streets, instead of being occupied by miners, were filled with beer drinkers, motorcycles, and throngs of tourists. More impressed by the colorful cliffs that soar above the narrow valley than by the snarled traffic and wailing police sirens, I continued up the road to Camp Bird Mine. This road—one of the Colorado's most spectacular, in places cut into overhanging limestone and poised above a precipitous drop to the stream below—was once a toll road to the mines above. Another toll road was built over 11,000-foot Red Mountain Pass from Ouray to Silverton, which was served by a narrow-gauge branch of the Denver and Rio Grande Railroad. The completion of the railroad in 1882 brought about an increase in mining activity in the area; during its first six months of operation, more than 6,000 tons of ore were shipped

from Silverton. About 700 miles of narrow-gauge track, with the steepest grades and sharpest curves in the United States, eventually circled and crossed the San Juans.

The Camp Bird Mine made Tom Walsh $5 million. Walsh acquired silver claims in 1895 for $20,000 but soon discovered gold in the ore. Rock was lowered from the mine—which was named for a Canada jay, a bird known colloquially as the camp robber, that helped himself to a miner's lunch—by a tramway to a mill, where the ore was pulverized.

In the San Juan region are more than 4,000 patented claims. Hillsides throughout the mountains are scarred by old shafts and mine roads. I continued driving, past the ghost town of Sneffels, the Revenue Mill, and relics of the Virginius and Mountain Top mines in a high basin to the southwest. Between 1881 and 1919, ore worth $27 million was extracted here; now mine shafts, yellow tailings, and decrepit buildings are everywhere, some in sight, some hidden by fir, spruce, and aspen. In the arid American West, the marks left by man are slow to disappear.

I parked in Yankee Boy Basin and began hiking along a jeep road. Evidence of prospecting pockmarked, it seemed, every square foot of hillside, in some places even above 12,000 feet. On Wilson Peak, in a western outlier of the San Juans known as the San Miguel Mountains, tunnels of the Silver Pick Mine extend as high as 13,200 feet. A tramway was built to bring ore—mostly gold, despite the mine's name—to a mill, from which mules carried the crushed ore to the valley. It is staggering to contemplate the hardships and risks of these early mining operations. More accidents have been related to mining in the San Juans than to mountaineering.

Hiking gave me the chance to observe the columbine, lupine, hellebore, and arnica growing on the hillside—and to note the vehicle tracks cut deeply in the grassy slopes. Alpine vegetation is easily damaged and recovers slowly, and water channeled into the tracks accelerates erosion. In a cold, high-altitude environment, soil is thin and, since decay is slow, also nitrogen-poor. For soil to develop again and new growth to occur may take thousands of years.

Right: **An easterly spur of Uncompahgre Peak seen from about 13,500 feet on the main peak. By David Sumner.**

Facing page: **Mount Sneffels and a picturesque rail fence, from the Dallas Divide, San Juan Mountains. By David Sumner.**

Finding a campsite behind a thicket of dwarfed fir trees, I sat back, relaxed, and admired the glow of the setting sun in the boulder-filled basin of Mount Sneffels. My own private meadow boasted cinquefoil, arctic sandwort, and miniature fleabane. Many plants that are tolerant of cold have migrated south from the Arctic along the mountain ranges of North America as far as the southern Rocky Mountains. Fewer arctic plants have migrated this far south in Europe or Asia, where most mountain ranges extend east and west.

Morning dawned clear and windy. I trod lightly across the lush but delicate meadows, my attention drawn successively to alpine sunflower, rosecrown, saxifrage, arctic gentian, marsh marigold, and alpine buttercup. Alpine phlox hugged the ground in a cluster of small white flowers and a compact leaf structure that acts as insulation against the cold air. Beyond an incongruous mining cabin at a small lake, I left the flowery meadows for a slope of boulders and a long gully filled with loose rock on the south flank of Sneffels. I wanted the feel of scrambling on rock, so I headed left to a shattered crag. At 13,800 feet I was surprised to see a tiny cinquefoil hidden in a rock crevice, but even higher, only twenty feet from the summit, I found a gentian growing in a rocky niche. The upper crags of the mountain were also adorned with a crust of black, orange, and yellow lichen.

Above: **A least chipmunk in the Weminuche Wilderness Area of the San Juan Mountains. By David Sumner.**

Facing page: **Columbine, paintbrush, and other wildflowers cover a meadow in Yankee Boy Basin, near Mount Sneffels. By David Muench.**

Lichen accelerates the process of erosion by secreting a substance that chemically decomposes the rock.

Sneffels was first climbed in 1874 by a pair of surveyors, Franklin Rhoda and Frederic Endlich, accompanied by a packer named Ford. Both the Wheeler and Hayden surveys explored Colorado during the 1870s. Ferdinand V. Hayden was such a zealous geologist that Indians called him "He-who-picks-up-stones-while-running." Because the surveys competed with each other to an extent, each largely ignored the massive sets of special monographs published by the other, and much duplication of work occurred.

Rhoda, Endlich, and Ford, of the Hayden Survey, approached Sneffels from the west, though they saw no feasible route and anticipated the most difficult climb of their season. It was during this approach that the mountain received its name. Jules Verne's *Journey to the Center of the Earth* mentions a giant hole below a certain Icelandic mountain named Snaefell. Endlich was reminded of this hole by an abyss and, pointing to the peak above, declared, "There's Snaefell." Mispronunciation by miners resulted in the peak's present less-elegant name. The trio climbed the southwest ridge, which Rhoda described as being "notched like a comb." They scrambled up the teeth, down into the gaps between, then "hand over hand up the steep bluff beyond." They built a five-foot-high stone monument on the summit that could be used in their survey work for sighting from other summits.

I could tell by the view from Sneffels' summit that it would have made a useful survey station. Uncompahgre poked into the sky, and farther to the northeast was the dim skyline of the Elk Mountains. To the south was the snow-plastered Grenadier group, beyond which was another San Juan subrange, the Needle Mountains.

The summit of Sneffels is also a good place for observing geologic features of the San Juans. The Needles are ancient granite, while the Grenadiers are sedimentary rock: quartzite and conglomerate. The San Miguels are volcanic rock overlying sedimentary rock. I was standing on volcanic rock.

Although the geology of the San Juans appears complex, the geologic history is in most respects typical of a Rocky Mountain range. Granite formed from molten rock more than a billion years ago. By 500 million years ago, erosion had flattened the terrain, and the land was submerged in a sea, where for millions of years sediments were deposited. Seventy million years ago, the Laramide Orogeny—the episode of immense crustal disturbance that created the

Rockies—reached Colorado. The San Juans were pushed up, first as a broad, arched dome, then as a more complicated structure as increased stresses led to folding and buckling and to blocks being thrust up along fault lines. Later, perhaps 30 million years ago, volcanos spilled lava over the existing rocks. Then, in an event of relatively minor geologic importance but of much significance to the human history of the San Juans, liquids rich in precious metals welled up into fractures and solidified into the veins that prospectors went to such trouble to locate.

The mountains may have once reached a height of 20,000 feet, but the period of violent mountain building was followed by one of relative calm, and erosion reduced the peaks to a gentle plateau. Continuing erosion, though, cut canyons into the plateau—precursors of today's rugged topography. The finishing touches were provided by ice-age glaciation. At least three times an icecap covered some 1,200 square miles of the central part of the San Juans, with glaciers radiating into the river valleys.

These glaciers deepened the valleys and sharpened the outlines of such peaks as Mount Sneffels.

The icecap is gone, and I had to be content with the sight of three cirques occupied by the unusual formations known as rock glaciers. These are glacier-like tongues composed of rock fragments, the spaces between rocks being filled with ice and perhaps the core being ice; they creep downhill in much the same way that true glaciers do. Rock glaciers occur below the summer snowline, where insufficient snow accumulates to form a true glacier.

I loped back to my camp, then continued down to my car. I wanted to spend the remainder of my San Juan vacation in the San Miguel Mountains. The Hayden Survey had been particularly impressed with this group of peaks; Rhoda and Endlich, joined by colleague Allen D. Wilson, had made the first ascent of the highest peak, which was subsequently named Mount Wilson. As I had done in the Sneffels area, I wanted to trace the surveyors' steps and again explore the legacy of the hardy Colorado miners.

Mount Moran

Impressive beyond any telling are those mornings when one awakens to find that in the night clouds have taken possession of the range. Daylight reveals them, poised over the cirques, wreathed about the peaks, or draped in festoons between them, settling into the canyons and trailing slowly along the mountain front. There are days when clouds sink even to the level of Jackson Hole.

Fritiof Fryxell
The Tetons, 1959

THE Teton Range, a relatively small group of peaks on the western edge of Wyoming, is one of the country's most ruggedly scenic regions. The product of the Rockies' most recent uplift, its jagged peaks rise abruptly some 7,000 feet above the level basin known as Jackson Hole.

Near the northern end of this forty-mile-long chain of mountains lies the most massive of all the Teton peaks, Mount Moran. Although this peak is not the range's highest—that honor is reserved for the Grand Teton—the bulk and isolation of Moran make it a prominent landmark, one visible from great distances. The 12,594-foot peak was named by the Hayden Survey in 1872 to honor the noted landscape painter Thomas Moran, whose portraits of the American West are still greatly admired.

Although the members of the Hayden Survey were the first to make a careful study of the Teton Range, the recorded history of the range goes back to the start of the nineteenth century. The Jackson Hole region had long been the hunting ground of the Teton Indians, a branch of the warlike Sioux. This tribe dominated the countryside so completely that other tribes named them the "Pirates of the Missouri." Needless to say, the Teton Indians were not pleased with the arrival of fur trappers in the early 1800s.

Trapper John Colter was a member of the historic Lewis and Clark expedition, but, unlike the other participants, he remained in the Rocky Mountains instead of returning to civilization. Traveling alone much of the time, Colter survived a number of misadventures, including a miraculous escape from a tribe of hostile Blackfeet Indians. In 1807 Colter discovered the geysers and hot springs now encompassed by Yellowstone National Park; he was also the first white man known to have entered Jackson Hole and gaze at close range upon the soaring Teton peaks.

Within a few years of Colter's discovery, fur trappers converged on the region. French trappers were responsible for naming the Tetons: the central group of three pointed summits, reminding the men of female breasts, became *Les Trois Tetons.* This name caught on immediately, appearing in print for the first time around 1812.

The towering peaks, so prominent from afar, became a well-known beacon for the trappers. During the late 1820s and early 1830s, great summer encampments at Jackson Hole and other locations attracted numerous "mountain men." A rendezvous, as the annual gatherings were called, allowed the men to sell their furs, stock up on supplies sent from St. Louis, and socialize with a rowdiness that became legendary.

In the late 1830s the market for beaver slowed;

simultaneously, the greedy trappers had almost annihilated the fur-bearing animals. The short-lived but exciting era of the trapper and fur trader was dying out by 1840—the year of the last rendezvous—and not many white men were to visit Jackson Hole for the next few decades.

Members of the Hayden Survey made a few serious attempts to climb the Grand Teton later in the century; these efforts will be described in the following chapter. But remote Mount Moran was ignored by mountaineers until 1915, when Jackson Hole rancher John Shive and three others reached a point only 600 feet below the summit. Time ran out on this attempt, and the party had to retreat.

Other assaults were made on Moran during the next few years, but all were unsuccessful. An article in the March 30, 1918, issue of *Scientific American* baldly stated that "the summit has never been attained and probably never will, as the last 3000 feet of the mountain are sheer perpendicular walls of rock."

A well-known eastern mountaineer named LeRoy Jeffers undoubtedly read this challenging statement, for he was a faithful contributor to the magazine. The following year Jeffers visited the Tetons with the goal of reaching the top of the "un-climbable" mountain. Jeffers displayed remarkable courage in climbing alone to the top of the Skillet Glacier, a distinctively shaped body of ice on the east face. Not far above this icefield, Jeffers had a bad scare. "I was greeted by a gigantic avalanche," he wrote later, "whose boulders, many tons in weight, came leaping at a terrific speed from the heights. They passed within a few feet of me, threatening to shake me from an insecure foothold."

Wisely, Jeffers retreated to the base of the glacier. A storm had arrived; it seemed like a propitious time to head for the valley far below. But, looking to the north, Jeffers spied a "concealed ravine" which led up onto the peak's northeast ridge. A lull in the storm convinced him to push on, even though it was after four o'clock in the afternoon.

The northeast ridge was not particularly difficult, but it seemed endless to Jeffers. At last, in waning daylight, he clambered onto the peak's northeast summit. But across a narrow gap, and rising 150 feet above him, stood the true summit. "At any other time," he wrote, "I should have crossed the *col*, but I had reached the extreme limit of human possibility. It was nine o'clock at night and darkness was upon me. Instead of moonlight, an electrical storm was sweeping toward me from the Grand Teton, and the gale was already driving its sleet furiously against me." This time retreat seemed

mandatory, and Jeffers spent the rest of the night slowly descending the 5,700-foot slope which led down to the valley.

Jeffers returned to Mount Moran three years later. This time climbing with Warren Loyster, he completed the ascent via the Skillet Glacier. But on the summit the pair were astonished to find the record of L. H. Hardy, Ben Rich, and Bennet McNulty, who had climbed the mountain just ten days earlier. This first-ascent trio had used stout sticks

Above: **Beaver feeding on a freshly cut willow. By David C. Fritts.**

Facing page: **Mount Moran from Jenny Lake, Grand Teton National Park. By Ed Cooper.**

and short shovels to aid them on the steep climb up the icy "handle" of the Skillet Glacier.

Beginning in the 1930s, mountaineering became a popular Teton activity, and Moran's great size and firm rock attracted many of America's most famous climbers. Nine separate ways to the top had been established by the time of the first truly ambitious route, the Direct South Buttress. The southern side of the peak displays numerous arêtes and ribs; the Direct South Buttress, the most obvious of these, shoots upward nearly 4,000 feet in several distinctive steps. In 1953 three distinguished Teton mountaineers, Don Decker, Dick Emerson, and Leigh Ortenburger, managed to work their way up past smooth walls and jutting overhangs; it was the most difficult rock climb yet done in the Rocky Mountains.

The remaining arêtes of the south face were climbed during the next decade; some of these climbs, like No Escape Buttress and the Blackfin, proved as hard or harder than the 1953 classic. The 1965 edition of Ortenburger's guidebook listed twenty-three separate ways to reach the top of Mount Moran.

One of the most remarkable of these routes ascends a feature clearly visible from Jackson Hole. Above and left of the Skillet Glacier rises a wide black band. Although many Teton visitors mistake this dark line for a deep cleft, the jet-black ribbon is actually a protruding dike composed of a fine-textured igneous rock known as diabase. The dike, about 125 feet in width and perhaps 800 feet high, offers climbers a rather straightforward technical route to the summit plateau; the dike was first climbed in 1931. Moran's dike, and the scattering of others in the range, was formed some 1.3 billion years ago when molten rock of basaltic composition surged upward through east-west fractures in the Precambrian rock.

The diabase dikes are certainly the most visible geological curiosities of the Tetons, but they form only an insignificant part of the range. Most of the Teton rock consists either of crystalline granite or foliated gneiss, both of which were formed during the Precambrian Era, some 3 billion years ago.

The great uplifting which took place during the

The skyline of the Teton
Range, with the Grand Teton
on the left and Mount Moran
on the right. By David
Muench.

Lone hiker on a rocky ridge, west slope of the Teton Range. By John I. Hendrickson.

crustal disturbance known as the Laramide Orogeny broke the various ranges of the Rocky Mountains into huge blocks along ancient fault lines. The large and almost undeformed block now called the Tetons, nearly forty miles long and one-third as wide, was bordered both on its east and west sides by faults. The deep-lying core of the Tetons was raised abruptly along the eastern fault zone when the weak sedimentary structure of the Jackson Hole block was let down during the formation of the Rocky Mountains. The Teton Range continued to rise, while nearby ranges did not. This movement probably began 75 million years ago and may still be continuing. Geologists estimate that the eastern edge of the Teton block underwent its principal uplift in the past 9 million years; the result is the youngest range of summits in the Rocky Mountains.

Jackson Hole, then, is a downfaulted basin containing a thick section of sedimentary rock, a result of the fracture of the Teton Fault, which displaced the two adjacent blocks. The absence of foothills along the eastern base of the Tetons indicates that rocks were clearly cut off along this fault.

As the Teton Range was uplifted, east-flowing streams cut deep canyons into the ever-steepening flanks of the mountains. Later, glaciers helped carve the resistant ancient rock of the peaks and canyons into their present spectacular shapes.

I first visited the remarkable summit of Moran in 1961, when I climbed the Direct South Buttress with Ken Weeks. After this lengthy and arduous ascent, it was a distinct shock to emerge upon the ten acres of flat rock which comprise the summit plateau. This tableland, an ancient Cambrian cover of sandstone laid down about 550 million years ago, slopes ever so gently up to the summit cairn.

From the top we looked west, where the sun was quickly setting behind purpling ridges in Idaho. One vertical mile down, the well-named Snake River wound sinuously through the lovely parklands of Jackson Hole. Signs of mankind were everywhere: streams of cars crept along the highways; boats scuttled down the river and across the surface of Jackson Lake; and buildings occupied many a glade or lakeshore. But on our lonely Cambrian plateau, it was easy to believe that time had stood still.

CHAPTER TWELVE

Grand Teton

*On gaining the ridge . . . we came in view of
the "Three Tetons," which we could see far in
the east, with their lofty tops covered with the
glistening snow, towering high in the clouds. . . .
The mountains in which these Tetons occur have
a direction of north and south, and have never
yet been ascended. They are represented as being
formed of rock from their base as far as they can
be seen towards the summit; and the tops are
covered at all seasons with snow to an
unknown depth.*

Lieutenant John Mullen
Pacific Railroad Reports
December 10, 1853

S O GREAT is the domination of the Grand
Teton over the remainder of the Teton Range
that one's eyes tend to focus on its summit,
despite the presence of Middle Teton, Mount
Owen, and Teewinot, in themselves peaks as magnificent as any in the American Rockies. Visible
from distances of more than 100 miles, the 13,770-
foot mass appears equally impressive from all directions—a rarity among North American mountains.
The eastern side of the peak, perhaps its most picturesque façade, has been viewed at close range by
millions of Americans, for it rises 7,000 vertical feet
in one sweep above the tourist mecca of Jackson
Hole.

Most visitors to Grand Teton National Park
regard this soaring peak simply as a pleasant backdrop to be gazed at while fishing or hiking the low-
lands. Mountaineers, on the other hand, have long
been fascinated with the mountain, regarding it as

the most desirable summit in the Rockies. As a
result of this attention, the peak has a colorful and
complex climbing history.

As mentioned in the preceding chapter, the early pioneers used the Teton peaks as a landmark. But
most of these men were far too busy trapping beaver
to make a try at reaching the heights. A trapper
named Michaud is said to have attempted the Grand
Teton in 1843, but nothing further is known about
this effort. It was not until 1872, more than six
decades after white men first saw the peaks, that a
determined attempt was made to reach the top of the
Grand Teton.

In late July of that year, James Stevenson of the
Hayden Survey led a party of fourteen men to the
mountain. A major goal of the expedition was to
ascend the Grand and determine its height baro-
metrically. Five of these men were able to struggle
from Pierre's Hole to the Lower Saddle, the 11,600-
foot gap separating the Grand Teton from Middle
Teton. Four of the men set out for the top, but two
eventually dropped out. Stevenson and Nathaniel
Langford continued upward, reaching the Upper Saddle, a smaller pass at 13,200 feet between the main
peak and its western spur.

Exactly what happened above the Upper Saddle
on that summer's day remains controversial even a
century later. The bulk of the available information
on this climb comes from an article Langford published in the June, 1873 issue of *Scribner's Monthly*.
In this account Langford claims the pair "stepped
upon the highest point of the Grand Teton." He also
wrote of finding flowers "of beauteous hue" at a
point only 125 feet below the top and of discovering
an odd, circular, man-made pile of rocks atop an

adjacent pinnacle "a little lower than the one we occupied." Describing the summit, Langford wrote that it was "an irregular area of thirty by forty feet." The account also mentions a sheet of ice "overlying the smooth shelving rock." In time these statements were to create problems for Langford, but for the next quarter-century few questioned the fact that men had climbed the Tetons' most spectacular summit.

Long before the eruption of the controversy about the success or failure of the 1872 climb, other mountaineers sought the Grand Teton's summit. The year 1878 saw an effort by the most proficient American mountaineer of the day, Allen D. Wilson. This surveyor, who earlier had made a bold, one-day ascent of Mount Rainier, started up from the Lower Saddle with two companions. At one point on the ascent Wilson heard an anguished cry from one of his friends. Turning, he saw the man clinging to the cliff like a "starfish hanging to a breakwater." Although encumbered by a transit, the agile Wilson cast down a rope and gave his companion a hoist.

Upon reaching the Upper Saddle, the trio scrambled up to the top of the peak's western spur. Here they discovered a structure of rocks—the same circular pile noted earlier by Langford. Later named the Enclosure, its origin remains unknown, but it seems likely it was a shelter built by Indians. Unable to find a passable route on the wall above the Upper Saddle, Wilson retreated; it was the first time during his twelve years of mountain exploration that a peak had defeated him.

During the 1890s a determined local man named William O. Owen made several attempts to climb the Grand Teton. Finally, success came. In company with Reverend Franklin Spaulding—who did most of the routefinding above the Upper Saddle—and two other men, Owen reached the summit on August 11, 1898.

Finding no evidence of the previous visitors, Owen immediately challenge the claims of the 1872 party. Within months a bitter controversy developed; at one point Owen sarcastically referred to Langford as a "truthful man who . . . has a monopoly on manhood, moral honesty and integrity. . . ." Deriding Langford's discovery of an "ice-sheet" and his description of the summit area, Owen wrote that this was "simply a lie—nothing more or less."

Obsessed with proving Langford's claim a fab-

Mount Owen and the Grand Teton as seen from Solitude Lake. By David Muench.

rication, Owen became suspicious of almost every facet of the 1872 climb. How, for instance, could a member of the prestigious Hayden Survey have failed to construct the traditional stone monument atop such a significant peak? If the ascent took as many hours as Langford claimed, where did the two men find time to detour over to the top of the western spur? And why did Langford describe an ice slope above the Upper Saddle when no such ice existed at the time of Owen's ascent?

Although the public controversy was short-lived and unresolvable, Owen remained convinced throughout his remaining years that Langford and Stevenson had failed in their attempt. Yet one can look in vain for any evidence that Langford changed his story on any point.

The controversy has an interesting sequel. In 1959 researchers discovered, among Owen's files, a letter written to him in 1899 by a Captain Charles H. Kieffer. This letter, which the crafty Owen never made public, describes Kieffer's ascent of the Grand Teton in 1893, five years before the Owen-Spaulding climb! Not enough information is contained in this letter to consider this ascent a certainty, and one must remain skeptical.

As for the Langford-Stevenson claim, it is my belief that the pair climbed only to the Enclosure, atop the western spur. Since neither man had any prior climbing experience, it seems preposterous to think they could have succeeded, in their first attempt on the mountain, in climbing the tricky section above the Upper Saddle, a problem that later defeated the far more experienced Allen Wilson. I would not wish to brand Langford and Stevenson liars; it seems far more likely that the pair—like many other persons who are not attuned to accepted mountain nomenclature and tradition—simply regarded any one of a mountain's high points as "the summit."

Most of the thousands of people who have climbed the Grand Teton use the route pioneered by Spaulding. This route, the easiest of the more than twenty routes on the mountain, is rated class 4, which indicates that ropes should be used to safeguard the climbers. The exposed part of the climb, where belays are necessary, is only a few hundred feet in length, but tired climbers, feeling the altitude, will welcome the protection offered by the rope.

The most notorious section of the Owen-Spaulding Route is found just above the Upper Saddle. At the spot named the Crawl, or Cooning Place, mountaineers traditionally wriggle along a narrow, thirty-foot-long ledge on their stomachs. Prentiss N. Gary, writing in the *Geographic Journal* (1934), commented on this novel problem: "While you could not possibly slip off, you could easily reach out an arm or leg and wave it over the 3,000-foot perpendicular drop." Geologist Fritiof Fryxell gave another interpretation: "One 'coons' along or wriggles like a snake, unable to rise even on the elbows." In actuality, one can discover excellent footholds a few feet below the ledge; by using these, one can traverse this section in a more dignified manner.

Considering the great controversy surrounding the first ascent of the Grand Teton, it seems odd that no one climbed the peak during the next twenty-five years. In 1923 three young men from Montana, inexperienced and without access to the previous accounts, climbed the Owen-Spaulding route in one day from Jackson Hole, without a rope. Shortly after passing the Cooning Place, the men used a three-man shoulder stand to overcome a steep section. When the two upper men arrived at a stable position, they lowered a pair of trousers to provide handholds for the last man!

The ascent became popular almost immediately after this 1923 adventure. A Sierra Club party in the summer of 1926 noted seventy names in the summit register. All of these climbers had followed the 1898 route; it was obviously the easiest way up the mountain. Some climbers undoubtedly considered it the *only* way up the mountain.

During the 1920s, mountaineering standards in North America lagged far behind those of Europe. But when Robert Underhill, a Harvard professor who had done severe routes in the Alps, decided to visit the Tetons in 1929, this situation changed. His ascent of the east ridge of the Grand Teton, climbed with Kenneth Henderson, was not only the mountain's first new route; it also marked the beginning of an era in which accomplished mountaineers were to establish dozens of high-quality routes throughout the Teton Range.

In the next few summers Underhill taught interested American climbers the rope-and-piton techniques he had learned in the Alps; soon the way was open for the ascents of the striking ridges and faces which abounded in the Teton. In 1931 Underhill himself pioneered a route still regarded as one of the finest alpine routes in the range—the north ridge of the Grand Teton.

The north ridge, averaging over sixty degrees in steepness for 1,200 feet, is an imposing feature of the Grand Teton. Shaded much of the day from the sun, the dank chimneys of the route usually harbor ice; Underhill and his companion, Fritiof Fryxell, were fortunate to have had a dry summer for their effort. Part way up the ridge, at a place now known as

Chockstone Chimney, the two men were stymied by a huge stone blocking the crack. Fryxell later wrote a thrilling description of what followed:

> [The] chockstone [was] so big that it extended well out over our heads. . . . I climbed to Underhill's shoulders, then to his head. I could touch the chockstone but nowhere find the slightest hold. When exhausted by futile efforts I lowered myself to Underhill's side and we resorted to pitons. . . . A ring was snapped into each. . . . Underhill mounted to my shoulders and, using the upper ring, launched an offensive. . . . At the third attempt he found a foothold well out to the right and, somehow, pushed himself over onto the chockstone. . . .

Easier climbing followed, and ten hours after leaving their camp the two men stood atop the Grand Teton. Underhill considered the route to be the culmination of his climbing career; at the time it was unquestionably the most difficult route in the United States.

It is difficult to determine whether certain ascents set new standards, styles, and trends in mountaineering. Yet both the 1931 climb of the north ridge and the 1940 ascent of the west face of the Grand Teton—done by Jack Durrance and Henry Coulter—demonstrated once and for all that American climbers could function superbly on the unpredictable and committing terrain of remote ridges and faces.

One Teton wall, the imposing north face of the Grand Teton, proved so intimidating that even the skilled climbers of the 1930s were unable to solve its mysteries. The range's most prominent wall, adorned with snowpatches and dripping with water, rises abruptly 2,400 feet above the Teton Glacier. Four diagonal ledges cut across the face at different levels, but the early pioneers feared the blank-appearing sections that separated them. The additional challenges would include rockfall and verglas, that dreaded veneer of ice which insidiously coats shaded slabs and cracks.

Considering these factors, it is amazing that Paul Petzoldt, Eldon Petzoldt, and Jack Durrance were able to climb five-sixths of the way up the great wall in 1936. This attempt by three of the finest Teton climbers required a degree of boldness that even Underhill did not possess. The trio solved the intricate routefinding problems as far as the Third Ledge; here, both the sheer wall above them and the waning daylight suggested an escape to the nearby north ridge.

Thirteen years passed before the steep cliff above the Third Ledge was surmounted and the

Sheathed with a dusting of snow, the Grand Teton and other high peaks tower above a basin of sagebrush and rocks. By René Pauli.

route completed. By 1949, of course, the great face had gained legendary status, an aura which kept climbers away. Full of confidence, however, Teton guides Dick Pownall and Art Gilkey agreed to venture onto the fearsome wall. On August 13 there was a combination of fine weather, free time, and the availability of a third climber, Ray Garner. As the trio progressed up the wall, discovering along the way the pitons left by the 1936 party, rocks occasionally fell from far above, whirring and crashing down the cliffs. The men did not reach Third Ledge until four in the afternoon, a discouraging sign.

Above Third Ledge rose a shallow crack system containing patches of ice. Pownall was able to struggle up this, but he soon reached an apparent impasse. A narrow ledge led up and left, but it inverted at a nearby corner. Still, it seemed to be the only possibility. Using pitons for aid and an innovative double-rope technique, Pownall worked his way around the frightfully exposed corner; not far above lay Fourth Ledge and the summit. The north face had finally been climbed.

In August of 1959 I found myself leading Pownall's famous pitch, trusting my safety to cold-stiffened fingertips and rusted pitons. A distant rumble of thunder heightened the tension. Summer storms high in the mountains can bring lightning—the most feared adversary in the Tetons—howling winds, and a slick coating of graupel on rock faces. On this climb, though, my partner and I were blessed, for the threatening storm never descended, and we soon were able to reach the small summit knob of the great peak.

The summit register was filled with the names of hundreds of climbers, and I realized that more people had signed the book during the past month than had reached the summit during the thirty years following the first ascent. Could the pioneers like Stevenson and Spaulding possibly have imagined that so many would duplicate and surpass their feats? The courage of these intrepid explorers, however, would be difficult to match.

Left: **A climber cautiously ascends the slabs of the upper Exum Ridge of the Grand Teton. By Galen Rowell.**

CHAPTER THIRTEEN

Gannett Peak

*Here a scene burst upon the view of Captain
Bonneville, that for a time astonished and
overwhelmed him with its immensity. He stood,
in fact, upon that dividing ridge which Indians
regard as the crest of the world; and on each side
of which, the landscape may be said to decline to
the two cardinal oceans of the globe. . . . The
peak on which the captain had taken his stand
commanded the whole Wind River chain; which,
in fact, may rather be considered one immense
mountain, broken into snowy peaks and lateral
spurs, and seamed with narrow valleys.*

Washington Irving
*The Adventures of Captain Bonneville, U.S.A. in
the Rocky Mountains and the Far West,* 1898

TRAVELERS who wish to obtain a good view
of the iciest summit in the American
Rockies will have to hike many miles to do
so, for Gannett Peak lies hidden in the
heart of a wide range surrounded by extensive high
ridges. Although the Wind River Range is by no
means as well known as the nearby Teton Range,
this 100-mile-long chain of alpine mountains in
west-central Wyoming contains scores of beautiful
lakes and classically shaped peaks. Gannett Peak
itself is the highest point in the Rockies north of
Longs Peak and Wyoming's highest point, though
barely: its elevation of 13,804 feet tops the Grand
Teton only by thirty-four feet.

Five glaciers grace the flanks of the massive
peak, and many of the dozen-odd climbing routes
which end atop the ice-clad peak cross or ascend one
or more of these icefields. Even the easiest route is
not to be taken lightly, as Joe Kelsey warns in his
*Climbing and Hiking Guide to the Wind River
Mountains:* "It is easy to forget in this seemingly
benign range that these are real glaciers, with crevasses, surrounded by alpine peaks that release
rocks. Respect these glaciers and know how to minimize the hazards of travel in glacial terrain."

Gannett's largest icefield, the appropriately
named Mammoth Glacier, is nearly two miles long,
an unusual length in a region where most of the
glaciers are small relics of a once colder climate.
Smaller but more accessible, the nearly flat Dinwoody Glacier covers some 860 acres of the peak's
southeast flank. Mountaineers cross this scenic body
of ice when doing the standard route on Gannett.

Since Gannett Peak lies astride the Continental
Divide, the meltwater from its glaciers ends up in
diverse locations. The creek that emerges from the
glacial debris below the Dinwoody Glacier rushes
down the mountain slope to join the Wind River.
Eventually these waters reach the Gulf of Mexico via
the Yellowstone, Missouri, and Mississippi rivers.
The peak's western glaciers spawn the huge Green
River, the Colorado's major tributary. In 1878 Or-
estes St. John wrote an eloquent description of the
beginnings of the Green:

Green River issues from the mountains at a
point eighteen miles northwest of Frémont's
Peak. Rising in the neighborhood of the latter
peak, its mountain course is eroded hundreds of
feet into the crystalline rocks which flank the
gorge with precipitous glacial-polished walls
scarcely inferior in height and grandeur to those
that have rendered famous the scenery of the
Yosemite. . . . Four or five miles above the

mouth a huge block of granite with nearly vertical sides and truncated summit, rises on the south side of the stream to a height of perhaps two thousand feet. Below this mountain the valley expands, and is occupied by a pair of beautiful lakes.

The colossal, flat-topped block described by St. John is a Wind River landmark now known as Squaretop; the beautiful lakes became the Green River Lakes. The Green River itself was once known to the Shoshone Indians as the Seeds-Kee-Dee Agie. The fur trappers of John Jacob Astor's company,

Above: **A climber traverses a narrow crack on the east ridge of Wolf's Head, a classic Wind River Range ascent. By Joe Kelsey.**

Page 110: **Glacier-clad Gannett Peak, in the left background, dominates the U-shaped valley of upper Dinwoody Creek. By David Muench.**

arriving in the area in 1811, called it the Spanish River, since it eventually ended in Mexico. Later, but only for a brief time, it was called the Colorado of the West. The Spanish knew it as Río Verde because its green banks stood out dramatically in reddish canyon country. This name, when translated, became the river's permanent name.

The first white men to approach the Wind River Mountains did not suspect that the interior of the range contained many glaciers, countless lakes, and intricately carved blocks of granite. The margin of the range, with its abundance of game and fur-bearing animals, satisfied the pioneers. The wide gap at the extreme southern end of the range, South Pass, was first crossed in 1812, but even though several high peaks are visible from the pass, no one seems to have made the effort to climb them.

Probably the first man to penetrate the interior of the range was a colorful adventurer named Captain Benjamin Bonneville. In the early 1830s this officer took a leave of absence from the military in order to establish a fur-trading business. Bonneville knew the perimeter of the range well by 1833, and in September of that year decided to seek a direct east-to-west route through the middle of the range.

What little is known about this epic trip comes from "Ascent of a Snowy Peak," a chapter in Washington Irving's biography of Bonneville. Probably ascending a branch of the river now known by its Shoshone name, Popo Agie, the men encountered herds of bison, some of which provided delectable meals for the expedition.

By the second day the party found themselves "in the midst of stupendous crags and precipices." In the afternoon the men reached two lakes surrounded by meadows. Above and beyond, they "beheld huge crags of granite piled one upon another, and beetling like battlements far above them." Bonneville and a few men climbed a minor prominence, then decided to try for a peak which looked to be the region's highest. After crossing an intervening valley, they began to scale this imposing peak. In Irving's words, "the ascent was so steep and rugged that he and his companions were frequently obliged to clamber on their hands and knees, with guns slung upon their backs. . . . They even stripped off their coats and hung them upon the bushes, and thus lightly clad, proceeded to scramble over these eternal snows." Irving states that Bonneville finally attained a summit upon that dividing ridge which Indians regarded as the crest of the world. The captain felt they had reached "the loftiest point of the North American continent," a delusion shared by more than one explorer.

From the top of the peak, according to Irving, Bonneville and his men could see the Sweetwater River, the head of the Wind River, the sources of the Columbia flowing past the three Tetons, and, almost at their feet, an enormous bend in the Green River. If this description was accurate, Bonneville could well have stood atop Gannett Peak, a theory put forth by more than one historian, for Gannett is the only peak from which this exact view can be obtained.

But other authorities remain skeptical, questioning Bonneville's mention of finding bushes not far below the top—an impossibility on glacier-clad Gannett. These dissenters theorize that Bonneville could easily have charted the Green's great bend when he later visited the range's northern end, and that his description was embellished by his biographer.

It is clearly impossible to ascertain exactly which peak Bonneville visited in 1833. The description of the view does point to Gannett, but the logistics and narrative do not. First of all, how could Bonneville have traveled from a branch of the Popo Agie all the way to Gannett in just two days? Second, and perhaps most telling, why does the Irving account fail to mention the difficulties of the ascent, difficulties that exist even on the peak's easiest route?

After Bonneville's climb of the mysterious peak, only a decade passed before the next mountaineering adventure took place in the Wind Rivers. John Frémont and his party of mountain men reached the top of a towering peak just south of Gannett. Again, it is not known exactly which peak was climbed; this controversy will be discussed in the following chapter.

The next visitors to the range left an infinitely more detailed record than did their predecessors. The famous Hayden Survey explored and charted the range carefully during the 1870s under Allen D. Wilson, whose exploits on the Grand Teton were described earlier. On August 1, 1878, he climbed a high peak in the Wind River Range and discovered a "very fine specimen of a living glacier."

Using an astronomical transit, a zenith telescope, and cistern barometer, Wilson and his men were able to carry out primary triangulation of the range accurately. A new invention, the telegraph, also helped the surveyors; using it to synchronize timepieces, the longitude of a place could be determined with far more precision than had been possible earlier. The maps that resulted from this survey were quite accurate in regard to the principal watersheds and mountain peaks. But areas in the interior of the Wind River Range had to be left blank. Later,

as these blank sections were filled in, one towering, ice-clad summit became Gannett Peak.

Among Wilson's contemporaries in the Wyoming surveys were William Henry Holmes and Henry Gannett. Holmes, a geologist and topographer, had remarkable artistic ability, carrying out his sketchwork with a precision lacking in earlier drawings of the range. In a sketch made from the summit of Fremont Peak when Holmes was with Wilson, Gannett Peak is clearly visible, unnamed but bearing the legend: "Snow capped peak north of Frémont's." Later, this imposing mountain was named in honor of Gannett, who was at the time making the first surveys and map of Yellowstone National Park, and who later became Chief Topographer of the United States Geological Survey.

The survey groups spent the majority of their time trying to decipher the geology of the region they were exploring. The scientists of a century ago seem to have been innovative and thorough; many decades later, however, geologists were to revise some of the concepts put forth by their predecessors. The present explanation of the origin of the Wind River Range is, of course, equally subject to change in the future as scientists become more knowledgeable.

The core of the range is an assemblage of metamorphic and igneous crystalline rocks which are overlain on the east side by marine sedimentary rocks. Along with most of the Rocky Mountains, the modern Wind River Range bowed upward during the Laramide Orogeny about 65 million years ago. The northwest-trending crystalline core of the range was folded by horizontal forces and broadly uplifted, this movement being accompanied by westward thrust-faulting where rock fractured along ancient weaknesses.

The sedimentary rocks that once mantled the core of the range were eventually removed by erosion—a beveling effect that reduced much of the range to a low-relief surface, or peneplain. According to a publication of the Geological Survey authored by H. C. Granger and other geologists, the last significant event to affect the range was a gentle arching sometime after the formation of the uplifted peneplain. The report speculates: "It is not clear whether the high peaks which form the spine of the Wind River Range were uplifted at this time or whether they are erosion remnants that resisted peneplanation."

The most recent uplifting of the range—that taking place within the past 10 million years—caused streams to vigorously carve the landscape. Glaciers formed on this scene about a million years ago, creating U-shaped valleys from stream incisions, and enormous cirques. The glaciers finally disappeared about 6,000 years ago; the few relics visible today date from the so-called Little Ice Age, which climaxed around 1850.

The observant hiker will everywhere discover signs of the range's geologic history. Moraines of several ages are quite obvious; less so are the subtle fault lines that cut across many parts of the range; sometimes these long faults contain strings of narrow lakes. Certain prominent parts of the range, best seen from the high summits, are composed of high tablelands—the peneplain remnants. Untouched by the glaciers, these are blanketed by angular blocks broken from the bedrock by the action of the frost. *Felsenmeer*, or "sea of rocks," is the term used by geologists to describe this odd landscape.

Although the early geologists and surveyors made their findings public, the Wind River Range remained relatively unvisited for many decades following the explorations of the 1870s. Hunters and fishermen eventually discovered this paradise, but, by and large, mountaineers ignored the range— perhaps because the nearby Tetons were so much more accessible.

Gannett Peak, for instance, was known to be Wyoming's high point, yet it was not climbed until 1922, when Floyd Stahlnaker and Arthur Tate made an unpublicized ascent. During the 1920s and 1930s

more mountaineers arrived, and most of the highest peaks were climbed, usually by their easiest routes. The region gained prominence when Kenneth Henderson, an eastern climber, wrote in 1927 that "here was to be found one of the best climbing centers in the United States." In July, 1929, Henderson and Robert Underhill—the same team that was to pioneer the Grand Teton's east ridge a few weeks later— spent a productive week in the Gannett Peak area. This strong pair, sometimes accompanied by Henry Hall, accomplished new routes on six peaks, including the icy north face of Gannett itself.

Climbers discovered many hidden faces and ridges during the next few decades; a few climbs done in the 1960s ranked with the hardest climbs yet done in North America. One superb Wind River climbing center, the Cirque of the Towers, in the southern part of the range, became so popular that it was overrun with climbers. Lake water became polluted, garbage peeked out from behind boulders, and tent platforms scarred fragile meadows.

Because of this overpopulation, it would be well if climbers redirected their attention to the huge and relatively untrammeled Gannett Peak region. Here is mountaineering at its best: above verdant meadowlands rise scenic glaciers leading to airy ridges offering unparalleled views of tablelands and glacier-scoured valleys.

Bighorn sheep are found throughout the Wind River region; here, two rutting males rush headlong at one another. By Ray Richardson.

Fremont Peak

The air at sunrise is clear and pure, and the morning extremely cold, but beautiful. A lofty snow peak of the mountain is glittering in the first rays of the sun, which has not yet reached us. . . . All the mountain peaks are gleaming like silver. Though these snow mountains are not the Alps, they have their own character of grandeur and magnificence, and will doubtless find pens and pencils to do them justice.

John C. Frémont
*Report of Expedition to
the Rocky Mountains, 1842*

I T WAS Lieutenant John Charles Frémont, backed by the influence of western Senators, who initiated the important work of the army in exploring the West. Frémont was a member of the elite Corps of Topographical Engineers, whose era of exploration in the West began with his 1842 expedition—a journey that included, among many other adventures, the ascent of the towering Wind River peak that now bears his name.

The Topographical Engineers formed a small but significant branch of the army in the mid-nineteenth century; the total complement of officers at any one time was only thirty-six. Concerned with recording western phenomena, exploring, and mapping, the men laid out territorial boundaries and constructed wagon roads to promote settlement in the West. Individual members of the Corps won great fame during the expansionist era of the 1840s after they examined the new country and reported their findings to a populace eager for information about the terrain, native peoples, and resources.

Frémont himself became a national hero, the most famous of all the Topographical Engineers, and the spirit of romanticism he exemplified influenced the scientific orientation of the Corps. The nation greeted Frémont's explorations with enthusiasm, partly because of his flowing narratives and comprehensive maps. Politically, the impact of Frémont's 1842 expedition was brilliant. His enthusiastic report of this trip, published during the Senate's debate on joint occupation of Oregon, was snatched up by anxious editors and readers. Congress then quickly agreed to a second expedition, this one to push west all the way to the Pacific.

Frémont's mandate of 1842 was far-ranging in scope, but he was charged to pay particular attention to the discovery of trade routes. However, unlike most explorers of the day, Frémont was not content just to find a route through the Rocky Mountains; his natural curiosity and his overriding desire to become a famous explorer drew him into a pursuit which was more ambitious. The feat of climbing the highest peak in the Rockies would add to his renown and further the promotion of his western explorations. The thought of placing his name atop some prominent point appealed to the young lieutenant's vanity and romanticism. And so, despite the fact that such an episode was not in the line of duty, Frémont ventured into the heart of the Wind River Range to seek his summit.

While studying the range from the west, the lieutenant spied a high peak, crowned with snow; it seemed to be the highest point of the range. His guide, Kit Carson, remembered that earlier frontiersmen had also considered this prominent peak the tallest in the region. Setting out through the foot-

115

hills, Frémont soon found that he had severely underestimated the distance to the peak; the competent party of guides and French *voyageurs* took several days to reach their soaring objective. From a lake near the foot of the peak, Frémont described the view: "The long mountain wall to the east, rising two thousand feet abruptly from the plain, behind which we see peaks, is still dark, and cuts clear against the glowing sky. . . . Water froze last night, and fires are very comfortable."

The expedition spent several days camped at Island Lake, a large body of water at the lower end of a beautiful valley now called Titcomb Basin. Besides Frémont, the group included a black servant, three *voyageurs*, several guides, and a German cartographer named Charles Preuss. The latter detested the rough frontier life and did not share Frémont's desire to reach the peak. But even the mapmaker could not resist the beautiful scenery for long, as one entry from his diary indicates: "Never before, in this country or in Europe, have I seen such magnificent grand rocks."

On the morning of August 15 the men rode their horses into upper Titcomb Basin, at the very foot of their objective; from here Frémont named it Snow Peak, "as it exhibited more snow to the eye than any of the neighboring summits." The climb progressed without incident up the mountain's flank to the tiny summit. Here, in the words of Preuss, "pistols were fired, the flag unfurled, and we shouted 'hurrah' several times."

"We had accomplished an object of laudable ambition," Frémont later wrote, "and beyond the strict order of our instructions. We had climbed the loftiest peak of the Rocky mountains, and looked down upon the snow a thousand feet below, and, standing where never human foot had stood before, felt the exultation of first explorers."

The peak, of course, was not the highest of the Rockies, or even of the Wind River Range. No one questioned that one of the range's high points had been reached. But which one? Wyoming seems to have had a disproportionate share of first-ascent controversies; the disagreements about who first stood atop the Grand Teton and Gannett Peak have already

been chronicled. Frémont's peak forms yet another chapter in the annals of mountaineering disagreements.

In 1878 Allen D. Wilson of the Hayden Survey reached the top of a high peak near Titcomb Basin. Wilson had not only studied Frémont's account carefully; he had ascended some two dozen Wind River peaks in 1877 and 1878 and thus qualified as an expert. His judgment: "We found no signs of any one having visited this point before; but I am of the opinion that this is the point Frémont ascended in 1842." Firm in this belief, Wilson named the 13,745-foot giant in Frémont's honor.

Many years later, mountaineer Orrin Bonney found that the latitude given by Frémont for the peak he climbed in 1842 did not correspond with the latitude of present-day Fremont Peak: it was two-and-a-half minutes off, or nearly three miles. Bonney also noted, while on a trip to Titcomb Basin, that Fremont Peak has so little snow on it that it would have been absurd for Frémont to have named it Snow Peak. Bonney then promulgated the theory that Mount Woodrow Wilson, snow-clad and lying directly on Fremont's latitude, had to be the peak reached in 1842.

Joe Kelsey, a contemporary authority, feels that Mount Woodrow Wilson is definitely not the correct summit. For one thing, it is totally invisible from the western plains, the region where Frémont and Carson first spied the peak. Although crediting Frémont with a high degree of accuracy, Kelsey believes that such latitude errors were common in the early days. As to the snow cover, Fremont Peak could easily have received a few inches of snow from a summer storm.

But perhaps the most significant factor in determining which peak was climbed lies in the relative difficulty of the two peaks. Preuss wrote that "the highest peak . . . looked so easy that we firmly believed that we could be back to our mules and our provisions before nightfall." The party had such confidence that they brought along brandy for the summit celebration as well as an American flag. Preuss describes starting the climb above a grassy lake, then continuing up "flat, smooth stretches of rock" to the summit. This description fits Fremont Peak quite accurately.

Mount Woodrow Wilson, on the other hand, proves to be a moderately difficult mountaineering venture when ascended from Titcomb Basin: one must climb either of two steep snow couloirs to a notch from which the summit is reached only by a steep dihedral where most climbers desire a rope.

When Craig Martinson, Bill Lahr, and I decided

High peaks of the Wind River Range from the air; Fremont Peak is the glacier-clad mass in the distance. Distinctive bergshrunds can be seen on the Heap Steep (center) and Dinwoody glaciers. By Russell Lamb.

Above: American elk ascending a barren ridge above the headwaters of the Wiggins Fork of the Wind River, Washakie Wilderness Area, Wyoming. By Jack Swenson.

Pages 118-119: Fremont Peak, the second-highest summit of the Wind River Range, from Island Lake in the Bridger Wilderness Area. By David Muench.

to visit Titcomb Basin in 1976, it was not to solve the lingering mystery, but rather to establish a new route on Fremont Peak. I had picked out a beautiful, un-climbed buttress on the mountain's west face seven years earlier; it was still unclimbed and the time had finally come to attempt it.

We flew in a private plane to the Pinedale Air-port, located very close to the spot where Frémont had caught his first glimpse of the peak later named in his honor. From the airstrip the grandeur of the Wind River Range rises in full perspective, and we knew we were embarking on a worthwhile adven-ture. Looking at our ropes and metallic rock tools, several passing pilots wondered aloud about our san-ity. Why, they asked, would anyone pack all the heavy paraphernalia into the far basins when one could simply fly over and see all the peaks in one vista? Our answer was this: the challenge of a climb is a combination of curiosity and the lure of the unexpected. In the Wind River Range, the drudgery of packing in comes first, but later the rewards are great.

Drudgery it was, for we faced a thirteen-mile hike from the roadhead to Island Lake. But the scen-ery was superb and made us forget our monstrous loads. Golden aspens lined the trail much of the way; limber and whitebark pines dominated the land-scape as we climbed higher.

As we approached Island Lake, the bold outlines of the peaks ringing Titcomb Basin stood before us; Fremont Peak looked as beautiful as I had remem-bered it. John Frémont had described this mountain scene: "Near by was a foaming torrent, which tum-bled into the little lake. About one hundred and fifty feet below us, and which, by way of distinction, we have called Island Lake. We had reached the upper limit of the piney region; as, above this point, no tree was to be seen, and patches of snow lay everywhere around us on the cold sides of the rocks."

Flowers glowed everywhere: rosecrown, gen-tian, cinquefoil, lungwort, fleabane, and the purple saxifrage. We paused to study the latter, for this plant is especially well adapted to withstand the extreme cold and dryness of the arctic-alpine environment. Its net of branches hugs the ground in order to escape the winds and to create a favorable microclimate.

Titcomb Basin displays ample evidence of the glaciers that long ago carved this enormous cirque from a formerly narrow valley. Jagged arêtes, similar to the famous ones of the French Alps, were formed after the glaciers scooped out vast amounts of rock from both sides of rounded ridges. Glacier ice dragged rock fragments across the bedrock, and we were able to find polished areas as well as long stria-tions which perfectly indicated the direction the gla-cier once flowed. Glacial erratics lay everywhere; these boulders, carried along by the icefields, were marooned when the ice finally retreated.

The ice ages in the Wind River Range resulted in a high-level accumulation of ice, from which gla-ciers spread out toward the plains on both flanks. Several glacial advances are now recognized by geologists; their sequences can be reconstructed by a study of moraines on the fringe of the range. Pinedale stage moraines, ending only about 10,000 years ago, now impound two large lakes. From about 7,000 to 5,000 years ago, an interglacial period with a warmer climate caused most or all of the range's glaciers to disappear. The present glaciers of the Wind Rivers, mostly clustered in the northern portion of the range, formed during the Neoglacial interval of the past five millennia. The fresh moraines beyond the present icefields are evidence that the glaciers have retreated from their mid-nineteenth-century max-imums.

From our lakeside camp we studied the west buttress of Fremont Peak with binoculars and be-came convinced that cracks and holds existed for its full sweep. On the first day's effort, a cruel wind caused us to flee back to camp after climbing one difficult pitch. But the next day was somewhat calmer, permitting us to finish a superb route con-sisting almost entirely of free climbing. Large crys-tals of feldspar and veins of firm pegmatite allowed us to move efficiently and with great pleasure. The exposure on the near-vertical wall was sensational, for the buttress fell away sharply on both flanks. But the climbing was so involved that the best psycholo-gical plan was to look upward at all times, studying the route and watching the leader. After we shared about 1,500 feet of serious and sustained climbing, the buttress tapered off into great blocks, easily climbed to the highest point of the mountain.

Having climbed where no humans had ever been, we totally understood Frémont's summit feel-ing: "the exultation of first explorers."

Mount Wilbur

To mountain climber and scenery lover alike the lure of Glacier Park is manifold. Its lakes, its dense forests and lovely alplands, and its rugged mountains, carved by glaciers into a bewildering array of picturesque and richly colored peaks, attract and challenge.

Norman Clyde
Appalachia, 1934

RETURNING from the Pacific Coast in 1806, Captains Meriwether Lewis and William Clark split their expedition in two to explore routes through the Montana Rockies. Lewis and Clark had succeeded in crossing the continent by ascending the Missouri River and descending the Columbia, but had failed to find an easy way through the mountains. Lewis took a northern route and led his group over the Continental Divide by what is now called Lewis and Clark Pass. From the Great Falls of the Missouri, he then set out on another quest—for a route connecting the Missouri to the fur country of Canada. He followed the Marias River north, but it soon curved west, and seeing the mountains from which it flowed, Lewis turned back.

These mountains, which the captain described as "very irregular and broken in their form" and "partially covered with snow nearly to their bases," are now named the Lewis Range and are the main scenic attraction of Glacier National Park. The Lewis Range traverses the park from northwest to southeast for fifty miles. The Continental Divide follows the crest of the range for most of this distance, though at the park's north end, the Divide swings west to the parallel Livingston Range.

The highest peak in Glacier Park, 10,466-foot Mount Cleveland, lies near the north end of the Lewis Range. The range also includes a large number of peaks between 8,000 and 10,000 feet in elevation. One of these, 9,321-foot Mount Wilbur, is a ragged limestone fin lying east of the Divide and thirteen miles south of the Canadian border. Selecting one peak to epitomize the complex alpine topography of Glacier Park is not easy, and Wilbur is not one of the higher peaks, but its dominance of the skyline west of opulent Many Glacier Hotel—the park's tourist haven—and its magnificent steep rise above Swiftcurrent Creek make it the mountain of choice.

Glacier National Park abuts the Canadian border, across which sits its sister park, Waterton Lakes. Indeed, the mountains of Glacier are continuous with the Canadian Rockies, and their geologic story is much the same.

The rock is mostly sedimentary—limestones and shale—that began as sediments deposited over a billion years ago in a shallow sea much like the present continental shelves. The 4,000-foot-thick layer known as the Siyeh limestone forms the main part of the walls of the high peaks. Within the Siyeh are two interesting formations. One is a dark, horizontal band 100 feet thick that crosses the faces of Cleveland, Wilbur, and several other peaks. This is a sill of diorite, a dark igneous rock that formed when molten magma was pushed between limestone layers, then solidified. The other formation is a blue-gray fossilized reef of algae that once inhabited the ancient shallow sea. The algae are grouped in colonies, giving the rock a texture that has been described as resembling heads of lettuce or cabbage.

Beginning 100 million years ago, these rock

Above: Mountain goat above
Gunsight Lake, Glacier
National Park. The prominent
peak in the background is
Going-to-the-Sun Mountain.
By Breck P. Kent.

Facing page: Waterfall, Glacier
National Park. By Russell
Lamb.

Page 122: Craggy Mount
Wilbur towers above a
lakeshore meadow in Glacier
National Park. By Ed Cooper.

formations were warped, folded, and finally broken by tensions in the crust. Then between 60 and 50 million years ago intense pressures thrust a great slab eastward along a surface called Lewis Overthrust Fault. The 300-mile-long slab, which includes the Lewis Range and the Canadian Rockies as far north as Banff, was thrust between thirty and forty-two miles out over rocks a billion years younger.

Rocks are part of the story of Glacier Park; water is an equally important part. The peaks cradle more than sixty glaciers. The largest is Blackfoot Glacier on the northeast flank of the Divide at the head of St. Mary River, though Grinnell Glacier on Mount Gould, seen south of Wilbur from Many Glacier Hotel, is more of a tourist attraction. Today's glaciers, however, contain but a small fraction of the ice that once covered the mountains, carved the innumerable cirques that separate the peaks, sculpted the deep U-shaped passes across divides, and gouged the lakes. Many of the cirques are classic examples of the effect of glaciation on topography, as are the lakes. Both flanks of the range are occupied by numerous long, thin fingers of lakes, the largest being Lake McDonald on the west flank and St. Mary Lake on the east. Lake Sherburne, the site of Many Glacier Hotel below Mount Wilbur, is a fine example of a glacier-gouged lake.

The Rocky Mountains lie in an arid region, and water is a valued resource. The northern ranges of the Rockies attract more precipitation than the mountains to the south; the glacier-fed streams of the Lewis Range provide water to a vast region. Toward the southern end of the Lewis Range is a mountain named Triple Divide Peak. From its slopes flow three streams. One, called Atlantic Creek, carries water east to the Marias and thence to the Missouri, the Mississippi, and the Atlantic Ocean. A second stream, Pacific Creek, flows west to the Flathead River, which occupies a segment of one of the world's great land depressions, the Rocky Mountain Trench. This trench follows a fault line for 800 miles, in Canada separating the Canadian Rockies from the Interior Ranges to the west. The waters of the Flathead eventually reach the Columbia River and the Pacific Ocean. Meltwaters from the small icefield under the north face of Triple Divide Peak feed Hudson Bay Creek, which in turn feeds the St. Mary River, finally reaching Hudson Bay by way of the Saskatchewan River.

Jutting out to the east of the main Lewis Range near the northern end of Glacier Park is an extraordinary formation named Chief Mountain. This mountain is the easternmost portion of the billion-year-old rock that was pushed out over the Lewis Overthrust, a monolith that is rootless in the sense of standing on younger rock. Chief Mountain is conspicuous by virtue of its isolated position and 1,500-foot prow; it was known to Meriwether Lewis from Indian reports.

According to Indian legend, a Flathead warrior ascended Chief Mountain with a bison skull. He fasted and spent four nights on the summit until he was able to make peace with the mountain's spirit. In 1891 Henry L. Stimson, whose long, distinguished career as a statesman was to include terms as Secretary of State and Secretary of War, ascended Chief Mountain with a doctor from New York and a Blackfoot Indian to satisfy his curiosity about the legend. On the summit he found the rotted remains of a very old bison skull.

The Flatheads lived west of the mountains, and among the dangers faced by the warrior during his expedition to Chief Mountain would have been the hostile Blackfeet tribe. The Blackfeet came to the east flank of the mountains from the Alberta prairies around 1700. They used horses for fighting the tribes to the west and for hunting bison. The Blackfeet now live a more sedentary existence on the eastern edge of Glacier Park.

The area now included in the park was little known to whites until the 1850s, when surveyors establishing the international boundary and exploring for rail routes first reached the mountains. By 1910 the beauty of this unique section of northern Montana was sufficiently well known that Glacier National Park was created. In 1933 the Going-To-The-Sun Road was completed, a highway that links Lake McDonald on the west slope to St. Mary Lake on the east side by crossing the Continental Divide at Logan Pass. The need to cut through the Garden Wall at the pass meant the Park Service had to balance its mandate to preserve the landscape against its wish to make the scenery accessible. The director of the Park Service, Horace M. Albright, gave this justification for the road: "Although Glacier will always remain a trail park, the construction of this one highway to its inner wonders is meeting its obligation to the great mass of people who because of age, physical condition, or other reason would never have an opportunity to enjoy, close at hand, this marvelous mountain park."

Traveling to Glacier Park in July, 1980, Eric Bjornstad and I stopped at the University of Montana's Biological Station at Whitefish Lake to chat with a friend about climbing plans. In the cafeteria we met a professor teaching courses in animal behavior. Because a couple had recently been mauled to death by a grizzly bear while camped on a sandbar near the park's east boundary, the talk naturally focused on *Ursus arctos*. About 200 grizzlies now inhabit the park, eating a wide range of foods varying from berries and grass to marmots and squirrels, which they dig from the ground.

Grizzlies were formerly hunted by Plains Indians armed only with bow and arrow. The Indians hunted in groups; nevertheless, the hunt must have been risky business requiring skill, coordination and discipline. Lewis and Clark first heard of grizzlies (which are distinguished from the more common black bear by their greater size and a characteristic hump between the shoulders) from Indians in North Dakota. Later, Lewis was chased for eighty yards by one he had wounded, escaping only by plunging into a river.

Six people have been killed by grizzly bears in Glacier Park, a statistic not easy to forget while hiking in the backcountry. Hiking through fir and spruce on the trail to Gunsight Lake, Eric and I carried a flare in case we met a bear; neither of us was inclined to walk first. But we saw no large animals, not even the elk that browse in willow thickets along the St. Mary River. We did see Lewis monkey-flower, and arrowleaf groundsel, bear grass, yellow

Russula mushrooms and lichen, McDonald Creek Valley, Glacier National Park. By Jeff Gnass.

columbine, gaillardia, false hellebore, showy fleabane, shrubby cinquefoil, thimbleberry, bog birch, and elderberry.

George McLean met us at our camp among boulders near the lake, which is tucked high under the Divide at the head of the St. Mary River and glows turquoise blue from suspended glacier dust. In the morning we followed the trail along the lake, where I saw the first specimens of rosy spirea I had ever seen, then scrambled up talus toward Mount Jackson. Here, amid small waterfalls draining the Jackson Glacier, were hardy, alpine plants: silky phacelia, stonecrop, alpine aster, moss campion and, highest of all, gentian.

We spent several hours ascending the small glacier that clings to the mountain's north side; its steepness dictated the use of rope, ice axe, and ice screws (the last, twisted into the ice and attached to the rope, are used to protect against long falls). Later, from the windy 10,052-foot summit, we came to understand the appeal of the peaks of Glacier Park; it lies not in their altitude, which is not exceptional, but in the variety of shapes, the remoteness, and the sheer number of peaks. Beyond the Blackfoot Glacier to the east we could see the great expanse of Montana prairie, where the cold, dry winds that have crossed the mountains and funneled through valleys like the St. Mary's blow at speeds of up to 100 miles per hour. Temperatures on this vast prairie fluctuate widely: from 100° F. to minus 40° F. The prairie meets the forest near St. Mary Lake; here, in a transition zone, or ecotone, the two plant communities overlap.

Descending, we nearly stepped on a pair of white-tailed ptarmigan. Then, rounding a point of rock, we abruptly met a long-haired, bearded fellow who appeared to be wearing knickers: *Oreamnos americanus.* The mountain goat—unofficial symbol of Glacier, official symbol of the Great Northern Railroad, which passes nearby—is abundant in the park. Our goat at first appeared unafraid, but suddenly sensed danger and quickly vanished around a ledge.

The nimble goats were virtually the only mountaineers in these rugged peaks until the arrival of Norman Clyde. Best known for his climbs in the Sierra Nevada, particularly in the Palisades, Clyde was attracted to the peaks of Glacier Park in 1923. He ascended thirty-eight peaks, ten of his climbs being the first ascent of the peak. Clyde climbed alone, but most climbers will wish for a rope on many of his routes.

One of Clyde's first ascents was of Mount Wilbur, and Eric and I wished to repeat his route. From Swiftcurrent Creek we clambered up steep, slippery grass slopes, feeling the spray of a nearby waterfall. The climb then led toward a right-slanting series of chimneys, gullies, and ramps. In a basin far below we spotted four bighorn sheep moving. We passed the reef of fossil algae, with its concentric rosettes, and reached the section that had worried Norman Clyde. "Almost sheer strata of limestone and argillite and the belt of diorite seemed to bar further advance," wrote Clyde. "The writer dropped rapidly down the side of the mountain until he encountered a broad limestone shelf, which he followed around to its eastern face. . . . There it was sufficiently broken to be scalable, and above it rose the two chimneys to an elevation at no great distance below the summit." Eric and I chose a variant of Clyde's route that is known as "Thin Man's Pleasure," for it involves a two-foot-square hole in the top of a cave. We used the rope, the rock here being steep and exposed, but the remainder of the climb proved easy for the most part.

On the summit we found ourselves in the midst of an exciting panorama of mountains and glaciers. We easily spotted Mount Cleveland, Mount Jackson, and Chief Mountain. Beyond nearby cirques loomed Mount Gould and Mount Siyeh, each boasting one of Glacier's largest rock faces. The wall of Gould was climbed in 1974, that of Siyeh in 1979. Below us to the east stretched Lake Sherburne; even the hotel on its shore did not seem to disrupt the primitive purity of the scene.

Mount Assiniboine

As with no other peak in this country, Assiniboine and Canada have become synonymous. When seen at a distance, Assiniboine exudes an elegance, a cleanness of line and symmetry of form rivalled by few other mountains in the world. At close quarters, however, the shape, form, and character of the peak change dramatically. The impression of firmness and airy solidity gives way to the crumbling reality of black, loose, sedimentary rock. Elegant lines disappear, dwarfed or blocked out by bands and bulges of friable stones interlaced with veins of ice and snow.

Randy Morse
The Mountains of Canada, 1978

THE LOCATION of the boundary between the United States and Canada at a latitude of forty-nine degrees is the result of a political compromise, not an indication of a sudden change in terrain. The mountains of America's Glacier National Park, such as Mount Wilbur, belong to the same range as the peaks north of the border that are known as the Canadian Rockies.

The Canadian Rockies extend northwest for more than 500 miles, forming the Continental Divide as well as the boundary between the provinces of Alberta and British Columbia. Rising in an unbroken chain from the Alberta prairie, the Rockies offered a formidable barrier to the few early explorers, fur trappers, and railroad surveyors who approached the mountains. And the mountains were known only to these occasional adventurers until

the completion in 1885 of Canada's first transcontinental railroad, the Canadian Pacific.

The sport of climbing was developed in the nineteenth century largely by British gentlemen who employed local guides in the Swiss Alps. When some of these mountaineers turned their attention to North America, it was the Canadian Rockies, snowier and more compact—thus more like the Alps than American mountains—that caught their eye. The Canadian Pacific Railroad, which had built a series of resort hotels along their line, took advantage of this similarity by billing the Rockies as the "Canadian Alps" and importing Swiss guides. These guides were more intimately associated with Mount Sir Donald, in the Selkirk Range, and will be mentioned at greater length in a later chapter, but guides stationed at the railroad resort of Banff played a major role in the development of climbing in the southern Canadian Rockies.

The Matterhorn was the Alps' most admired peak, and it was inevitable that a Canadian peak resembling the Matterhorn would gain quick renown. Such a peak was found situated on the Continental Divide thirty-two miles south of Banff: Mount Assiniboine. With a pointed 11,870-foot limestone summit that towers 1,500 feet above its immediate neighbors it is, indeed, the highest point between the railroad and the American border. By 1900, striking photographs of the mountain taken from the north had made Assiniboine the "Matterhorn of the Rockies" and, according to British mountaineer Sir James Outram, "the most talked of mountain in the Rockies." Outram himself spoke of the mountain in glowing terms, describing it as a mass that "rises like a monster tooth when seen from the N." and mentioning such features as magnificent cornices overhanging tremendous precipices.

With a mountaineer's eye, Outram also noted more mundane details—that Assiniboine "is formed of the usual limestone of the Cordilleran range, much eroded and disintegrated," and that the banding of the strata is nearly horizontal, forming steep cliff belts alternating with slopes of ice. For, despite "the N. face having been pronounced probably inaccessible, and the only supposed feasible route consid-

Above: Red fox, Banff National Park, Alberta. The fox's long snout enables it to burrow through snow for mice and other rodents. By Brian Milne.

Facing page: The final section of the classic North Ridge Route leads to the summit of Mount Assiniboine. Dawn sunshine lights the ice flutings of the east face. By John Cleare/Mountain Camera.

Page 128: Mount Assiniboine from the northeast over the waters of Magog Lake, with the north ridge facing the viewer. Mount Magog is on the left. By John Cleare/Mountain Camera.

ered a serious problem," Outram hoped to make the first ascent. "It was to attempt to disprove these theories that my expedition was undertaken."

Outram was aware of three previous attempts on Assiniboine: one in 1898 and two in 1900. One of the 1900 parties, which included Walter D. Wilcox and guide Edouard Feuz, reached the highest point of the three, about 10,900 feet on the southwest face. The dangerous conditions that turned back these climbers were described vividly by Wilcox:

> The roar of avalanches became more and more frequent, and the long, serpentine streams could be seen, from time to time, pouring down the amphitheatre on our left. Echoed and re-echoed amongst the cliffs, the sound of these snow slides appeared to come from every point of the compass. . . . Thus every distant booming roar was startling, and most trying to the nerves, and from time to time Feuz stopped to listen in an endeavor to detect danger at the earliest possible moment.

Wilcox and party were lucky to escape: "As the great slabs of stone came rattling down the *couloir* with metallic, almost bell-like sound," Wilcox wrote, "we hugged close to the rocks, but even so we were both struck several times by dangerously heavy stones."

Outram could find no competent amateurs to join him in an attempt in 1901, so he took the Swiss guides Christian Häsler and Christian Bohren. A forty-mile march with pack animals was necessary to reach the base of Assiniboine from Banff. Early on the morning of September 2 the mountaineers were finally ready to begin climbing. Not knowing what obstacles they would encounter, they carried a light tent, blankets, and food for two days, in the event they had to spend a night on the mountain. From camp below the north face they climbed to a jagged col northwest of Assiniboine, then to a second col at the base of the west arête. Outram later described their situation at the col:

> We were now 9,600 ft. above the sea, 2,400 ft. higher than our camp, and the time 9 A.M. A fine view of the lower portion of Assiniboine's south-western side was opened out, and, much to our satisfaction, we perceived at once that nothing formidable lay between us and the S.W. ridge, by which we hoped to make our way towards the summit. The face itself was mainly a long succession of sheer or almost perpendicular cliff-belts for some considerable distance, intersected by steep gullies, every one of which

seemed to be a much-used channel for stones and ice and snow, and of extreme steepness. Narrow ledges, sometimes with slopes of débris, ice, and snow, stretched away almost horizontally, and after 10 min. rest we embarked upon the traverse.

Their satisfaction at finding a way onto the face, however, was short-lived, for clouds were piling up to the west. Soon the climbers were engulfed by a thick mist, but, constructing cairns, or "stone-men," to help locate the route on their return, they continued up to the base of a cliff at 10,750 feet. Uncertain of their position because of the poor visibility, they tried skirting the cliff to the right but were stopped when "a huge abyss, with wreathing clouds, yawned at our feet." Retracing their steps, the trio found a cleft in the wall, which they ascended by "a gymnastic scramble." They reached a subsidiary summit at about 11,000 feet, which made them realize they were lost, so they decided to descend to their 7,000-foot camp.

To Outram's surprise, the sky cleared during the night, the moon and stars shining brightly. With new enthusiasm, he and his guides set out for another attempt and quickly regained their previous high point. Above, hard ice slopes necessitated the chopping of many steps. According to Outram, "quantities of snow and solid ice filled almost every cavity and rift; the rocks were very brittle and extremely insecure; and to the ordinary difficulties was added the abomination of *verglas*, which covered all the rocks, from the night's frost after the rain and sleet of yesterday."

Outram, Häsler, and Bohren climbed a steep, icy gully to the south ridge and found themselves 300 feet from the summit, "with only an easy slope of snow between us and victory."

Clouds were again gathering by the time the trio had reached the top, so they quickly took a few photographs and considered the descent. Outram persuaded the guides to descend the unknown north ridge. Steps had to be cut in ice, and cliff bands forced searches for clefts, but a route always was found, and the half-circuit and traverse of Assiniboine was accomplished in only fourteen hours. Outram correctly considered this the most difficult climb yet done in the Rockies.

The Englishman could not resist comparing his ascent of Assiniboine to routes in the Alps:

The climb itself reminded me more than anything of the Dent Blanche in fairly bad condition with *verglas*. On the S.W. side it cannot be called a very severe ascent; only about 700 ft. are difficult at all for practised mountaineers; but the northern side will always, I think, provide a climb equal in interest (though only 1,500 ft., perhaps, of the highest order) to almost any peak in Switzerland.

Assiniboine, despite its loose and often ice-plastered rock, remained a coveted mountaineering objective, and continued to inspire eloquent prose from those who visited it. "Assiniboine," wrote a climber of a later generation, "is a simple pyramid, and in that lies its charm." The route descended by Outram's party became the peak's most frequently taken line of ascent: a glacier; broken rock on the right side of the north ridge; two cliff bands seen from afar that constitute the crux of the ascent; and, finally, the narrow crest of the north ridge. The climb is not difficult by modern standards, yet treacherous ice and cornices preclude Assiniboine being taken lightly.

In 1910 Tom Longstaff and guide Rudolf Aemmer climbed what was reported to be Assiniboine's north face, an ascent involving much step-chopping in ice. In 1967, Yvon Chouinard, Joe Faint, and Chris Jones were relieved to discover that what had been climbed was actually the northwest face—the face between the two cols crossed by Outram—for these three Californians, also inspired by photographs, hoped to make the first ascent of the true north face. Encouraged by fine weather in Banff, they hurried to their objective. They began climbing in the afternoon, up a snow couloir that led to a shoulder on the left flank of the face. To escape a strong wind, they built a stone wall and disappeared into bivouac sacks, with skies so threatening they assumed they would be forced to retreat. But the three climbers awoke to a glorious dawn, the clouds that had hovered on the mountain now hugging the valley. The snow was perfect for crampons as they began climbing, but higher they encountered ice that required the delicate placement of the front points of the crampons and the use of short ice axes held in each hand. Rather than belaying one another, the trio

moved together, for in the mountains, speed means safety. In this situation it meant better, early-morning ice and less risk of being hit with falling rocks. By the time stones loosened by the sun began rattling down the face, the climbers were safely on the summit ridge, above rockfall. They reached the summit by noon, having completed Assiniboine's first route requiring today's techniques and equipment.

The Assiniboine country not only provides challenging climbing; it also offers outstanding powder snow for skiing. Erling Strom built a camp near the mountain in 1928 and for many years guided patrons over his favorite runs, some many miles long over terrain mostly above timberline. Strom left his cabin unlocked when he was away, so visitors could light a fire, brew a pot of tea, and make themselves comfortable.

Although I have been intrigued by Assiniboine for years, the nearest climb I have made was eighteen miles to the southeast, on the northeast face of Mount Queen Mary, which is tucked away in the almost unknown Royal Group. Lured by a description of the face by Rudolf Aemmer, who made the first ascent of the 10,600-foot mountain in 1922, and my own observations during a reconnaissance flight, Jim Kanzler, Doug McCarty, and I made the long approach three times in September, 1975, before having suitable weather. We cramponed quickly up the lower ice slopes until the steepening face encouraged the use of rope and ice axe. Fresh snow made the scene wintry. A loose, awkward rock pitch led to the craggy, castlelike summit. For an hour we basked in the welcome warmth of the sun, admiring the peak that dominated the scene, Assiniboine. We could begin to imagine how James Outram felt so long ago when, on the evening after the first ascent, he looked up at his peak:

> Before turning in, we took a last look at the great obelisk above us, brilliant in the moonlight beneath the dark canopy of a star-strewn sky; and next morning awoke to a world of snow, which lay thick and soft around, whilst whirling masses of storm clouds drifted across the mountain and wrapped its summit, giving but an occasional glimpse of its steep flanks, covered with freshly fallen snow.

Mount Robson

On every side the snowy heads of mighty hills crowded round, whilst, immediately behind us, a giant among giants, and immeasurably supreme, rose Robson's peak. This magnificent mountain is of conical form, glacier clothed and rugged. When we first caught sight of it, a shroud of mist partially enveloped the summit, but this presently rolled away, and we saw its upper portion dimmed by a necklace of light feathery clouds, beyond which its pointed apex of ice, glittering in the morning sun, shot up far into the blue heavens above, to a height of probably 10,000 or 15,000 feet. It was a glorious sight, and one which the Shushwaps of the Cache assured us had rarely been seen by human eyes, the summit being generally hidden by clouds.

William F. Milton and Dr. W. B. Cheadle
The North West Passage by Land, 1863

Toward the northern end of the Canadian Rockies, and dominating its setting like no other mountain in the range, stands Mount Robson. Robson's 12,972-foot summit surpasses by 700 feet the Rockies' next highest summit, Mount Columbia, which lies far to the southeast, and towers nearly 2,000 feet above nearby peaks. Complex, massive, snow-mantled Robson is spectacular from all sides, and the difficulty of an ascent by any of its long, risky routes makes its summit one of those most highly prized by mountaineers.

Kamloops Indians called the mountain *Yuh-hai-has-kuh*—"the mountain of the spiral road"—no doubt referring to the conspicuous bands formed by the ancient sedimentary strata. The origin of the white man's name is less clear. It appears as long ago as 1827, when western Canada was the exclusive domain of fur traders, in the diary of George Mac-Dougal:

> Tête-Jaune Cache is a place where one, an Iroquois Indian half-breed, who was fair-haired, had made a Fur-Cache, or a place to store his Catch of Furs, and was known as Tête-Jaune Cache. It is near the meeting of the Grand River—which flows from the base of Mt. Robson—and the Fraser River. Here I rested for two days and made repairs to our snow-shoes, which were nearly worn out and in bad shape.

A Hudson's Bay Company official, H. J. Moberly, gave the most plausible explanation for the early existence of the name Robson:

> Years before the Hudson's Bay Co. and the Nor'-West Co. joined (1821), it was the custom for the Nor'West Co. to outfit a party for a two years' trip, hunting and trading. . . . One party, under the charge of Peter S. Ogden, some two hundred men, chiefly Iroquois and French Canadians. When west of the Rockies, he scattered his hunters in different parties under the charge of a foreman, to hunt for the season. One of his camps, under the charge of a man named Robson, was somewhere in the vicinity of this mountain, and it was the rallying point where all other parties came together for their return east.

Mount Robson's unique grandeur has been appreciated for more than a century. Travelers cross-

Mount Robson as seen from
Berg Lake. Immediately below
the summit is the 2,600-foot
ice wall of the north face; from
it the Berg Glacier tumbles
into the lake. The right skyline
is the Emperor Ridge, with the
recently ascended Emperor
Face below. By John
Cleare/Mountain Camera.

ing the mountains by Yellowhead Pass invariably described the peak using adjectives like noble and majestic. An 1898 survey seems to have been sufficiently impressed with Robson to determine its elevation as 13,700 feet—an error of a magnitude far from the usual standards of accuracy. Nor did the weather attracted by the isolated giant go unnoticed. An 1862 traveler commented that "the guide told us that out of twenty-nine times he had passed it he had only seen the top once before the time we passed it, and as the day was very clear we could see the top quite plain." The storms that regularly assault the mountain, often when other parts of the Rockies are enjoying more benevolent weather, are a recurring theme in Robson's climbing history.

It was inevitable that Robson would intimidate men—but equally inevitable that the mountain would prove an irresistible lure to mountaineers and that its history would be one of heroic endeavors. The first climbers to approach Robson were Arthur P. Coleman, who was a geologist at the University of Toronto, his brother L. Q. Coleman, and the Reverend George Kinney. The Colemans and Kinney set out in 1907 from Lake Louise, its water an exquisite blue-green from the light reflected by minute particles of glacier-ground sediments.

Before the construction of the Canadian National Railroad, which passes through the resort town of Jasper, over Yellowhead Pass, and down the Fraser River, a long approach march—usually beginning from Banff—was necessary to reach the northern Canadian Rockies. As J. Monroe Thorington pointed out in an early guidebook to the range,

> Conditions under which mountaineering is carried on in the Canadian Rockies differ from those prevailing in the Alps or other inhabited mountain areas. Along the railroads alone are there places that can be regarded as climbing centers. Depart from these but little and a pack-trail must be employed, so that often far more time will be spent in travel than in actual climbing.

The Colemans and Kinney took a month to trek from Lake Louise to Robson—much of their route now followed by countless tourists on the Banff-Jasper Highway—and reached their destination in September, only to be stopped by bad weather. "Almost always," Coleman later wrote, "we were watching Mount Robson, or gazing at the clouds in his direction, sometimes catching a gleam of sunshine through the slanting raindrops, while blue gloom hid the mountains down the Grand Forks. At other times the top of Robson was caught by winds from the southwest, tumbling over its summit a grey cowl of flying clouds."

The three, accompanied by a man named Yates, returned to Robson in 1908. But before recounting their climbing efforts it is necessary to sketch the mountain's main architectural features. Robson's north face rises 7,500 feet from Berg Lake, the upper 2,000 feet being a steep ice wall. A prow forms the left edge of this wall and separates it from the broad east face. Two glaciers provide access to the mountain's east side: Berg Glacier, which falls into Berg Lake, and Robson Glacier, which terminates in alluvial gravel bars beyond the lake. A strip of ice extends the full height of the 1,300-foot east face, meeting the crest of the long south ridge where the ridge abuts the glacier-hung south face of the summit pyramid.

The right edge of the north face is the Emperor Ridge, and to *its* right, towering nearly 10,000 feet above the Robson River and the lake now known as Kinney Lake, is the west face. High in the center of this face a pair of ribs converge, and sweeping up to the summit through this convergence is the rib named the Wishbone Arête. To the south of the Wishbone Arête the snow slopes of the summit pyramid are guarded by icefalls and rock bands.

The Coleman/Kinney party first approached the peak from Robson Glacier, reaching the top of a 10,098-foot ice outcrop called the Dome. Kinney then made an attempt from the northwest, spending a night out alone, before snow squalls forced him back. The entire group then tried the east face, reaching the bergschrund formed by the glacier pulling away from the steeper ice frozen to the face, before turning back a third and final time.

Kinney was obsessed. In 1909, when his expected partners did not materialize, he left Edmonton alone, with three horses, three months' provisions, and less than three dollars. The flooded Athabasca River brought Kinney a partner, a young trapper and prospector named Donald Phillips, who also was waiting to cross the swollen river. Phillips was a handy fellow in this rugged country, but on the Big Smoky River he failed even to wound a large bull caribou with nine shots fired at less than fifty yards, while the caribou trotted up and stampeded the horses. Later, the rifle barrel was found to be bent. Such unlikely problems were part of mountaineering early in the century.

Arriving beneath Robson, Kinney and Phillips were awed by the steepness of the west face; they noted that a snow cornice could fall 7,000 feet from the crest of the Emperor Ridge. Nevertheless, from a high camp at about 10,000 feet they started up the face—apparently between the Emperor Ridge and the Wishbone Arête. Kinney, leading, chopped steps with his ice axe, while Phillips, with no climbing experience and a stick instead of an ice axe, followed. But stones loosened by the sun "whistled past," according to Kinney, and avalanches threatened, so the pair retreated. A second attempt was also thwarted by the threat of avalanches, and two more tries were frustrated by storms. But the weather cleared on August 12, and they returned from Kinney Lake to their high camp, where they cleared new snow to make beds among the rocks.

On the next day they passed their previous high point and continued up rock that Kinney estimated to be as steep as sixty degrees. "On all that upper climb," he later wrote, "we did nearly the whole work on our toes and hands only." They also encountered cornices that were apparently on the Emperor Ridge, for they could see a glacier descending to Berg Lake. But clouds soon obscured the mountain, and the climbers found themselves enshrouded by mist and sleet. Within 500 feet of the summit, according to Kinney's estimate, they met the bizarre ice formations—the gargoyles and mushrooms—that have proved an obstacle to all climbers high on Robson. "The snow," Kinney wrote, "driven by fierce gales, had built out against the wind in fantastic masses of crystal, forming huge cornices all along the crest of the peak."

Finally, according to Kinney, "we stood on the needle point of the highest and finest of all the Canadian Rockies, and the day was Friday, August the thirteenth, 1909." He added, "I doubt if ever a peak was fought for more desperately, or captured under greater difficulties." Kinney gave a prayer and proclaimed, "I capture this peak, Mt. Robson, for my country, and for the Alpine Club of Canada."

In mountaineering circles, however, some of Kinney's statements about his ascent were greeted with disbelief. And Phillips later admitted that "we reached, on our ascent (in mist and storm), an ice-dome fifty or sixty feet high, which we took for the peak. The danger was too great to ascend the dome." So, despite the valiant efforts of Kinney and Phillips on what some consider the mountain's most dangerous route, Robson had not been climbed after all.

When Englishmen Arnold L. Mumm, Leopold S. Amery, and Geoffrey Hastings, with guide Moritz Inderbinen, met Kinney and Phillips in Jasper on August 23, they heard Kinney's account, offered congratulations, and continued to Robson, hoping to reach the summit by the east face. Led by Inderbinen, this Alpine Club party found a way over the bergschrund but were slowed by a loose rock gully made slick by melting snow. Mumm later recalled

their difficulties: "Those who frequent the English Lakes at Christmas or a snowy Easter know the kind of thing I am trying to describe, but they do not get it in such large doses." Mumm was "impressed by the continuing steepness. . . . The rocky belt above appeared literally to overhang, like the eaves of a roof." Eventually the climbers, having started from too distant a base camp, were compelled to retreat because they ran out of daylight, but they had found a feasible route.

Taking advantage of the completion of the railroad, which passed within five miles of Robson's base, Arthur O. Wheeler led an Alpine Club of Canada camp to Robson in 1913. Anxious that Robson be climbed by his club, Wheeler invited Canada's most notable guide, Austrian-born Conrad Kain, to join the camp. Kain had seen the east face and recognized the avalanche danger, but he felt that much of the climbing could be done on rock to the left of an avalanche's likely fall line and that a dawn start would get a party above the worrisome lower slopes before the snow was loosened by the sun. On July 31, Kain crossed the bergschrund via a collapsed snow bridge, accompanied by William Foster and Albert MacCarthy, two strong mountaineers who were destined in 1925 to make the first ascent of Canada's highest peak, Mount Logan.

Swinging his heavy ice axe with one hand, Kain cut steps in a zigzag pattern to a rock ledge. But the rock that had promised a safe, rapid ascent proved difficult, and Kain was repeatedly forced to chop steps in the fifty-degree ice. Often, minutes elapsed before a move could be made; standing in small steps on a steep ice slope, exposed to rockfall and buffeted by a strong wind, was the most trying part of the climb.

At noon, after four hours on the hazardous wall now known as the Kain Face, the three reached the south ridge. The terrain was no longer so dangerous, but deep, loose snow made the going strenuous. On the slopes of the summit pyramid the climbers encountered the notorious hoarfrost formations, which Kain described as resembling "ostrich feathers" and which necessitated additional step cutting. According to MacCarthy, "Conrad cut steps as though inspired. The flying ice combined with drifting snow blown off the higher slopes, froze upon the clothing, and the rope, which had been wet earlier in the day, became hard and difficult to handle." Altogether Kain cut more than 600 steps during the climb. Finally, he turned to his comrades and said, "Gentlemen, that's as far as I can take you." They were on the summit.

After retracing the steps down the south ridge,

A climber stands just below
the summit of Mount Robson,
on the final few feet of the
south ridge, gained via the
Kain Face. By John
Cleare/Mountain Camera.

Bighorn lamb, part of a herd of fifteen ewes and their young, grazing near a snowfield in Jasper National Park, Alberta. By Richard and Ruth Pontius.

Kain, wishing to avoid his treacherous ascent route on the east face, chose instead to descend the unknown southwest face. At one point the trio was stopped by a steep drop and had to reascend, and one couloir was menaced by an ice cliff above, but by 10 P.M. they reached the safety of rock ledges, and there they bivouacked. As the climbers settled down for a cold night, an avalanche thundered down a nearby glacier, prompting Kain to remark, "If that goes on, it will spoil my good night's rest."

Kain, Foster, and MacCarthy returned to camp having performed the outstanding mountaineering feat yet accomplished in Canada. Basil Darling, a participant in the camp, declared the ascent "an exploit performed with a judgment, dash, and finish that should place it in the category of historic climbs."

Darling's evaluation has stood the test of time, but a few days later he nearly participated in an even more notable exploit. One morning, Darling, Harley Prouty, and guide Walter Schauffelberger began climbing the right-hand fork of the Wishbone Arête. The narrow crest, rising like a gigantic staircase,

necessitated continual rock climbing, though the difficulties were never exceptional. After twelve hours they reached an elevation of 12,500 feet and the array of awesome ice pinnacles that top the narrow ridge crest. Forced by the gargoyles—which these climbers likened to "a host of white-cowled monks"—to traverse on one side or the other of the ridge, the audacious Schauffelberger began chopping steps. But he could only strike short blows on the steep ice and in an hour had chopped fewer than sixty steps. The summit had been in view, but storm clouds rolled up the icy slopes, and the cold became intense. The rope froze as stiff as wire. Wind and snow made a night on the summit unthinkable, so the intrepid trio turned back, reaching 11,000 feet before being overtaken by night. Darling recalled that "snow fell all night, and thunder, lightning and the roar of the gale were continuous."

The Wishbone Arête was not climbed until 1955, when Donald Claunch of Seattle became interested in the gargoyles. "A feeling of admiration, irresistible attraction, and cold hostility is produced in the ambitious climber gazing at this spectacle,"

Claunch later wrote. He interested Harvey Firestone and Michael Sherrick in the challenge, and in early August the trio ascended the lower ridge, ice-plastered from a recent storm, and pitched a tent below the gargoyles. A day of climbing over, around, and through the bizarre ice formations left the climbers still 300 feet from the summit, facing the prospect of a second cold, cheerless night. "This perch was high, remote, and lonely in a strange ice world," wrote Claunch. On the third morning a very steep ice chute had to be surmounted, while ice chips swirled in a cold wind, but after a few more leads by Claunch, the climbers were on top, having completed the 1913 route forty-two years later.

Ice gargoyles also adorn the Emperor Ridge, and this northwest ridge of Robson was not climbed until July, 1961, when Ronald Perla and Tom Spencer found themselves in the midst of what they described as "tooth-like ice blocks" with "a translucent quality." Perla and Spencer traversed the ridge for thirty rope-lengths. Their technique, according to Spencer, "was to establish a solid axe belay on one ice block and thread our 150-foot rope alternately on the left and right side of subsequent blocks. It was occasionally necessary to chop away overhanging portions of blocks, and several ice pitons were used for direct aid." They bivouacked near the end of the ridge and in the morning reached the summit in a fantasy world of wind and snow.

The classic, steep ice of the north face was first climbed in 1963, by Patrik Callis and Dan Davis, and Robson was first climbed in winter in 1965, by a team composed of Leif Patterson, Alex Bertulis, Tom Stewart, and me, by way of the Kain Face. But the most difficult route yet done on the mountain lies on the Emperor Face—the right-hand facet of the north face, which rises in one great sweep to the Emperior Ridge. The weather must be stable and the face itself free of excessive snow for an attempt to be warranted on this dangerous wall. Several expert parties made attempts and either found conditions unsatisfactory or found themselves climbing too slowly. Finally, in the summer of 1978, Jim Logan and Terry Stump spent several days overcoming the face's numerous rock and ice bands and emerged on the Emperor Ridge unscathed. Logan later wrote that "the real key to climbing the Emperor Face was making a firm decision to try, regardless of the obstacles that nature and our imagination might place in our path."

No easy routes reach the summit of Robson, and Logan's remark applies to any climb of the mountain and to any climber who would confront the aura and the dangers of this monarch of rock and ice.

Howser Spire

And now a still grander view lay before us: a broad, more or less circular glacier stretched out and rounded up to rest on the sides of several beautiful spires along its south edge, one of them with its outline capped by an image of a pouter pigeon; at its west side it ran up high on the walls of a lofty ridge that stood in a semi-circle with five sharp peaks vying with each other for leadership.

A. H. MacCarthy
Canadian Alpine Journal, 1917

A STREAM, by erosion, deepens a valley, but but the valley's location is determined by the character of the bedrock—by fractures and faults, for instance. West of the Canadian Rockies, five rivers flow parallel to the range's crest, separating the Rockies from the Interior Ranges of British Columbia. These rivers—including the Columbia and the Fraser—are aligned as segments of one remarkably straight crease in the earth, the Rocky Mountain Trench, indicating that the trench existed before the streams. In fact, it marks a deep break in the crust. The origin and significance of the Rocky Mountain Trench are not fully understood, but it separates mountains of vastly dissimilar geologic history. The Rockies, east of the trench, are a folded and faulted range; the Interior Ranges on the west consist chiefly of great masses of ancient metamorphosed rock intruded by granite.

The Columbia flows northwest in the trench but then bends sharply south. Within this bend, two of the Interior Ranges are themselves separated by another linear depression, the Purcell Trench, which is occupied by the Beaver and Duncan rivers. East of this trench lies the Purcell Range, west of it lies the Selkirk Range.

When the great Welsh explorer David Thompson was in the region in 1807, he heard the news of Admiral Nelson's victory at Trafalgar and named a nearby peak Mount Nelson. On his map all the peaks within the Columbia's loop were Nelson's Mountains. Fifty years later, a surveyor named the Purcells for a professor of his, and geologists, judging the Purcells a separate range from the Selkirks, adopted the name.

Thompson, unraveling the complex geography of the Canadian mountains for the North West Company, discovered Howse Pass through the Rockies in 1807, followed the Columbia upstream through the Rocky Mountain Trench, and near its headwaters built a fur-trading post he called Kootenae House. Thompson circled the Purcells and Selkirks in 1811 but did not penetrate the mountains.

A cluster of large rock spires—a granite stock, geologists would learn, that intruded into billion-year-old metamorphosed sediments deposited at the edge of an ocean—had been seen from the Rockies and from Mount Sir Donald in the Selkirks. But these granite spires were a mystery until 1910, when surveyors Tom Longstaff and Arthur O. Wheeler, accompanied by a young Austrian guide named Conrad Kain and photographer Byron Harmon, took a sternwheeler up the Columbia and continued on horseback, ascending a stream that had been called Bugaboo Creek by disenchanted miners. At the head of Bugaboo Creek they crossed Bugaboo Pass and descended Howser Creek to the Duncan River on the west flank of the Purcells. Wheeler and Kain opted to

Above: The slabby east face of Pigeon Spire, a classic example of a nunatak. By Galen Rowell.

Page 140: Triple-peaked Howser Spire, the crown of the Bugaboo group in the Purcell Range. The South Tower is on the left. By Galen Rowell.

turn back when the horses could not descend a canyon, but Longstaff and Harmon, continuing, were surprised to meet a trapper heading *into* the mountains in late September. The avalanche danger would be too great for him to leave the mountains before the spring melt, but this self-sufficient fellow was equipped to spend a solitary winter in a wilderness as elemental as any on earth.

Longstaff's account of "remarkable nunataks or aiguilles rising out of Harmon's big glacier" and Harmon's photographs taken during the traverse of the Purcells interested climbers in the remote, unnamed peaks.

Six years later, Kain returned to the mysterious nunataks with a climbing group organized by Albert MacCarthy. A nunatak, according to one geological dictionary, is "an isolated hill or peak which projects through the surface of a glacier," but what MacCarthy, Kain, and party beheld from the head of Bugaboo Creek was something more than the usual nunatak, which is a single rock outcrop. It was the group that, after being named the Bugaboos, would offer the most popular wilderness rock climbs in Canada. MacCarthy later described the view from Bugaboo Creek:

> From there we received our first impressions of the vastness of this granite region and the great number of climbs it offers. To the northwest in a row the three spires referred to by Doctor Longstaff as "The Nunataks," shot out of the glacier, so we designated them from south to north, Numbers 1, 2, and 3; to the west beyond this line several other peaks shown between these three, and several more rose on the east of them. All these spires presented more or less the same appearance and several seemed to be of about the same height, so at Conrad's suggestion we crossed the glacier to the east of the three and ascended to the summit of the saddle between Nos. 2 and 3.

To determine "which peak was the ruler of this mighty array," the explorers walked onto the Vowell Glacier, MacCarthy "devoutly hoping that No. 2 would not be chosen; for, with the sheer cliffs on all sides we had seen, it seemed clearly impossible." Flanked to the east by the numbered nunataks, to the west by a compact three-peaked ridge—five-peaked by MacCarthy's count, as he included two minor summits—the party chose, correctly, the high point of the ice-plastered ridge. They named the entire ridge Howser Spire, a source of some confusion, as the massif may be considered to have three spires. These three, however, are today called towers—the

North, Middle, and South towers of Howser Spire.

Having located the high point of the Bugaboos, Kain, MacCarthy, his wife Bess, John Vincent, Mrs. George Vincent, and H. O. Frind continued across the glacier to the North Tower. They ascended a steep slope of snow-covered ice—MacCarthy measured it as fifty-two degrees—toward the notch between the North and Middle towers. The snow led to a six-inch-wide crack between a "blank wall" and a "smooth slab," years before crack-climbing techniques became a standard item in a climber's repertoire. By improvising a variety of foot jams and twists of the knee and shinnying up the edge of the crack, the climbers reached a series of snow cornices, a section of loose rock, and steep ice up which Kain, as guide, cut steps.

During lunch, eaten at the notch, MacCarthy was "amused at the frank curiosity of a small mountain squirrel which ran about on the rocks chattering at us in a most friendly manner, finally coming within a few feet to enjoy its noonday meal of lichen, thus showing it did not believe man's treachery would carry to such heights." MacCarthy had discovered the notorious Bugaboo "snafflehound," a species of ground squirrel which, apparently quick to forgive man's treachery, makes regular meals of climbers' unguarded food, tents, leather boots, and climbing ropes.

In mid-afternoon the Kain-MacCarthy party climbed an arête, wriggled through a tight window behind a large boulder, and reached the 11,150-foot summit of Howser Spire. They crossed the summit and descended the north ridge, then, at 7 P.M., the snow of the east face. The steepness forced the weary climbers to face in, toward the snow, and kick steps. Kain, ever the responsible guide, lowered the others by rope from the bergschrund's upper lip, then rigged a rappel for himself from a protrusion of snow.

A few days later, Kain, the MacCarthys, and John Vincent turned their attentions to "No. 3 peak," a 10,420-foot pyramid which will always be associated with Kain and was considered by the great Austrian guide to be his most difficult climb in Canada. About 1,200 feet of scrambling up the south ridge took the climbers to the *pièce de résistance*, to again quote MacCarthy, a few hundred feet below the top. "Our route was completely blocked by a most formidable gendarme," wrote MacCarthy, "whose base completely spanned the width of the ridge. The way to the west was blocked by cliffs. The gendarme, "which immediately suggested to our minds the appropriateness of the name 'Bugaboo' for this spire," rose hornlike to a sharp point that abutted the sheer, 2,000-foot east wall. Kain decided the gendarme's face offered the only hope and gradually worked up diagonal cracks, finally crawling over an edge, much to the relief of MacCarthy, who "supposed the difficulties were ended."

"But," continued MacCarthy, "they had really just begun." A crack seven feet to the left was the only possible way, but the intervening slab lacked holds for either hand or foot. A very audacious series of moves was required, and Kain retreated twice, feeling the holds insufficient. For a half hour he probed the rock, then retreated to "survey the situation." Kain was too far above his belayer to afford to fall; the belayer could only tend the useless rope, paying it out or pulling in slack. Kain recalled an obstacle in the Tyrol he had overcome by using an ice axe. He tried jamming his axe in the crack to take the weight off a foot, but this proved useless. Finally, he jammed his left arm in the crack and found a hold for his right hand. Moving delicately, he was able to continue.

The seventy-foot Gendarme Pitch was the crux of this memorable ascent. The pitch is considered only moderately difficult today, but modern climbers wear rubber-soled climbing shoes, are belayed with trustworthy nylon ropes, and are protected on the crux move by a nearby piton. Kain's daring, under the circumstances, was remarkable. Kain's followers climbed the gendarme with the aid of a doubled rope. Soon, Bugaboo Spire had been conquered.

The ascent of Bugaboo Spire required climbing of a difficulty extreme by the standards of 1916, and MacCarthy's assessment of No. 2 as "clearly impossible" was realistic. Even Kain declared it to be beyond his ability. "After carefully searching with powerful binoculars," he later wrote, "I came to the conclusion that this pinnacle will prove very hard to conquer. Since then I have had the opportunity to study the peak from different angles, and I have not changed my opinion. I feel inclined to prophesy that this pinnacle will be the most difficult in the Canadian Alps." Not until 1940 was a route found up No. 2, by then renamed Snowpatch Spire. The ascent by a team of Californians required equipment, such as pitons, not available to Kain and MacCarthy.

Snowpatch Spire was the prize of the Bugaboos, but the South Tower of Howser Spire had not yet been climbed. Although some 300 feet lower than the North Tower, it was obviously more difficult and was not even attempted until 1941, when a Seattle party composed of Lloyd Anderson, my brother Helmy, Lyman Boyer, and Tom Campbell faced the problem of crossing the immense bergschrund at the base of an ice sheet on the east face.

Three climbers traverse a
snowfield beneath the
imposing east face of
Snowpatch Spire in the
Bugaboos. Pigeon Spire looms
behind the snow col; the
skyline of Bugaboo Spire is
seen on the right. By Art Wolfe.

144

The climbers had driven twenty-five miles on dirt roads from the Columbia River valley, then backpacked five miles to timberline. They had read about the South Tower, studied photographs, and speculated about it; setting up base camp, they had been anxious to see their spear-shaped objective. Boyer later remembered the first view: "Sprawled on a rocky promontory high above the last trees, we gazed intensely at a cloud. Hail blew in our faces. Reluctantly the cloud lifted, revealing the last unclimbed giant of the Bugaboo group."

Helmy recalled that "the ice wall behind the 'schrund was very steep, and Boyer, who led, chopped lots of steps and used a few ice pitons to protect himself until he reached a rock outcropping." While Boyer cut steps up the sixty-degree ice, his comrades tried to cheer him by pointing out that "at least no one has been this far."

While the Seattle climbers ascended a broken granite face interspersed with ice, an interested audience appeared below on the Vowell Glacier. They were a Sierra Club group who had also come to make the first ascent of the South Tower. The coincidence was remarkable, and the Sierrans' disappointment at finding a rival team must have been deep.

At 7:00 P.M., Helmy crossed an ice mound at the head of the main couloir and "with a glad whoop," according to Boyer, "informed us that he had found a fine, level ledge." Here the four worked until dark to build a windbreak and a rock floor on the underlying ice. "With all our spare clothing on," Boyer later wrote, "we took off our boots and put our feet into our rucksacks, huddled together, and tried to keep warm." During the night a "snafflehound" found the food the climbers were saving for the next day's lunch.

The morning began with a false start to the left. Traversing right, the climbers found ledges leading to more promising terrain, but they had to return to the bivouac site, because of a snowpatch, for nailed boots and ice axes. By 11:00 they had gained only thirty feet. Boyer gave Campbell a shoulder stand to reach past a smooth spot. A jam crack led to a series of pitches that were a pleasure to climb in soft-soled shoes. A wall that ended in an overhang required each climber to stand in stirrups suspended from pitons. But soon they reached the summit, where Helmy casually mentioned that it was his sixteenth birthday. Moonlight aided the descent, but the climbers stumbled into their base camp after a forty-hour absence.

Albert MacCarthy, having seen the west flank of the spire from the notch between the North and Middle towers, observed that "it dropped in one sheer cliff for several thousand feet to a small, nearly flat glacier at its base, presenting a face that would defy any sort of attack." In 1959, I made a circuit beneath the west faces of Howser Spire and was astounded. I found giant columns of rock soaring upward for 2,000 feet or more. I was particularly drawn to a buttress on the South Tower that from any vantage point swept up in architectural loveliness. Here was a climb of the high standards being set in Yosemite Valley, but in an alpine setting. It would be the most spectacular route on the western Howser walls.

Bad weather prevented an all-out attempt, but two years later I returned with Yvon Chouinard. After carrying loads and setting up camp at the col between the South Tower and Pigeon Spire, we dropped to the base of the buttress and, to test ourselves and the rock, climbed a few pitches on perfect rock. To make the reascent of these pitches easier, we left two ropes hanging from pitons and returned to camp for a good night's sleep.

Ascending the ropes in the morning, Chouinard found to his horror that two of the three strands of the upper rope had been severed, chewed by a "snafflehound." Fortunately, we had an extra rope and did not resort again to climbing anchored ropes left overnight. We climbed thirteen pitches that have since been described by Steve Roper and Allen Steck as "the landscape of a rockclimber's dream." Our experience in Yosemite cracks served us well, and we needed to employ little direct aid.

We bivouacked in soft granite sand at the base of the Great White Headwall. This exposed prow, as we had anticipated, proved to be the crux of the ascent, but by the next afternoon, we stood on top of the South Tower. The climb was almost too good to be true: perfect summer weather and clean, continuous cracks requiring a variety of techniques on a pillar soaring like a giant white fin into the sky. And best of all, we could look down upon a vast wilderness. The same scene inspired Galen Rowell, climbing the west face of the North Tower ten years later, to wonder,

> What is wilderness? Is this wilderness? If not, is there any wilderness? These thoughts rushed through my mind as I remembered my personal definition: a place where the current of evolution, which quite incidentally led to the creation of man, goes on little interrupted by his presence. Below me was the wildest country I had ever seen. At my back was a virgin granite wall and in the vast panorama I saw no place where there could be a trail, a road, or other evidence of man.

Mount Sir Donald

Above the forest-clad slopes, precipices almost we might call them, and rising above the top of the waterfall, the crags of Eagle peak stand up 5,000 feet from the track. Running our eye along this high rocky rampart, towards the right, that is towards the south, we behold the huge obelisk of Sir Donald 10,629 feet high, the face towards us a sheet of bare rock inaccessible to man or beast. Sharp jagged arêtes *meet it on either hand and suggest possibilities of ascent. Farther to the right the lower part of the* arête *loses itself in a saddle of snow-covered glacier which forms the sky-line for about a mile. From this saddle, which we have called the Great Illecellewaet Nevé, descends in a single plunge of over 2,500 feet a fine glacier of pure white ice.*

W. S. Green
Among the Selkirk Glaciers, 1890

IN 1857, the British government sent an expedition under Captain John Palliser to explore the possibilities for a transcontinental railroad across the colony of Canada. The Palliser expedition found a feasible route through the Rockies but not through the more heavily forested mountains to the west, in what is now British Columbia—mountains designated on the Palliser map as the Selkirk Range, named for Lord Selkirk, a patron of the Hudson's Bay Company.

In 1865, surveyor Walter Moberly approached the Selkirks from the west and followed the Illecillewaet River into the mountains. Six years later, Moberly discovered a pass through the Selkirks farther north, but it was a crossing found by Major Albert B. Rogers that became the route of the Canadian Pacific Railroad. In 1881, Rogers, with his nephew and a few Kamloops Indians, ascended the Illecillewaet to the pass at its head and climbed Mount Avalanche. The next year he completed the route by reaching the pass, which is now named Rogers Pass, from the Beaver River to the east. He called the finest peak seen from the vicinity of the pass Syndicate Peak, for the group financing the railroad.

Sir Sandford Fleming, the engineer-in-chief of surveying, traveled the railroad line to the Pacific in 1883. Fleming was perhaps the first, though by no means the last, to give a vivid account of the flora of the moist Selkirk country. After three days along the Illecillewaet during which the party traveled only ten miles, Fleming wrote, "Rain! Rain! Rain! . . . The walking is wretchedly bad, we made little headway, and every tree, every leaf is wet and casts off the rain. In a short time we are as drenched as the foliage. . . . Skunk cabbage here is indigenous and is found in acres of stinking perfection. . . . We try another course, only to become entangled in a windfall of prostrate trees."

The final railroad spike was driven on November 7, 1885, by financier Donald A. Smith (later Lord Strathcona) and Rogers' Syndicate Peak was soon renamed Mount Sir Donald. The next year a hotel called the Glacier House was opened near Rogers Pass, within sight of the Illecillewaet Glacier and in the shadow of Mount Sir Donald, which, with an elevation of 10,818 feet, towered 7,000 feet above the hotel a mere four miles away. So closely did the Selkirk slopes impinge on the hotel and railroad that "snow sheds" had to be constructed to carry avalanches over the tracks.

Above: **The sheer quartzite face of Mount Dag towers above Mulvey Basin, in the Valhalla group of the Selkirk Range. By Pat Morrow.**

Facing page: **A white-tailed ptarmigan on rocky terrain in the Selkirks. The red comb above the eye indicates that this is a breeding male. By David Sumner.**

Page 146: **The distinctive pyramid of Mount Sir Donald, in the Selkirk Range of British Columbia, looms above a field of paintbrush. By Ed Cooper.**

Mountains so accessible quickly attracted visitors, whose extravagant praise of the Selkirks attracted still more visitors. Otto J. Klotz, a British surveyor and astronomer, described Rogers Pass in 1886: "The climax of grandeur in the Selkirks is at the summit: Mountain, rocks, peaks, ice, snow, glaciers, cascades, streams and richly clothed valleys present a panoramic scene that can never be effaced from the memory."

In 1884, English clergyman and mountaineer Henry Swanzy had made a photographic excursion to Canada and had ventured by horse to Rogers Pass. The Selkirks' striking rock peaks, glaciers, and wet forests reminded Swanzy of the Alps. In 1888, he persuaded his cousin, William Spotswood Green, who had climbed in Switzerland and New Zealand, to accompany him to the Selkirks. The Royal Geographic Society loaned the pair a number of surveying instruments, and Swanzy and Green not only were the first climbers in the Selkirks, they did valuable topographic mapping as well. Swanzy and Green climbed several peaks, of which the most impressive was 10,194-foot Mount Bonney, five miles southwest of Glacier House. Sir Donald, however, eluded them, an attempt from the Illecillewaet Glacier to the south ending at a minor 9,729-foot summit.

In 1890, Green published his delightful *Among the Selkirk Glaciers*, in which he described the view from this peak:

> On all sides were vast precipices, and down these precipices our eyes ranged to the green, forest-clad valley of Beaver Creek, the river being visible for many miles, winding with an infinity of curves 6,000 feet below us.
>
> Beyond the river rose a range of hills with flattish plateaux on the top, flecked with snow. Still further to the eastward, range rose upon range, fading into purple and blue. Above them all, the Rockies, bearing silvery white glaciers, formed a sharply defined sky-line, and were visible for over 150 miles. . . . To the southward it was totally different; in that direction the undulating fields of glacier lay like a great soft white blanket, covering up everything for ten miles, beyond which other snow-seamed crags rose, rivalling, probably in some cases surpassing, Sir Donald in elevation.

Green also described a creature that must be closely related to the Bugaboo "snafflehound": "To our great disgust [we] found that some beast had got at our packs, and with a most depraved taste had breakfasted off my Alpine rope. It was on the outside of the pack, tied on in a coil, and the wretched creature had nibbled through every bight of the coil, thus cutting up the rope into a number of short lengths."

Sir Donald was first climbed in 1890, by Swiss Alpine Club members Emil Huber and Carl Sulzer, who ascended the southwest face and southeast arête in only six hours from a high camp.

Returning home, Huber and Sulzer visited with members of the Appalachian Mountain Club, and soon these Bostonians, led by Professor Charles Fay, were visiting Glacier House. Accounts of this charming hotel during its early days portray a pleasantly rowdy atmosphere, with horses bolting in fear of trains, "Mother" Young at midnight salvaging soggy railroad tickets from the laundry, and a pet bear cub squealing for its mother.

The Canadian Pacific also built the Glacier Circle Cabin several miles south of Glacier House in an amphitheater south of the Illecillewaet Névé. With this cabin serving as a base, ascents were made of peaks rising from the surrounding complex of glaciers and icefalls. The most notable climb was the 1899 first ascent of 11,123-foot Mount Dawson, highest point of the Selkirks south of the railroad, by Professor Fay and two guides who were to distinguish themselves on Mount Assiniboine, Edouard Feuz and Christian Häsler. Surveyors J. J. McArthur and Howard Palmer also relished the exploratory nature of British Columbia mountaineering and made many first ascents, often encumbered by a packful of surveying instruments. Palmer even probed the defenses of remote, 11,590-foot Mount Sir Sandford, highest point in the Selkirks, finally effecting its first ascent in 1912.

The arrival, in 1899, of skilled Swiss guides employed by the railroad company ushered in a new era in Canadian mountaineering. The railroad gave its guides a good deal of publicity, even displaying them in Montreal and London. It often seemed that their main function was to be seen in full climbing costume on the train platform.

Mount Sir Donald, so impressively visible from Glacier House, received a disproportionate share of attention. In 1900, when the peak had been scaled four times, George Vaux and Swiss guide Edouard Feuz and Karl Schluneggar pioneered a variant of the 1890 route on the southwest face, a variant that became the standard route for ascending Sir Donald.

Mount Sir Donald was first climbed by a woman in 1901, when Mrs. E. E. Berens celebrated her honeymoon with an ascent of the Vaux route with two guides. Proper clothing was an important question in this unliberated era; a council of ladies at the hotel decided upon her husband's best pair of

knickers. Mrs. Berens doubted her guides' assertion that as much as five hours would be required to reach the summit from the first rocks. Later, she was to write, "I thought to myself, what nonsense! I am sure we can easily get there in an hour or so. Alas! my conceit was very quickly taken out of me, as I found that it was not such an easy climb as it looked. Be wise, my friends, and never despise a mountain."

Feuz regularly guided the Vaux route, but he was intrigued by the other possibilities on Sir Donald, in particular on the northwest arête. Seen in profile from Glacier House, this arête rises to the summit in one smooth, razorlike sweep. But Feuz, familiar with the peak's angular quartzite, knew the rock, in detail, was not as smooth as the distant profile appeared.

Late in the summer of 1903 Feuz had as a client a competent German mountaineer named Erhard Tewes and with another guide associated with Assiniboine, Christian Bohren, set out for the northwest arête. The trio began climbing unroped on the solid quartzite, but the dramatic exposure down the north face on the one side and the west face on the other soon encouraged the use of the heavy hemp rope. On the easier sections, the three climbed simultaneously, the guides tied to either end of the rope and Tewes in the middle; on the more difficult pitches, Feuz and Bohren belayed their client. Feuz and his companions veered onto the west face for the final third of their climb, but in 1909 the great ridge was climbed in its entirety by Val Fynn and A. M. Bartlett.

The northwest arête became the classic climb of the Selkirks. Howard Palmer, who made the fourth ascent, termed the arête a "masterful, clean-cut sweep." He also described the character of the climbing: "It is impossible to narrate the ascent in detail. The obstacles were all so much alike and so numerous that in retrospect they blend into a confused impression, a hodgepodge of chimneys, cracks, corners, caverns, ledges, and ridges."

One of my two adventures on Sir Donald took place on the north face, the other on the Vaux route. In August, 1961, Yvon Chouinard and I, fresh from the north face of Mount Edith Cavell in the Rockies, took a train to Rogers Pass, then sulked while rain soaked the forest. One day our only amusement was watching a bear swim the raging stream that drains the Illecillewaet Glacier. A bright dawn, though, coaxed us out of camp the next day, and we hiked quickly to the col between the northwest arête and Uto Peak to the north. Here we descended to a small glacier under the north face and began our ascent. We chose to travel light, exchanging the security of extra ropes and bivouac gear for the freedom to climb rapidly that is not possible with cumbersome, heavy packs. We were in shape to climb boldly, and the sharp holds provided by the quartzite made our choice a good one. On some pitches we coiled the rope, carrying it over our packs and ice axes. On more fearsome sections, we belayed with piton anchors and moved out on long, piton-protected leads. At the end of each pitch I gauged our progress by sighting past the skyline of 9,620-foot Uto; when its summit was below the peaks north of Rogers Pass, I knew the climb would be ours. It was a day of perfect weather, firm rock, confidence, and fast climbing. After a short rest at the top, we descended the northwest arête, a great experience in itself, and were in the meadows below by sunset.

In March, 1965, I had made a winter ascent of Mount Robson, and conditions were promising for a winter climb of the great pyramid of the Selkirks. Donald Liska, Alex Bertulis, Dave Beckstead, and I drove from Seattle to Rogers Pass, then skied to the base of the Vaux route. To the southwest the great Illecillewaet Glacier tumbled 4,000 feet in a mile-wide ice cataract. In summer, a narrow couloir we ascended is often the pathway of falling rock, and, despite its frozen condition, we climbed with anxious upward glances and hurrying feet. Fortunately, crampons bit well into the ice that covered the slabs and broken blocks.

The sun reached us by late morning, but we took only a brief lunch break, for, having no bivouac equipment, we had to be off the mountain by dark. As we moved quickly and efficiently along the narrow summit ridge, the sky clouded over. One of the pictures I took shows us huddled on the summit, having completed the first winter ascent of Sir Donald, with down parka hoods drawn tight, pile mittens, double boots, gaiters, and crampons. We looked cold, and we were. As we began descending, the first snowflakes of an approaching storm whitened the air.

Mount Timpanogos

Crossing the next day a slight ridge along the river, we entered a handsome mountain valley covered with fine grass, and directed our course towards a high snowy peak, at the foot of which lay the Utah lake. On our right was a bed of high mountains, their summits covered with snow, constituting the dividing ridge between the Basin waters and those of the Colorado.

. . . It [Utah Lake] is almost entirely surrounded by mountains, walled on the north and east by a high and snowy range, which supplies to it a fan of tributary streams. Among these, the principal river is the Timpan-ogo— *signifying Rock river—a name which the rocky grandeur of its scenery, remarkable even in this country of rugged mountains, has obtained for it from the Indians.*

John C. Frémont
Report of Expedition to the Rocky Mountains,
1844

THREE-FOURTHS of the population of Utah is concentrated in the valley of Great Salt Lake and Utah Lake. It is not by chance that the chain of prospering cities in this valley lies at the base of the bold front of the Wasatch Range. Utah is the nation's second-driest state, and the water needed to support the population, its agriculture, and its industry is a precious commodity. The mountains draw scarce moisture from the atmosphere; from their heights flow streams that provide fresh water for Salt Lake City, Provo, Ogden, and other cities. In addition, two streams—the Provo River, which was once known as the Timpanogos River, and the Weber River—cut through the range,

bringing water from the range's eastern slopes to the populous valley.

The spine of the Wasatch Range extends for 160 miles down the center of Utah's northern half. The Wasatch averages twenty-five miles in width and is nearly joined to another range to the east, the east-west trending Uinta Mountains. The highest summit, 11,928-foot Mount Nebo, rises at the range's southern end, but peaks to the north, being more alpine and nearer population centers, are the Wasatch's main attractions. On the skyline east and southeast of Salt Lake City loom Mount Olympus, Twin Peaks, and Lone Peak, while towering more than 7,000 feet above Provo stands the most impressive and the second highest in the range, 11,750-foot Mount Timpanogos.

The Wasatch Range receives ample precipitation because of its north-south orientation and its elevation, averaging 10,000 feet. Weather in these mountains can be extreme. Violent winds down the canyons may accompany the arrival of arctic air. During summer thunderstorms, torrents of water running off steep slopes collect quickly in narrow stream cuts; streams occasionally rise with the sudden, dangerous surge known as a flash flood.

But most of the precipitation occurs as winter snow. At Alta, a Wasatch ski resort located near the head of Little Cottonwood Canyon and noted for its powder snow, seventy percent of the fifty inches of annual precipitation falls in winter. Twenty years ago one storm, caused by a cold arctic front colliding with moist Gulf of Mexico air, dropped one hundred inches of snow at Alta.

Such large quantities of snow in such steep terrain create dangerous avalanche situations. Alta's

A wintry view of Mount
Timpanogos in the Wasatch
Range, Utah, from the north
fork of the Provo River. By
David Muench.

hundred-inch storm resulted in more than a hundred avalanches crossing the canyon road. During the late nineteenth century, when the lure of gold for a time outweighed the common sense needed to survive the mountains in winter, more than 170 deaths were caused by sliding snow. Basins at the head of both Big and Little Cottonwood canyons offer easily accessible ski touring, but snow depths of ten and fifteen feet and treacherous wind slab may make conditions hazardous.

The hazard is greatest on steep slopes and in gullies; any Wasatch slope steeper than thirty degrees must be distrusted. But slides dropping over mountain walls may gain enough momentum to run out onto flat terrain or even continue up a valley's opposite slope. Unconsolidated snow of early winter can create dangerous situations: in time, structural changes occur within a snowpack; crystals become interlocked, and under some conditions snowflakes are transformed to smoother granules, or depth hoar. Depth hoar may have the effect of ball bearings, creating a surface along which a slab of snow above may slide.

While water in its various forms is an important part of the Wasatch's present, water of a more extraordinary sort has an important place in the history—geological and human—of the region: a lake that is no longer and a river that never was.

The Wasatch forms the eastern rim of a geophysical region that stretches across western Utah and Nevada to the Sierra Nevada and is known as the Basin and Range province. This vast area is characterized by a series of parallel, north–south trending mountain ranges separated by broad valleys. Each basin and each range represents a fault block, a segment of the earth's crust separated from adjacent blocks by north-south trending faults. Along these faults the ranges were thrust upward and the basins dropped downward. The Wasatch Range is itself a young fault-block range. The Wasatch Fault, which is manifested in the range's abrupt western front, is one of America's great fault lines. The faulting that elevated the Wasatch to its prominent position above the valley of Great Salt Lake and Utah Lake began 35 million years ago and has continued intermittently to the present. The most rapid uplift has been during the past 4 million years.

The rocks exposed by this massive uplift vary from granitic to sedimentary, from very ancient to geologically young. Little Cottonwood Canyon and Lone Peak are granite; Big Cottonwood Canyon is quartzite; Timpanogos is limestone and sandstone. Prior to the Wasatch uplift much of the sedimentary rock had been severely folded during the Laramide

Orogeny, the episode of crustal disturbance in which the Rocky Mountains as an entity were created. The aggregate thickness of the exposed rock formations, 50,000 feet, make the Wasatch escarpment of special geologic interest.

Stream erosion carved a series of V-shaped valleys into the Wasatch block, valleys that have since been modified to the U-shaped cross-section characteristic of glaciation. The Wasatch Range is too far south to have been covered by the continuous ice sheets that spread over the northern part of the continent during the ice ages of the past million years, but smaller glaciers formed on much of the range. At one time at least fifty glaciers that were over a mile long descended the western slope; the longest, extending twelve miles, occupied Little Cottonwood Canyon. Moraines deposited during three major glaciations are conspicuous near canyon mouths.

Great Salt Lake owes its saltiness to the absence of an outlet: water evaporates and salt accumulates. During the ice ages, when temperatures were lower and precipitation greater, the landlocked area of Utah and Nevada was occupied by numerous lakes, which were fed by the mountain glaciers of such ranges as the Wasatch. At one time 123 of these lakes covered twenty per cent of the region. The largest has been called Lake Bonneville, after the nineteenth-century explorer who tried to attach his name to Great Salt Lake (and who made the first ascent of a disputed peak in the Wind River Range). This ancient lake, nearly the size of present-day Lake Michigan, lapped the base of the Wasatch, and discharged north, into the Snake River in Idaho. Utah Lake and Great Salt Lake are mere remnants of this immense body of water.

The first white visitors apparently assumed that Utah Lake and Great Salt Lake were one body of water, and also gave it an outlet. An expedition led by the Spanish missionaries Escalante and Domínguez reached Utah Lake in September, 1776, hoping to discover a feasible route from New Mexico to northern California. A soldier accompanying the padres, Miera y Pacheco, drew a generally accurate map of their journey, but he combined the two lakes into a Lake Timpanogos and invented an outlet, which he named the San Buenaventura River, flowing west off the edge of his map.

Subsequent mapmakers thought it reasonable that Miera's river would reach the Pacific; thus a myth was created that played a significant role in the history of the fur trade. Jedediah Smith, the greatest explorer among the fur trappers, traveled from Great Salt Lake to the Mojave Desert in southern California in 1825, and returned by a more northerly route,

153

but his failure to find the San Buenaventura did little to extinguish the myth. A party of California emigrants in 1841 were advised to take boat-building materials on their long trek across the Great Plains and through the Rockies, so they could float to their new homeland from Great Salt Lake.

It took an official reconnaissance, an expedition led by Lieutenant John C. Frémont, to finally eradicate the San Buenaventura from maps. Having traveled west to Oregon, south to the southern tip of the Sierra Nevada, then back to the foot of the Wasatch, Frémont sat at Utah Lake on May 24, 1844, and wrote in his journal that the rivers of California

do not breach the Sierra; that the region he called the Great Basin has no outlet to the sea; that, in short, the San Buenaventura does not exist.

I had in past years made some rock-climbing ventures to challenge the steep granite walls of Lone Peak, though I had never set foot on the higher Mount Timpanogos. But the opportunity finally came, after a night drive along the aspen-lined canyon of the American Fork to the 7,400-foot Timpooneke trailhead. My headlights caught the common sight of a skunk, then a less-common one—a cougar. Encountering this rare, crafty cat in other circumstances would have been more pleasurable, but to see this beast at night, near where I would soon be sleeping out in remote, wooded mountains, was hardly a comforting experience. I changed my plan and slept in my car.

Setting out in the morning on a trail that ascends the mountain's east side, I could see to the south the canyon of the Provo River. The foothills of Provo Canyon were covered with oak and maple scrub, the oaks present up to 9,000 feet on the mountainside. The trail took me through an aspen forest, the light breeze making the leaves quiver—or quake—on their long, flexible stems. It was early September; the leaves, now light green, in a few weeks would turn to shades ranging from luminous yellow to deep red. The aspen stands were interspersed with parklike meadows. Higher, I entered a forest of pine and fir.

The trail climbed to a large east-facing gully, which even in early autumn held snowfields. A chaos of firs lying in the snow showed the gully to be swept by winter avalanches. At one time, glaciers filled the cirques on this side of the mountain, coalescing downhill to form a continuous body of ice that descended to 6,000 feet. Today Timpanogos shelters only one small glacier on its southeast flank, which drains into Emerald Lake.

The trail makes use of the sedimentary bedding planes to gain elevation by long, gentle switchbacks, and I could admire the abundant wildflowers. Amid the bewildering variety I recognized familiar flowers: paintbrush, larkspur, Parry's primrose, columbine, and stonecrop. Certain of the flowers—bistort, lupine, mountain bluebell, and showy fleabane— have flexible stems that allow the plant to bend with the wind. Several species concealed butterflies, but the ubiquitous bees concentrated on the phacelia. Soon I reached tundralike slopes where plants grow as low, thick mats to minimize exposure to the wind, which evaporates valuable moisture. Here were pink moss campions and penstemons of several sizes and colors.

Elk herd in the Wasatch Range.
By Steve Solum/Bruce
Coleman, Inc.

Ski touring in the Wasatch
Range, near the south fork of
Provo Canyon, Uinta National
Forest. By Dick Stum.

The south end of the summit block of Timpanogos, as seen from near the true summit. By Ed Cooper.

Plants of this high alpine zone have the benefit of more intense solar radiation, ironically, than the warmer, more fertile valley 7,000 feet below. However, the shortness of the snow-free growing season, in addition to wind and cold, limits life at this elevation to specially adapted plants.

A path continued to the summit, where a metal building, marked with a county survey sign, reminded me that Timpanogos, within sight of a string of cities, is a popular objective for hikers. Most urban centers have been situated far from mountainous country, but Mormon leader Brigham Young chose this Utah valley for his followers because of its proximity to the Wasatch and the life-giving water it provides.

Below me were ribbons of concrete, the rec-tangular town blocks of Pleasant Grove, and, held in the valley by a temperature inversion, gray smoke from a steel plant. Pollution from automobiles, trucks, smelters, and oil refineries also hovers over the valley. Young wrote that "water is more important than meat or bread," but in the same passage he wrote that "good pure air is the greatest sustainer of animal life." The water pouring down the Wasatch's massive escarpment made possible the thriving industries, but by deflecting the winds, the range also causes the pollution created by industry to be trapped over the cities.

I dozed briefly, sharing the balmy summit with a throng of ladybugs. Several hawks circled over the valley. When I awoke, I could see Utah Lake glistening, albeit gray through the smog, in the noon sun.

Ship Rock

Shiprock, fabled monument, rises before us in splendor and silence, a tableau from the genesis of the Southwest, historical remnant of a unique volcanic violence which has created a collage of mountainous fluted columns, jagged arêtes and sheer orange walls that intimidate us into silence.

Chuck Pratt
Ascent, 1970

OF THE many formations that punctuate the American desert, none commands more attention than Ship Rock, a volcanic plug soaring 1,700 feet above the plains of northwestern New Mexico. This landmark reminded the early Anglo-Americans of a gigantic schooner under full sail; the shiplike skyline is enhanced by three conspicuous summit towers, easily construed to resemble masts of a schooner.

The great fluted grooves on the walls of Ship Rock make the architecture look saintly, and it would be easy to ascribe religious forms of some great temple to this isolated geologic phenomenon. According to Navajo legend, Ship Rock was originally a great bird which carried the tribe's ancestors to the present site from the rocky ground where they were being besieged by the fearful Ute tribe. The bird sailed away to leave the enemy behind, alighting later on the San Juan plains, where it turned to stone. This legend has bred a sacred tradition, and Ship Rock is known to the Navajos as *Tsa-Beh-Tai,* "the rock with wings."

The rock of this immense desert landmark is a yellow-tan tuff-breccia, formed during active volcanism some 50 to 40 million years ago. Tiny mineral fragments cemented into the matrix form the essence of monolithic walls, whose outer shell is often decomposed. Black gullies and dikes of basalt were formed when magma was forced into the tuff-breccia during later eruptive action. Despite an appearance of impregnability, some day the ramparts of Ship Rock will crumble on the desert's dusty floor, for here the wind gnaws and sculptures incessantly.

The Old Spanish Trail, which began in Santa Fe, passed to the north of Ship Rock, but it seems possible that some of the early western travelers spotted the craggy, 7,178-foot summit. William Wolfskill, who in 1830 was the first to lead a group of trappers along the Old Spanish Trail, may have seen the impressive landmark, for some of the country he crossed was characterized as having huge monoliths.

Coloradans were the first to plan the ascent of the great desert structure. Robert Ormes was the instigator of the first few attempts, making two reconnaissances in the mid-1930s with Mel Griffiths. Finding no obvious climbing route, the two men were baffled by the problems: the ridges had terrible notches, easy-looking bowls overlooked perpendicular walls that dropped 1,000 feet to the desert, and chimneys were merely rounded, overhanging troughs.

In 1937, returning with Griffiths, Gordon Williams, and Bill House, Ormes devised a plan to ascend a steep and exposed basalt rib which led to the north summit tower. Although there seemed to be no logical route joining the north tower to the middle tower—Ship Rock's highest point—perhaps something would turn up. But a foothold broke when Ormes was attempting the difficult rib, and he fell

some twenty feet before a piton held his plunge. Ormes and House returned to the challenge two days later, and although there were no further incidents, progress ended not far above the point where Ormes had fallen. The route ahead would require pitons for direct aid, and neither man had experience in this little-known technique. Ormes never again went back on Ship Rock, though he soon penned a story entitled "A Piece of Bent Iron" for the *Saturday Evening Post.* This article, describing Ormes' experiences on the desert skyscraper and his close call, was read avidly by other climbers.

By the late 1930s Ship Rock was known as the number one climbing challenge in America. Its impregnability became notorious, and climbers from distant regions were increasingly aware of its reputation. But only birds had reached Ship Rock's summit when a new age of technical climbing was ushered in by Bestor Robinson, David Brower, Raffi Bedayn, and John Dyer. These innovative California climbers, who called themselves "rock engineers," had honed their skills in Yosemite Valley. This foursome tended to become riveted to the intricacies of a climbing problem, and kept the emotional aspects of a challenge in the background. The Californians were a practical, self-taught team who owed little allegiance to past methods of climbing, instead depending on their route wisdom and free-climbing skills.

It was the overall skill of this party, as well as their commitment to the ascent, that led to the first climb of Shiprock in 1939. Choosing October, the best month for climbing in the American Southwest, showed wisdom, as did the planned bivouac high on the route during the third day of their adventure. The climbers were not only concerned about safety, but they also organized their efforts and individual abilities to good fashion. For instance, to put a minimum of weight on questionable holds, John Dyer, who weighed only 135 pounds, was put in the lead on some of the baffling pitches, belayed by Bedayn, the husky anchor man.

The cleverly planned route at first followed the one Ormes had chosen, but at the base of the basalt rib the Californians made an innovative rappel down onto the eastern flank of the formation. This rappel led to a shallow, exposed bowl and the key to the climb: the Traverse Pitch. In an article in the *Saturday Evening Post,* Brower later recalled his lead across this crux section:

> I was traveling over a slope with an average angle of about sixty degrees. This was too steep for friction alone. . . . In such situations every instinct demands that you hug the rock and clutch for handholds. To do so, however, is just a mild form of suicide. Leaning toward the rock tends to force the feet off the minute holds. So one must stand vertically, relying for salvation upon balance, augmented by touch; aiding balance with the finger tips of one hand. . . . Balance climbing does not allow much margin for errors in judgment, and a mistake would send me swinging over the gully with a turning radius of eighty feet. I scouted around for a piton crack.

On the third climbing day the summit formation was scaled via the "Horn," a striking feature that has been described as resembling a sightless reptile. This last serious obstacle to coveted success was surmounted with the aid of a rope thrown over

Above: Cactus wren at its nest in a cholla cactus. By Lynn M. Stone.

Facing page: Ship Rock, the immense volcanic plug that stands alone above the desert in northwestern New Mexico. By David Muench.

Overleaf: Ship Rock from the south. The Southwest Buttress Route ascends to the right-hand tower; the highest point of the formation is the left-hand tower. By David Muench.

the Horn; later this was described as a "job for a cowhand."

On several occasions when piton cracks were either poor or absent, the Californians had resorted to expansion bolts, devices never before used in American climbing. Traditionalists had argued for years that bolts and even pitons had no place in mountaineering, but the four successful climbers rationalized the use of this specialized equipment by claiming that safety took precedence over ethics. To the men's credit, only four bolts had to be placed; all of these were used for anchoring purposes only, not for upward progress.

In the ensuing years numerous parties used the spectacular 1939 route to Ship Rock's summit. Many of these climbers showed little respect for the achievements of their predecessors; by the mid-1960s thirty additional bolts marred the rock.

During the 1960s climbers began to speculate about other routes to the summit of Ship Rock. The 1939 route, classic though it was, wound around the formation in a very circuitous manner. Was there a more direct route? In April, 1965, my enthusiasm brought me to this problem.

As Eric Bjornstad and I drove slowly along the bumpy road leading to Ship Rock, we stopped many times to marvel at the grandeur of the formation. It became readily apparent that a classic new route might be forced up the huge southwest buttress to the final arête that soared to the south summit tower. Never had I been able to drive a car so close to the foot of a major climb. We unloaded my pink and black Thunderbird—its flamboyant shape and colors in seeming defiance of the natural environment—and organized our array of ropes and technical equipment. The same afternoon we squeezed up a tight chimney that opened up into a basin below the buttress. The rock was rhyolite, pink-yellow in color; its outer surface was scaly, but underneath it was basically solid. Everywhere the wind had sculptured the rock into a myriad of tiny hollows and horns, making it difficult to decipher a route pattern. We scampered upward several hundred feet into a basalt basin in order to survey the great buttress above.

The view was sobering, and the absence of a really natural route and the apparent necessity of placing many bolts took away some of the appeal. Closer inspection, however, showed a few connecting ledges and a hidden chimney. Our chosen line would have tremendous exposure, but it would be a real classic.

The next morning we began climbing. Above the hidden chimney I tackled a thin rock nose. Finding the right combination was unnerving, for the gap was too wide to use my feet for stemming. I had to back down three times before I gained emotional control and took a chance on desperately small holds. Although I was certain I would fall backward as handholds gave way, I kept my grip and managed to pull myself onto a stance. Here I was able to hammer in a large piton and study the next section, a chimney which widened into a short overhang. It seemed wisest to tackle this obstacle the next morning, when we would be fresh.

The next day dawned without a sunrise; it seemed Earth's seasons had reversed and winter was coming. Nevertheless, we returned to our high point—using the fixed ropes we had left the previous day—and spent the day climbing wild, overhanging rock with the aid of numerous pitons and a few bolts. The wind shattered our spirits that afternoon, and as a sandstorm raged below, we descended back to camp. Sleep was vital and welcome.

The following morning we were back on the buttress again, but only for a short time. The unreasonable weather brewed a special threat: sunlight filtered through swirling snowflakes. After retreating, we drove to the nearby town of Shiprock as an afternoon consolation.

A great windstorm robbed us of the next day, as sand blotted out most of the desert. Worse luck came the day after that, when a large chunk of rock broke off while Eric was climbing the fixed ropes. He was able to avoid the rock, but in the process suffered a severely bruised elbow. We made a side trip into the canyon country of Arizona.

Fighting the elements was as much a problem as the climbing itself. When we returned to the buttress in a few days, the wind howled and sand worked its way into our clothing and eyes. Sick at heart, we quit for the time being, as Eric had to return to work.

Four days later I returned, this time with Alex Bertulis. The capricious weather had turned calm and sunny, but as we prepared to launch a new assault, torrid sun baked Ship Rock. Whereas we had earlier suffered from the wind and cold, this time it seemed we were destined to be tortured by the heat. To save on our meager water rations, we barely drank the first day, a fact that undoubtedly delayed our reaching the high point of the fixed ropes. It was a great strain to haul the bags of sleeping gear, ironware, and food, for our ropes continually became stuck in cracks.

On a sloping ledge large enough for only one person, the two of us spent a disquieting night hanging against our anchor ropes. Looking down through our legs, we saw my Thunderbird directly below; it seemed we could hit it with rocks if we so chose. The evening shadow of Ship Rock stretched far to the east; Robert Ormes had once considered it "as long as Manhattan Island."

The next day was a study in patience and deprivation. The merciless heat so dried our mouths that we could hardly speak. The climbing proved to be tedious and difficult; we made only a few hundred feet that day. The second bivouac was more comfortable than the first, even though our throats were still parched.

The night seemed to reduce our troubles to their proper scale as well as fortifying our spirits. The solitude gave us time to reflect; by a struggle with a tangible objective man can learn those essential qualities in himself. Socrates stated that happiness is greater after an experience of discomfort. In the discovery that there is a penalty for too much comfort, man longs to escape from the artificial to the natural order, to escape from the social, religious, and political creeds of the material world. The codes and regulations men lived by just a few miles away did not apply to us. We had made a complete escape from civilization, within full sight of it.

On the following day we reached a point not far below the south summit. But here, so close to victory, our acute shortage of water and Alex's commitments elsewhere forced a retreat. We had underestimated both the heat and the final difficulties. Leaving our ropes fixed in place, we returned forlornly to civilization.

The third time on the southwest buttress had its charm, as if to compensate for the earlier miseries. When I joined forces with Harvey Carter a few days after Alex had departed, nature began to apply kind blessings, and, in a sense, the near-certainty of success diminished the remaining adventure. The air became crisp and cool in the mornings, and a comfortable breeze kept the temperature perfect. The mountains far to the west stood sublime in the sunshine, their snows sparkling in the splendor of a clear sky. As we began to ascend the ropes, it seemed the spirit of restlessness that had brought us to Ship Rock would soon be fulfilled.

After a pleasant bivouac high on the buttress, Harvey and I worked our way up the intricate passages of the final tower. Late on the afternoon of April 29, some three weeks after Eric and I had begun the route, Harvey and I stood atop the south summit. It seemed sad that my other two companions could not share in the final reward, but they were along in spirit when in the morning we surmounted the Horn Pitch of the true summit. Soon we were enthralled by the magnificent panorama of Navajoland. It was easy to visualize the legend of Ship Rock's southward flight. We daydreamed and relaxed, thankful for the stature of the bird that had turned to stone.

San Francisco Peaks

To the casual observer the San Francisco Mountain forms a most impressive feature of the scenery which surrounds it, not only from its symmetrical and striking outlines but also from its isolation. . . . It is volcanic throughout and is, in fact, a huge volcano whose fires have been but recently extinguished.

John S. Newberry
Report upon the Colorado River of the West, 1861

THE LANDSCAPE of much of northern Arizona was created by volcanos. A terrain of lava flows, lava-capped mesas, and more than 400 cinder cones, the volcanic field is one of the most extensive on the continent. Near the center of this area lies northern Arizona's largest city, Flagstaff. Just north of Flagstaff stands the dominant landscape feature, the San Francisco Peaks. Towering 5,000 feet above their surroundings, these extinct volcanos are visible from the entire vast volcanic plateau.

The birth of the San Francisco Peaks began 1.8 million years ago, when hot lava from deep in the earth burst through vents in the surface, and continued until 400,000 years ago. Episodes of violent eruption, with ash, cinders, and gas being blown into the atmosphere, alternated with quieter periods, when molten rock poured down the slopes of the growing mountains; this sequence has been deduced from the alternating layers of ash and lava. At one time the volcanic mass rose to more than 15,000 feet, and its base covered an area of 110 square miles.

Erosion has reduced the massif's elevation by a few thousand feet, and the once-symmetrical cone is now breached on its northeast flank by a bowl called the Interior Valley. The San Francisco Peaks today are a semicircular rim from which rise Humphreys Peak, which at 12,633 feet is the highest point in Arizona, 12,356-foot Agassiz Peak, and 11,969-foot Fremont Peak. While the mountain was built by fire, it was sculpted by ice. The formation of the Interior Valley may have begun with the collapse of a section of the ancient volcano, but it was ice-age glaciers that enlarged the valley and carved the two-mile-wide cirque at its head. Glaciers occupying the Interior Valley left a series of moraines as far as four miles below the basin's head. Humphreys Peak also sheltered a glacier which carved a cirque and deposited prominent moraines up to one mile from the cirque headwall.

The San Francisco Peaks, at a latitude of about 35° 20', were one of the southernmost sites of glaciation in the United States. And while average temperatures have risen and glaciers vanished, the present local climate is also noteworthy. On many a summer day, moist air from the Gulf of Mexico, forced clockwise around a high-pressure cell in the central United States, reaches the Southwest. This moist air is pushed upward by Arizona's high plateaus and the San Francisco Peaks, where it cools and condenses into clouds. This sequence, typical of July and August, leads to thunder, lightning, and a brief but heavy rainstorm. Autumn is generally dry, but winter can bring heavy snows. In 1973, about 200 inches of snow fell on Flagstaff.

It was snow, as well as the isolated eminence of the San Francisco Peaks, that beckoned to me in March, 1973, after Hooman Aprin and I had been frustrated by poor climbing conditions on Charleston Peak in Nevada. Our trek began on touring skis one sunny morning at the base of the Arizona Snow Bowl, a ski area situated on the forested western slope of Agassiz Peak. Dodging downhill skiers, we ascended from the 9,600-foot base into the basin north of the lift, then, using kick-turns, made a series of traversing zigzags up a spur of Humphreys Peak's southwest ridge, which we gained at about 12,000 feet. Packed spring snow made the ascent easier than we had anticipated, so we could savor our magnificent position under a cloudless sky. Leaving our skis in a rocky area, we headed northeast along the summit ridge, often kicking steps in the wind-packed crust and plunging our ice axes firmly to counteract unexpected gusts of wind. Cold northern air made the summit of Humphreys Peak an uncomfortable spot, and we lingered only long enough to admire the north and east slopes of the mountain dropping away to the Little Colorado River and to note, in the distance beyond the river, the volcanic landscape giving way to the sedimentary rocks of the Painted Desert.

Because of their great relief and the variation in local climate from plateau to summit, the San Francisco Peaks host an unusual variety of plant communities. It was this region's impressive diversity of habitat that inspired biologist C. Hart Merriam, in 1890, to propose a classification system for distinguishing various "life zones" at different elevations. Systems for identifying broad ecological bands from south to north across the continent were already in use; Merriam observed that during an ascent such as that of the San Francisco Peaks, one encounters a sequence of plant communities comparable to what would be seen traveling between the southern and northern ends of the continent. Merriam identified five of his eventual seven "life zones" on the slopes of these isolated volcanos: a belt of ponderosa pine up to 8,200 feet; a Douglas fir belt up to 9,200 feet; an Engelmann spruce zone from 9,200 to 11,500 feet; a narrow timberline zone of dwarf spruce; and, near the summit, a bare, rocky, alpine zone. The timberline zone is an eerie landscape that also features limber pine and mats of dwarf juniper and gooseberry currant. Boulders of the alpine zone disintegrate in time into soil, which in moist, sheltered niches supports certain plants that can tolerate such lean conditions. An alpine tundra of sedges, rushes, grasses, and flowering plants is scattered between rocks. Some fifty plants inhabit this alpine zone, though the only bird to nest above timberline is the water pipit. The pine siskin, Steller's jay, Clark's nutcracker, mountain chickadee, and junco also visit the high slopes in summer, though such mammals as the mule deer, coyote, and the rare bobcat prefer the cover of the lower forest.

The names Merriam assigned to these "life zones"—Upper Sonoran and Hudsonian, for example—are no longer in vogue, since the change in flora going north and the change going uphill are only superficially similar, though both are caused by lower temperatures. Nevertheless, Merriam's concept of differentiating vegetation zones in a mountain environment was important to the development of the science of ecology.

The name San Francisco is a legacy of Spanish missionaries who came to the Southwest for the dual purposes of converting Indians to Christianity and making them subjects of the King of Spain. The name was bestowed, about 1629, by Franciscans at the Hopi pueblo of Oraibe, situated atop a mesa northeast of the Painted Desert. The Hopis themselves called the mountain *Nuvátukaóvi*—"the place of snow"—and believed that certain supernaturals, called *kachinas*, came to them from the peaks. Kachinas were benevolent spirits, with some control over nature, especially the weather, and from the San Francisco Peaks brought the Hopis rain, prosperity, and happiness.

Other names for the mountain appear in early Spanish accounts and on old maps: Sierra Cienega and Sinagua, Sierra de los Cosninas, and Sierra Napac. Each of these names refers to a tribe that has been associated with the San Francisco Peaks.

The Sinagua were prehistoric people who lived along the Little Colorado, near the mountain, as long ago as the sixth century. Residing in pithouses—structures of sloping, earth-covered poles surrounding central firepits—the Sinagua specialized in pottery and carried on an extensive trade with tribes that lived as far away as the Gulf of California. The most important article they could offer in trade was obsidian flakes, obtained from the volcanos and used for projectile points and various tools. Other items

Page 164: **The San Francisco Peaks seen from the vicinity of A-1 Mountain. Agassiz Peak, on the left, hides the highest peak, Humphreys; Fremont Peak and Shultz Peak are to the right of Agassiz. By Peter L. Bloomer/Horizons West.**

Facing page: **The San Francisco Peaks, with the sandstone formations of the Painted Desert in the foreground. By David Muench.**

that have been found are arrows, stone-bladed knives, grinding stones, bowls of volcanic tuff, and ornaments of stone, wood, and bone.

Indian life was altered by an event that, according to the precise dating possible by counting tree rings, occurred during the winter of 1064–65. Ten miles east of the San Francisco Peaks is a volcano that was named Sunset Crater by John Wesley Powell, ascender of Longs Peak and explorer of the canyons of the Colorado River, because the red cinder at the top of the cone makes the volcano appear to be catching the final rays of a sinking sun. The eruption of Sunset Crater destroyed nearby Sinagua habitations, but otherwise brought prosperity to the region. Indeed, Hopi mythology attributes the eruption to the dancing of the kindly kachinas. For the volcanic ash that covered 800 square miles of adjacent country retained moisture, making the soil more fertile. Several tribes were attracted to the area; each learned from the others. Prosperity faded, however, as the soil became exhausted, and following a drought around 1225, the Sinagua drifted south to the Verde Valley.

The Cosninas were the Havasupai. These Indians once made their homes in caves on the San Francisco Peaks, but the arrival of the Apaches forced them to seek refuge in more protected canyons. The name survives as Coconino, the county of Flagstaff and the San Francisco Peaks, and as Cohonino, which the caves they once occupied are called.

Sierra Napac is apparently an error made by a scribe copying the journal of Francisco Garcés, the most notable explorer of the Spanish missionaries,

for "Napao" was Garcés' usual spelling of Navajo. The Navajos, who came to the area after the Hopis and Havasupai, made the San Francisco uplift, *Dook 'o'oslid,* one of their sacred peaks: the western boundary of their world, a home to spirits, and reservoir of all plant and animal life. The Navajos are still active in an effort to preserve the region from encroachment by civilization.

Ever since the members of a group from Colorado each paid $140 to the Arizona Colonization Company of Boston for transportation to the Flagstaff area, land development schemes have been part of local life. During the past decade, schemes have involved the west slope of the San Francisco Peaks, bringing the development ethic into conflict with the preservation ethic. In opposing developing in the mountainous area, Navajos have been joined by environmentalists—those who believe, to borrow the words of Wallace Stegner, that "we simply need that wild country available to us, even if we never do more than drive to its edge and look in." In 1970, this coalition prevented a development that would have concentrated a population of 3,000 on a site valuable to wildlife and susceptible to fire and erosion. More recently, the Indians have opposed plans to expand the Arizona Snow Bowl's skiing facilities and, further, have called for the dismantling of all man-made structures in the mountains. Stegner could have been speaking for these Navajos when he wrote: "Something will have gone out of us as a people if we ever let the remaining wilderness be destroyed. . . . The reminder and the reassurance that it is still there is good for our health."

North Palisade

*Such a stupendous view I never expect to see
again in the Sierra. We were on the edge of a
precipice which sank for a thousand feet
absolutely sheer to the head of a splendid glacier,
the largest in the Sierra Nevada, but never before
described. Just to the left our ridge joined the
Palisade ridge not more than a hundred yards
from the summit, and that last portion was a
serrated knife-edge. The only possible route was
along this edge, and this might have been
feasible had it not been gashed in one place
by a notch a hundred feet deep.*

Joseph N. LeConte
Sierra Club Bulletin, January, 1904

I N THE spring of 1776 the Anza Expedition,
which had traveled north from Mexico through
California, reached San Francisco Bay. Missionary Pedro Font, looking east from a hill near the
Bay, saw *"una gran sierra nevada"*—a range of
snowy mountains. Father Font was merely describing the view, but his phrase gave California's greatest
range its name, Sierra Nevada.

The Sierra Nevada is a chain of peaks 400 miles
long, longer than any one range of the American
Rockies. The range stretches from Tehachapi Pass in
the south nearly to Lassen Peak in the north, where
the Sierra block disappears beneath sheets of younger volcanic rocks. The Sierra's western flank rises
gradually from one of the world's richest agricultural
areas, the great Central Valley, while to the east the
mountains rise in a magnificent abrupt escarpment
to soar 7,000 to 10,000 feet above the arid basin of
the Owens Valley. With not a single river passing
through the range, the Sierra forms a formidable
mountain barrier.

The name Sierra Nevada notwithstanding, the
mountains are not especially well endowed with
glaciers and permanent snowfields. An exception,
though, is the Palisades group, located south of the
range's midpoint. Here, along an eight-mile section
of the range's crest, stand five 14,000-foot peaks,
culminating in the Sierra's third highest, 14,242-foot
North Palisade. Past glaciation has produced an
alpine topography that features sharp peaks and
ridges, deep cirques, and numerous lakes.

Tucked under the peak's north face, in a cirque
whose base is above 12,000 feet, lies the Palisade
Glacier. More than a mile wide and a half-mile long,
it is the largest body of ice in the Sierra. A few miles
to the southeast lies the Middle Palisade Glacier,
second largest in the range, while several smaller
glaciers and icefields occupy other north-facing
cirques. The Palisades is the most alpine section of
the Sierra, even though moraines down-valley from
present glaciers are a reminder that much larger
bodies of ice existed a few centuries ago.

The glaciation of the Palisades is a recent chapter in a geological story that began long before. The
oldest Sierra rocks were deposited as oceanic sediments nearly 475 million years ago. During most of
the next 250 million years and possibly longer,
deposition continued, with the deposits becoming
compressed and cemented to form such sedimentary
rocks as sandstone and limestone.

About 225 million years ago the North American plate—presumably driven by thermal currents
in the mantle beneath the earth's crust—began to
move westward. It met the Farallon plate, which,

being composed of heavier oceanic crust, slid under the westbound plate. Melting in the diving Farallon plate produced magma, liquid that rose into the older rocks at the edge of the North American plate and eventually solidified to granite. By 80 million years ago more than 100 bodies of granitic rock had been formed in this manner; this rock constitutes the core of the Sierra Nevada.

Meanwhile, for a period about 150 million years ago the two plates collided more violently. The intense pressures and heat generated caused the rocks on the edge of the continent to be intricately folded and altered to metamorphic rocks. Then came a time of relative quiet in the ancestral Sierra: older rocks were stripped by erosion, and some of the granite core was exposed in the low ridges to which the ancient mountains had been reduced.

About 30 million years ago the North American plate overrode portions of the Farallon plate and began to collide with the next plate to the west—the Pacific plate. This collision marked the birth of the San Andreas Fault, a giant sheer line along which the Pacific plate moves northwest relative to the North American plate. This movement, as the plates grind against each other, causes most of the state's earthquakes. In fact, eighty percent of the world's earthquakes occur along the boundary between the Pacific plate and other plates.

The intense stresses generated in the earth's crust by the plate movements also created cracking in the ancestral Sierra. In the Sierra these weakened zones, or faults, trend north to south, and the present Sierra block has been upthrust along them along its eastern margin. Like the Tetons and the Wasatch, the Sierra is a tilted fault-block range: the faulting is vividly indicated by the range's great eastern escarpment. On the west slope, no faulting took place in the north and only minor faulting toward the south, so that the Sierra has been tilted to the west. Uplift has been greater toward the south; here the eastern escarpment is as great as 10,000 feet and the Sierra's highest elevations are found.

The rise of the present Sierra Nevada was probably underway by about 25 million years ago. Recent studies indicate that uplift and tilting proceeded more rapidly during the latter part of this period. Uplift along east-side faults continues today, and its rate may still be increasing. Accompanying earthquakes have caused considerable damage in the Owens Valley, though losses have been small in human terms because the population is sparse. Earthquakes jolted the Mammoth Lakes region in 1927, 1941, and 1980, triggering rockfall and snow avalanches in the vicinity of the quake's epicenter.

While the Sierra block has been rising, the Owens Valley has been sinking. Owens Lake, on the valley's flat floor, has been left without outlet to the ocean. Water from the Sierra's east slope once flowed into Owens Lake, though it is now carried by an aqueduct out of the valley to Los Angeles.

Volcanic activity during the past 30 million years is another sign of crustal instability in the Sierra and in the Owens Valley. Mammoth Mountain is a volcano that formed within the past 200,000 years, while the crescent-shaped chain of Mono Craters—obsidian plugs in volcanic cones of pumice—formed between 60,000 and 1,600 years ago just south of Mono Lake.

Mono Lake also lies in a landlocked basin, and its feeder streams also are diverted to supply water to Los Angeles. Since 1941, when diversion began, the lake level has fallen forty-five feet, exposing 15,000 acres of alkali lake bottom. Mono Lake has been important to migratory birds—800,000 eared grebes have been counted there at one time—but unless diversions are curtailed, the lake will shrink to a sterile alkaline sump unable to support birds or other life.

The western slope of the Sierra offers a wider variety of habitats than the eastern escarpment. The foothills, which gained prominence during the 1849 gold rush, feature a chaparral that includes such shrubs as manzanita, chamise, ceanothus, yerba santa, and scrub oak. The life zones above the foothills are dominated by conifer forests: ponderosa pine at elevations ranging up to 6,000 feet; Jeffrey pine, white fir, and red fir at somewhat higher elevations, and lodgepole pine typically on subalpine ridges and in glacial basins. Such mammals as bighorn sheep, the grizzly bear, the marten, and the wolverine have been exterminated or had their numbers reduced by the coming of white man to the Sierra forests, but birds have been little affected by man's presence. Steller's jay, the most conspicuous bird of the Sierra forests, will venture boldly into camp, and its harsh cry is heard often. Clark's nutcracker, a large, noisy, black-and-gray bird of higher elevations, seems to be constantly in search of insects, pine nuts, and tidbits left unguarded by campers. Other birds are active in the sparsely forested high country: the mountain chickadee, rosy finch, and rock wren.

Within the forest belt are meadows rich in

Aerial view of the southwestern ramparts of North Palisade in the Sierra Nevada. By Galen Rowell.

vegetation. Typically, these meadows occupy sites once covered by lakes. Streams have been responsible for the transition, by carrying soil from mountain slopes above and depositing these sediments in the lakes, in time filling them in. Commonly seen in alpine and subalpine meadows are such wildflowers as asters, corn lilies, paintbrush, shooting stars, lupine, buttercups, cinquefoil, Sierra gentian, monkshood, and marsh marigold.

A California Geological Survey party which was surveying the Sierra's unexplored western slope saw and named the Palisades in 1864. These pioneers were studying the complex and then unknown topography and geology of the country below the range's crest, rather than climbing high, difficult peaks. However, their report described the serrated alpine group and charted approaches that later adventurers could follow. In July, 1903, when a small Sierra Club group reached the Palisades, some of the major peaks were attempted for the first time. These

Above: The author during the first ascent of a difficult route on Clyde Peak in the Palisade group. By David Black.

Facing page: The rock-strewn surface of the Palisade Glacier, largest in the Sierra Nevada. In the background is North Palisade, displaying a distinctive horizontal snowfield. By David Muench.

stalwart mountaineers first climbed 14,162-foot Mount Sill, second highest of the Palisades, but the deep notch known today as the U-Notch prevented them from continuing along the crest to North Palisade. The leader, James S. Hutchinson, felt discouraged about their prospects for success on the higher summit, but the next morning, with Joseph N. LeConte and James K. Moffitt, he tried again and found a broad couloir leading from the basin southwest of the crest to the U-Notch. LeConte discovered a ledge bearing left from the couloir, a ledge that proved to be a key passage on the route. LeConte later recalled the section above the ledge:

> We were now on the rocky front of the mountain, and a glance above showed a narrow chimney parallel to the big one below. Up this we climbed with the greatest care. Sometimes it was only wide enough to admit a man's body, and we had to work up with knees and elbows. In some places it was filled with clear ice, and great icicles hung directly in the way from some lodged boulder above. . . . After about five hundred feet of this we suddenly came to a widened portion, and there, towering almost in the zenith, a thousand feet above us, was the summit we had so long worked for. Up to that moment we had not hoped for success.

They saw no difficulties ahead greater than those they had overcome. LeConte's exclamation, "Oh, the excitement of the minutes that followed!" expresses their feelings as they surmounted the final obstacles.

In 1921, Hermann Ulrichs completed the route from the U-Notch that had stalled the 1903 party, then in 1928 Norman Clyde reached the U-Notch from the north, via the Palisade Glacier. The dominant force in Sierra climbing between 1920 and 1940, Clyde made over 1,000 ascents in his long career. He was a distinctive figure with his immense pack filled with cooking kits, cameras and books; a contemporary, Jules Eichorn, who described Clyde as a "jut-jawed, blue-eyed, ruddy-complexioned, animated block of granite, somewhat resembling a soldier," believed him to be a man who, having made up his mind to accomplish something, would not swerve from his objective.

Clyde was especially fond of the North Palisade. He once wrote that "there is no more spectacular peak in the Sierra Nevada, none more alluring to the mountaineer, than the North Palisade." In 1929, Clyde climbed the peak by a slanting snow-and-ice chute leading to a notch just northwest of the summit, and in 1934 he climbed it from the gap adjacent to North Palisade's northwest satellite, Thunderbolt Peak.

Clyde described a climb on North Palisade in these words: "The crest was narrow and broken by numerous pinnacles. We hastened along it sometimes over the pinnacles, more frequently, however, along ledges skirting their bases, soon reaching the actual foot of the summit. . . ." The jagged, serrated ridge depicted by Clyde is typical of the Palisade crest as it extends from Mounts Agassiz and Winchell in the northwest through Thunderbolt Peak, North Palisade, and Mount Sill to Middle Palisade and Split Mountain to the southeast.

The numerous pinnacles owe their existence to closely spaced sets of joints in the rock. Water enters these cracks and chemically alters the feldspar and mica present in granite. The resulting expansion enlarges the joints, and a repeating cycle of freezing and thawing further wedges the rock apart.

The intricate jointing of Palisades rock adds character to the numerous attractive routes of moderate difficulty, as well as to the more demanding technical routes, notably those on Temple Crag, a monolith standing east of the crest, high above Big Pine Creek.

Early Palisade climbers also commented on "suncups"—a scalloped texture seen on snowfields and glaciers during the summer, when days are warm and nights cool. Moving air evaporates snow from any raised areas on the surface, while solar radiation melts snow in any hollows. Snow vanishes more rapidly from the hollows than from the raised areas, and the irregularity of a surface becomes progressively more pronounced.

The last 14,000-foot peak in California to be climbed was Thunderbolt Peak, first ascended in 1931. A winter ascent of Thunderbolt Peak became an elusive quest for me during several ski tours to the foot of Palisade Glacier. Dale McCauley and I encountered fine weather and firm snow on January 22, 1976, and we made the trek from the road to the glacier in one long day. Despite the shelter of a tent and warm sleeping bags, we shivered half the night, and an early start was difficult in the morning shadows. Deep snow forced us to plunge above our knees as we approached the twin couloirs that were used by the 1931 party and lead to the summit ridge. We had misgivings about our chances of success, but as the slope steepened, the snow became firmer. Steep snow climbing and an awkward pitch on snow-covered rock led to the crest. Here the sun warmed our numbed bodies, and we were rewarded with feelings of delight and freedom as we clambered up the quintessential Sierra granite. We were further rewarded for our adventure with a summit view that encompassed the White Mountains beyond the Owens Valley and, westward, canyons that eventually faded into the indistinct foothills of the gold-rush country. There was not a track or sound of any human to interrupt our reverie.

Mount Whitney

The Sierra here is a bold wall with an almost perpendicular front of about three thousand feet, which is crowded by sharp turrets, having a tendency to lean out over the eastern gulf. . . . Mount Whitney itself springs up and out like the prow of a sharp ocean steamer. Southward along the summit, my sketch is of a confused region of rough-hewn granite obelisks and towers, all remarkable for the deep shattering to which the rock has been subjected.

Clarence King
Mountaineering in the Sierra Nevada, 1872

LESS THAN 120 years ago, not a single person in the United States even suspected that a remote peak in California's Sierra Nevada was the country's highest point. Surveyors of the time believed that the high point was either Mount Shasta or Mount Rainier, those lofty, isolated beacons of the Cascade Range. This guess was not too far off; 14,494-foot Mount Whitney, far less conspicuous than either of the two volcanos, tops Rainier by less than a hundred feet.

The early history of Mount Whitney—from its discovery to its first ascent—is a complex and fascinating story, one covering nearly a decade. In essence, it is the story of one man's efforts to reach the mountain and climb it. Clarence King was fresh out of the Yale Scientific School when he traveled west in 1863 to begin his career as a geologist. On a California riverboat he encountered William Brewer, the field leader of the California Geological Survey. This survey, established a few years earlier to chart the state's topography and mineral resources, was popu-

larly known as the Whitney Survey, after its leader, Josiah Whitney.

Impressed with King's credentials, Brewer hired him on the spot. It was too late in the year to explore the unknown High Sierra, but in July, 1864, Brewer, King, and several other men worked their way into the southern portion of the range. The party climbed Mount Silliman, then continued to a campsite at the western base of a huge, symmetrical peak soon to be named Mount Brewer. The group had thought that this peak lay astride the main Sierra crest, but upon climbing it they beheld the main divide and the loftier mountains a dozen miles to the southeast. In his journal Brewer described the view from the top of Mount Brewer: "Such a landscape! A hundred peaks in sight over thirteen thousand feet—many very sharp—deep canyons, cliffs in every direction almost rivaling Yosemite, sharp ridges almost inaccessible to man. . . ."

The twenty-two-year-old King persuaded Brewer to let him set out on an adventurous quest toward the highest of the newly discovered crest peaks. This massive peak, King believed, should prove to be the range's highest point; anticipating this, the group had named it in honor of their leader, Josiah Whitney.

King's adventure with packer Richard Cotter, occurring at a time when rugged mountainous terrain was generally shunned, stands out as a true pioneering effort. King was to relate the details of this expedition in his acclaimed 1872 book, *Mountaineering in the Sierra Nevada,* a classic of mountaineering literature. King wrote in the current literary style, which demanded emotional adventures, and his vivid tale is often embellished with death-defying incidents. Still, we should not denigrate the

Above: Climber on the east face of Keeler Needle in the Mount Whitney group. By Galen Rowell.

Page 174: Clearing storm over the Mount Whitney group. Lone Pine Peak dominates the center; Whitney and its satellites are to the right. By James Randklev.

Facing page: From the summit rocks of Mount Whitney, climbers look northwest across the plateau country of the upper Kern River toward the peaks of the Great Western Divide. By Galen Rowell.

trip's difficulties, for the country the two men traversed is truly rugged and remote.

The two men crossed the serrated barrier separating the Kings and Kern rivers and worked their way toward the crest. Spotting a high peak, they assumed it was Mount Whitney and started for its summit. King was later to report that they progressed by "clinging" to the "cracks and protruding crystals of feldspar." Higher on the mountain, further difficulties arose: "I was obliged to thrust my hand into the crack between the ice and the wall, and the spire became so narrow that I could do this on both sides; so that the climb was made as upon a tree, cutting mere toe-holes, and embracing the whole column of ice in my arms." Soon, however, the two climbers reached an easy rock slope which led to the uppermost rocks. There, much to their chagrin, they realized they had climbed the wrong mountain: six miles to the south loomed the distinctive outline of Mount Whitney.

After descending from their peak—which King had christened Mount Tyndall—the men decided the correct mountain was too far away to attempt. On the fifth day of their adventure, the pair arrived back at the survey group's main camp to find Brewer composing a letter to King's family. He had written only a few words: "It becomes my painful duty to inform you. . . ."

King tried to climb the true Mount Whitney a week or so later, and this time he found the correct target. But he chose the steep southeastern flank of the mountain and failed far below the summit.

Seven years later, in 1871, King decided to try once again, this time from the Owens Valley, east of the range. He reached the top of a huge mountain, but clouds obscured the views of the nearby peaks. Nevertheless, King claimed the first ascent of Mount Whitney, and so matters stood for two years.

King received a special shock when a paper read at the California Academy of Sciences in 1873 indicated that he had *not* climbed Mount Whitney in 1871 but rather a lower summit (Mount Langley) five miles to the south. Making a special trip from the East, King finally completed the climb on September 19, 1873. But the flat summit rocks contained a surprise: King was astounded to find records of two earlier parties, both of which had reached the top just that summer. The first climb had been accomplished by a vacationing group who wished to escape the heat of Lone Pine, a nearby village. This trio, Charles D. Begole, Albert H. Johnson, and John Lucas, were more interested in fishing than in mountaineering, so their August 18 ascent resulted in a christening of "Fisherman's Peak." This name was received well by the locals, for Josiah Whitney had made himself unpopular in the Owens Valley. But the influence of the California Geological Survey prevailed during the resulting nomenclature decisions, and the peak officially became Mount Whitney.

As evidenced by his three failures to climb Mount Whitney, King was not a very good mountaineer. Sierra historian Francis Farquhar felt that the explanation for this lay "very largely in King's character. His boldness and impetuosity led him to a frontal attack, to rushing tactics and rash expedients, where careful study and more devious ways might have succeeded better."

Clarence King, of course, possessed other talents. At the age of twenty-five—just a few years after his climb of Mount Tyndall—he presented to Congress a bold plan for a full survey of the Fortieth Parallel from Colorado to the California boundary. King himself was appointed to head this survey, the

most important one of its time. Later in his life he became the first director of the United States Geological Survey, a prestigious job indeed. Historian Henry Adams, a close friend, eulogized King in *The Education of Henry Adams.* "His wit and humor," Adams wrote, "his bubbling energy . . . ; his personal charm of youth . . . ; marked him almost alone among Americans. . . . One Clarence King only existed in the world."

The first parties to reach the top of the highest spot in the Lower 48 had all ascended the easy ribs and gullies of the peak's southwestern flank. The fifth ascent, however, proved to be a unique one, both because of the man who did it and the route he chose. In October, 1873, just a month after King's ascent, naturalist John Muir pioneered a solo ascent up a steep and narrow couloir on the northern side of the precipitous east face. Years later, Muir was to describe this route in wry terms: "Well-seasoned

The eastern flank of the Mount Whitney group at night, with Venus setting. Left to right are Third Needle, Day Needle, Keeler Needle, and Whitney. By James Peter Stuart.

limbs will enjoy the climb of 9000 feet required by this direct route. But soft, succulent people should go the mule way." Muir's gully remained unvisited until 1930, when Norman Clyde, the legendary figure mentioned in the preceding chapter, scrambled up it; he named it the Mountaineer's Route.

In the decades following the adventures of King and Muir, Mount Whitney became extremely well known. A crude path was built to the summit in 1881 by members of a scientific expedition led by Professor Samuel Pierpont Langley, director of the Allegheny Observatory. Clarence King had suggested to Langley that Mount Whitney would be the logical place to carry out experiments in solar radiation. Mules transported supplies—including a quarter of a cord of firewood—to the summit, and the party spent several nights enduring the wind and cold. The experiments proved only moderately successful, for, as Langley later wrote, "The great drawback in our case was the inability to remain at the very summit, for to do this requires a permanent shelter. . . ."

Langley's idea became a reality in 1909, when the Smithsonian Institution constructed a stone cabin on top to house members of an expedition intent on discovering whether or not Mars had water vapor in its atmosphere. Two other Smithsonian expeditions, in 1910 and 1913, also used the shelter during the course of their experiments. One member of this latter party remained on top for fourteen days straight. A decade later, other scientists studied cosmic rays in the vicinity of Whitney.

By the mid-1920s scientists had abandoned Mount Whitney as an observation point. But the mountain was soon to attract another dedicated group, the rock climbers. John Muir had once written that "almost any one able to cross a cobblestone street in a crowd may climb Mt. Whitney." But mountaineers continually seek more challenging routes, to set themselves apart from hikers. Certain ascents become landmarks, reference points in the tradition of the sport. Such an ascent was the 1931 climb of Whitney's east face, a feat inspired by the presence of Robert Underhill, whose ascent of the north ridge of the Grand Teton has been chronicled elsewhere in this book. On the invitation of Francis Farquhar, then vice president of the Sierra Club, Underhill headed for California after his successful season in the Tetons. Prior to his visit, early Sierra Club parties had been using manila ropes for safety, but their belaying techniques were primitive in comparison to Alpine standards. Those climbers exposed to the teachings of Underhill during his visit quickly changed their techniques and attitudes.

After a few warm-up climbs, Underhill joined Glen Dawson, Jules Eichorn, and Norman Clyde for an attempt on one of the range's most prominent walls, the 1,500-foot-high east face of Whitney. In mid-August the climbers worked their way to the base of the great cliff. The right-hand margin of the wall looked promising, although there was some question of linking certain obvious crack systems. Rating their chances of success at only fifty-fifty, the pioneers set foot on the rock.

Climbing in two roped teams, the men quickly reached a tier of rippled granite slabs known today as the Washboard; it proved easier than it had looked from below. But higher, a sheer wall presented an apparent impasse. An attempt to surmount this obstacle failed, but Underhill and Clyde noticed an exposed traverse across narrow ledges that overhung "a thousand feet of fresh air," as Clyde later wrote. This crucial section, which proved only moderately difficult, later became known as the Fresh-Air Traverse.

Above this passage lay a 400-foot section of steep, broken rock called the Grand Staircase. Soon the difficulties were over, and the foursome continued unroped to the summit plateau. "The route we had followed," Underhill proudly wrote later, "was exactly that which we had mapped out originally. . . . Much of the fascination of our climb lay, in fact, in seeing the sections we had marked out for ourselves. . . . The beauty of the climb . . . lies chiefly in its unexpected possibility, up the apparent precipice. . . ."

Without question, the three-hour ascent of the east face was a tribute to the men's routefinding skills; it was a clever route up a big feature of the mountain, a route flanked by greater difficulties. But one of the joys of establishing a great route is to find a safe way through demanding terrain.

I have yet to climb the east face of Mount Whitney, but in 1963 Rick Reese and I obtained a fine view of it as we made the first ascent of the east face

of Day Needle, a southern abutment of Whitney. On our route, joints in great granitic blocks showed us the way; we shared leads and hauled our packs as we progressed. At the end of the first day we reached a tiny bivouac niche two-thirds of the way up and anchored ourselves to the wall with ropes tied to pitons. Ours was a magnificent prospect: we could look down and see the twinkling lights of Lone Pine, some 9,000 feet below; we could look up and see stars glowing especially brightly because of the lack of atmospheric pollution. It was easy to see why the early scientists had chosen this austere region to carry out their experiments.

Rick and I completed our climb by mid-morning of the following day, emerging from a vertical wall onto a vast field of boulders—the "back side" of the Whitney massif. The trail was visible only a few yards away; hikers were plodding along it, unaware of our presence. Caching our gear, we wandered over to the trail and followed it on its last quarter-mile to the top of Mount Whitney.

The summit of the highest peak in the contiguous United States can hardly be termed a "summit," for it consists of several acres of rocks on a nearly flat surface—the product of frost-heaving. This remarkably ancient surface, perhaps 60 million years old, may be the remains of a lowland surface. While ice carved at Whitney's flanks, reducing ridges to craggy pinnacles, the summit platform escaped glaciation, for most snows were blown away by the wind before accumulating.

Rick and I spent nearly an hour at this historic summit, absorbing the panorama which stretched endlessly in all directions. Peaks were piled together in titanic confusion; many of them plunged precipitously into the Owens Valley. Lakes and tarns shone everywhere, and we spotted many of the 700 that lie in the 250 square miles represented on the Mt. Whitney quadrangle. One of these bodies of water, lying just over a mile northeast of Whitney, is the highest lake in North America: Tulainyo Lake lies at 12,802 feet.

With evidence all around us of glaciation, frost-heaving, and faulting, we could easily agree with Clarence King's assessment of Mount Whitney: "A great monolith left standing amid the ruins of a bygone geological empire."

Mount Ritter

How glorious a greeting the sun gives the mountains! To behold this alone is worth the pains of any excursion a thousand times over. The highest peaks burned like islands in a sea of liquid shade. Then the lower peaks and spires caught the glow, and long lances of light, streaming through many a notch and pass, fell thick on the frozen meadows. The majestic form of Ritter was full in sight, and I pushed on over rounded rock-bosses and pavements, my iron-shod shoes making a clanking sound, suddenly hushed now and then in rugs of bryanthus, and sedgy lake-margins soft as moss.

John Muir
The Mountains of California, 1894

THE WESTERN slope of the Sierra Nevada is the largest single piece of uplifted and tilted earth surface in the United States This vast slope, in places sixty-five miles from foothills to crest, is deeply dissected by streams. The San Joaquin River, one of the principal watersheds of the western slope, has three major branches and numerous tributaries that drain an enormous area in the central portion of the range, not far south of Yosemite Valley.

Many of the San Joaquin canyons display a distinct two-story form, with wide benches located on the canyon walls far above river level. Geologist François Matthes reported that these upland benches are remnants of a Miocene erosion surface. The exceptional preservation of the uplands is due to the durability of the massive granite that underlies them. Granitic rocks of the San Joaquin basin tend to be sparsely jointed, with long intervals between frac-

tures. This characteristic has played a major role in determining the character of the landforms by governing the manner and rate of weathering processes and of erosion by streams and glaciers.

The Middle Fork of the San Joaquin is the deepest and grandest river of this particular watershed. Along its course, walls of exfoliating granite, here and there streaked with cascades, tower 3,500 feet above river level. One impressive section of this canyon is located just above the junction of the South and Middle forks. Here the Middle Fork rushes through a narrow slot overlooked by a huge monolith known as Balloon Dome. This glacier-smoothed formation was seen at close range by members of the California Geological Survey in 1864. William Brewer wrote that the rock looked looked like "the top of a gigantic balloon struggling to get up through the rock." The report of Josiah Whitney, the Survey's leader, in the following year termed it "a most remarkable dome, more perfect in form than any before seen in the state." Such massive domes as Balloon Dome, Tehipite Dome, and Half Dome appear to be formed by a process called pressure-release exfoliation, in which rounded sheets of granite peel away from the underlying rock.

In vivid contrast both in color and in shape to the pale, smoothly rounded domes of the western slope is the craggy Ritter Range, a high subrange upstream from Balloon Dome but still six miles west of the main Sierra crest. Unusual in that its sharp peaks—Mount Ritter, Banner Peak, and the Minarets—far overtop the main crest in altitude, this alpine cluster also is distinguished by the dark tones of the peaks.

Josiah Whitney was quite aware of the turrets

181

and spires of the twelve-mile-long Ritter Range, even though he never obtained a close glimpse of them. Basing his report on the observations of Clarence King in 1866, Whitney wrote that south of Mount Ritter are "some grand pinnacles of granite, very lofty and inaccessible, to which we gave the name 'Minarets.' Here are numerous peaks, yet unscaled and unnamed, to which the attention of mountain climbers is invited."

Whitney was wrong in thinking that the rock of the Ritter Range is granitic like most of the Sierra Nevada. Rather, it is metamorphic. Vast eruptions, particularly during the Jurassic Period (150 to 110 million years ago), took place here as rising magmas reached the surface. Rocks from this time were later metamorphosed and are seen today in the Ritter Range. The closely jointed metavolcanic rocks are mostly tuffs and breccias, tilted on edge to form shapes not found elsewhere in the Sierra.

The serrated Ritter Range was probably not seen by white men until 1851, when troops of the Mariposa Battalion directed a campaign against the Chowchilla tribe in the upper San Joaquin basin. But it was Clarence King, that ubiquitous surveyor whose exploits on Mount Whitney have been described earlier, who was the first person to set foot on the range's highest peak, 13,157-foot Mount Ritter. King and James Gardner scrambled up the western side of the huge peak until stopped by a combination of bad weather and "inaccessible" cliffs some 500 feet below the top. Yet another failure for the luckless King! The two men named the peak after Karl Ritter, a lately deceased German geographer who was much admired by Josiah Whitney.

King and Gardner had seen snow and ice high on Mount Ritter, but they had been so influenced by Whitney's scorn of the possibilities of living Sierra glaciers that they mentioned the icefields to Whitney only as a curiosity. It remained for another great Sierra figure, John Muir, to "discover" these glaciers when he made the first ascent of the peak in 1872.

Muir contributed conspicuously to the literature and the origins of mountaineering in America, and his observations on natural history resulted in some of the most eloquent writings ever published about our mountains. To Muir, the mountains were alive; in particular, the peaks, slabs, waterfalls, and forests of the Sierra Nevada possessed a nobility unmatched anywhere. He called Cathedral Peak, that superb formation near Tuolumne Meadows, "a temple, displaying Nature's best masonry and sermons in stone." He revered Half Dome as if it were divine: "a most noble rock, it seems full of thought, clothed with living light, no sense of dead stone about it."

Glaciers so fascinated Muir that he was to seek them out most of his life. A few miles west of Mount Ritter, in 1871, Muir discovered a body of ice reposing under a steep north face; it was the first of many glaciers he was to describe. Studying the composition of moraines and measuring the movements of various glaciers, Muir correctly concluded that these were indeed living, not just residual, snowfields. It was on Mount Ritter that Muir became convinced of the sculpting powers and carrying capacity of the ice. "I have seen," he wrote, "the north Mount Ritter glacier in the act of grinding the side of its channel, and breaking off fragments and rounding their angles, by crushing and rolling them between the wall and ice."

Muir soon came to believe that glaciers had been responsible for shaping the wondrous domes and immense U-shaped canyons of the Yosemite region. This concept was in direct contradiction to the ideas put forth by eminent scientists such as Josiah Whitney. Whitney felt that earthquakes had formed the canyons, and he dismissed Muir as "that shepherd" and an "ambitious amateur."

However, Muir's theories were far more carefully thought out than Whitney's, and eventually they became accepted. Present-day geologists, of course, have refined Muir's ideas and placed them into the context of the ice ages. It is now thought that the cold wave which gripped the earth several million years ago formed the first small Sierra glaciers. The oldest major Sierra glaciation dates back 2.7 million years, and from then until some 10,000 years ago the range was often overwhelmed by ice. Vast icefields mantled the range and gave birth to great trunk glaciers which descended far down the western canyons, excavating rock as they progressed. The ancient San Joaquin glacier attained a maximum length of forty-seven miles; the Tuolumne glacier, the largest in the range, extended some sixty miles into the foothills.

Muir's ascent of Mount Ritter in October, 1872, is a classic example of solo exploration. After guiding a party of artists to Tuolumne Meadows, he decided to hike south and try for the huge peak he had cov-

Page 180: **Mount Ritter and Banner Peak rise above Ediza Lake in the central Sierra Nevada. By Ed Cooper.**

Facing page: **Winter camp at frozen Ediza Lake, under the Minarets. By Galen Rowell.**

eted for several years. The naturalist set up his camp not far from Thousand Island Lake, a large body of water dotted with hundreds—perhaps even a thousand!—isles. From this idyllic campsite near the headwaters of the Middle Fork of the San Joaquin River, Muir could gaze straight up at the jagged crestline of Mount Ritter and its satellites. It was an unforgettable view and clearly made an impression, for he was to praise the peak highly in an article in the January, 1875 issue of *Overland Monthly:* "Though not the very loftiest, Ritter is to me far the noblest mountain of the chain. All its neighbors stand well back, enabling it to give full expression to its commanding individuality; while living glaciers, rushing torrents, bright-eyed lakes, gentian meadows . . . combine to irradiate its massive features, and make it as beautiful as noble."

Leaving his camp at dawn, Muir ascended a long, narrow glacier on Ritter's north flank; the ice ended at the broad saddle separating the mountain from its high neighbor, Banner Peak. Above the saddle rose steep cliffs and gullies, and the naturalist scrambled up blocky terrain until the situation became perilous. After passing several dangerous spots, he dared not think of descending. In his *Mountains of California,* Muir described a few anxious moments:

> After gaining a point about half-way to the top, I was suddenly brought to a dead stop, with arms outspread, clinging close to the face of the rock, unable to move hand or foot either up or down. My doom appeared fixed. I *must* fall. There would be a moment of bewilderment, and then a lifeless rumble down the once general precipice to the glacier below.
>
> . . . But this terrible eclipse lasted only a moment, when life blazed forth again with preternatural clearness. I seemed suddenly to become possessed of a new sense. . . . Then my trembling muscles became firm again, every rift and flaw in the rock was seen as through a microscope, and my limbs moved with positiveness and precision. . . . I found a way without effort, and soon stood upon the topmost crag in the blessed light.

Muir had climbed one of the Sierra's most significant peaks alone and with no specialized mountaineering equipment such as nailed boots or an ice axe. Relying mostly on verve and ingenuity, Muir was surely one of the country's finest mountaineers of the last century.

During the next twenty years only one party revisited Ritter's airy summit, but by 1900 the peak was a popular goal, one still sought after today by climbers. Muir was the first writer to praise Ritter, but other writers have followed suit. Joseph N. LeConte, the range's most active explorer in the early twentieth century, wrote: "I doubt if in the whole Sierra there is a more noble mountain. . . ." Ansel Adams was fascinated by the landscapes of the Ritter Range, taking some of his most famous photographs in the vicinity. He once called the range "the Olympus of the central Sierra."

Despite the fact that the striking summits of the Ritter Range lie in the heart of a magnificent wilderness area, they can be reached in a weekend. The approaches to the lakes and cirques nestled under the great peaks are easy and scenic: giant lodgepole pines line the trails at the lower elevations, and the graceful mountain hemlock—a tree Muir called "the very loveliest in the forest"—makes its appearance near timberline. The lakes themselves are of startling beauty, for in their cobalt-blue waters are reflected soaring pinnacles and jagged ridges. The majestic range and its natural wonders stand as a legacy to John Muir's intrepid spirit.

CHAPTER TWENTY-SIX

Mount Shasta

The one great point in the landscape is the cone of Shasta; its crest of solid white, its vast altitude, the pale-gray or rosy tints of its lavas, and the dark girdle of forest which swells up over cañon-carved foot-hills give it a grandeur equalled by hardly any American mountain.

Clarence King
Mountaineering in the Sierra Nevada, 1872

O F ALL the dominant mountain masses in the West, Mount Shasta was the last to be discovered. An Indian tribe called Shas-tí-ka once lived below the huge volcano, referring to it as *Wai-í-ka,* or "snowy mountain." Various tribes living in the vicinity had myths telling of the spirits which lived on the summit, but the Indians probably knew little about the howling winds and subzero temperatures that can occur on Shasta.

The Spanish were undoubtedly the first white men to spot the 14,162-foot volcano, but the year of discovery is uncertain. The diary entry of Fray Narciso Duran—a member of Luis Argüello's expedition—for May 20, 1817, gives this description: "At about ten leagues to the northwest of this place we saw the very high hill called by the soldiers that went near its slope Jesús María. It is entirely covered by snow." Historians have questioned whether this was Mount Shasta, but it is probable that the mountain was seen on Argüello's second expedition, in 1821.

Mount Shasta's name took many forms in the early 1800s. Peter Skene Ogden's journal entry for February 14, 1827, states that he found "a mountain equal in height to Mount Hood. . . . I have named it

Mount Sastise." In 1841 came the overland party of the Wilkes Expedition. Lieutenant Charles Wilkes was impressed: "The Shaste Peak is a magnificent sight, rising as it does to a lofty height, its steep sides emerging from the mists which envelop its base. . . . Its cleft summit gave proof of its former active state as a volcano." John C. Frémont passed by the mountain five years later; he referred to the peak both as Shastl and Tsashtl. By midcentury the great mass bore the name Shasta Butte, and it was not long until this name evolved into the present one.

The first ascent of Shasta was made in August, 1854, by Captain E. D. Pearce, the superintendent of a local sawmill. His ascent route lay on the relatively gentle southwest flank of the mountain. Pearce's party reached the summit at noon, unfurled the stars and stripes, and built a huge monument. Into this cairn they placed a New Testament, several newspapers, and the constitution of the Independent Order of Odd Fellows. On the descent, Pearce later reported, they encountered a snow gully that was seventy-five degrees in steepness. Thousands of Shasta climbers have followed, with minor variations, the pioneering route of 1854, but none of them have reported that the steepness even approaches Pearce's estimate: it was undoubtedly a case of nineteenth-century embellishment.

In 1862, Josiah Whitney, head of the California Geological Survey, became anxious to determine which of the state's peaks was the highest. Shasta, he knew, might well be that point, so in September he, William Brewer, and a companion arrived at its base. Local inhabitants told conflicting stories about the difficulties one might expect on the huge volcano. Brewer was later to describe these contrary stories in

Mount Shasta and its satellite, Shastina, as seen from the north; in the foreground is a field of snowbrush. By Bob and Ira Spring.

Appalachia: "Many told us that it could not be ascended; others told us that it was perfectly easy; one man said the grass grew nearly to the top, yet the fact that its snows are seen at a distance of one hundred and fifty miles made me doubt his word."

The only way to learn the truth was to set foot on the mountain, and so the three scientists began their ascent. "We found no great difficulties," Brewer wrote, "no crevasses, no fearful precipices, only an exceedingly hard climb." On top, using their specially made barometers, the party made the first relatively accurate measurement of a high mountain in the United States. The calculation of 14,442 feet convinced Whitney that he had discovered the supreme mountain in the nation. (Twenty years later, surveyors put the height at 14,380 feet; shortly after the turn of the century, the estimate was further reduced, to 14,200 feet. By 1913 the Coast and Geodetic Survey established its present elevation, 14,162 feet.)

The most eminent geologists of the 1860s—Josiah Whitney, James Dana, and Louis Agassiz—had all published statements claiming that no true glaciers existed in the United States. But when the irrepressible Clarence King climbed Shasta in 1870 he looked over a cliff to see a startling sight: "There, winding its huge body along, lay a glacier, riven with sharp, deep crevasses yawning fifty or sixty feet wide, the blue hollows of their shadowed depth contrasting with the brilliant surfaces of ice." There could be no doubt; King had discovered a bona fide glacier.

Mulling over this discovery, King and his cohorts spent a memorable night atop Shastina, the 12,330-foot volcanic cone attached to Shasta's western flank. King eloquently described this austere bivouac in *Mountaineering in the Sierra Nevada:*

Upon cold stone our bed was anything but comfortable, angular fragments of trachyte finding their way with great directness among our ribs and under shoulder-blades, keeping us almost awake in that despairing semi-consciousness where dreams and thoughts tangle in tiresome confusion.

. Just after midnight, from sheer weariness, I arose, finding the sky cloudless, its whole black dome crowded with stars. A silver dawn over the slope of Shasta brightened till the moon sailed clear. Under its light all the rugged topography came out with unnatural distinctness, every impression of height and depth greatly exaggerated. The empty crater lifted its rampart into the light. I could not tell which seemed most desolate, that dim moonlit rim with pallid snow-mantle and gaunt crags, or the solid black shadow which was cast downward from southern walls. . . . Naked lava-slopes and walls, the high gray body of Shasta with ridge and gorge, glacier and snow-field, all cold and still under the icy brightness of the moon, produced a scene of Arctic terribleness such as I had never imagined.

On the following morning, the geologists reached the top of Shasta, discovering several more glaciers from nearby vantage points. The men had climbed the mountain by a route farther to the north than the standard route used by Whitney and Brewer, and as he followed the standard route back down, King realized why his predecessors had not discovered the glaciers themselves: they were invisible from this side of the peak. Upon his return from this expedition, King made public his discovery of living glaciers in the United States, an announcement greeted with mixed feelings by scientists back east. But King's evidence proved indisputable, and soon some geologists were claiming that *they* had known about the existence of living glaciers long before King's discovery. King shortly published a series of articles in *The Atlantic Monthly*, telling of his adventures and discoveries. At age twenty-nine, Clarence King was firmly embarked on a career of science and writing.

John Muir was the next famous figure to climb Mount Shasta. Caught in an April blizzard while making observations for the Coast and Geodetic Survey, the naturalist endured a miserable thirteen hours at the hot springs located just below the summit, freezing on one side of his body while roasting on the other. Later, he was to describe these fumaroles as "the last feeble expression of the mighty force that built the mountain." But, Muir cautioned, "volcanoes work and rest, and we have no sure means of knowing whether they are dead when still, or only sleeping."

By the 1920s Shasta was such a popular goal of mountaineers that a race was scheduled for the Fourth of July, 1925. Beginning from the Sierra Club lodge—a one-room stone cabin built in 1922—the contestants faced a 6,200-foot, trailless ascent up lava and snow slopes tilted at angles of up to thirty-five degrees. The legendary Norman Clyde had set the record for this ascent in 1923, having reached the top in a fine time of two hours and forty-three minutes; the contestants of 1925 would be anxious to beat this record. An eighteen-year-old named David Lawyer managed a time of two hours and twenty-four minutes, a remarkable effort involving ascending 2,600 feet per hour at high elevations.

Racing up a peak is hardly what mountaineering is all about, although many a time I have climbed a significant peak in the space of a single weekend. Bill Hildebrand recalls one such trip very well. I called him at noon on a Friday in May to inquire about a tent he was making for me; that business finished, we discussed doing a climb together some day. Within minutes we had agreed to leave in a few hours for a spring ski ascent of the north flank of Mount Shasta.

"I cain't understand what you guys love about them big mountains," exclaimed the waitress who served us the next morning's breakfast at a cafe under Shasta's flanks. We had told her of our plan but, obviously thinking we were demented, she went back to gossiping with the burly loggers whose tastes she could better appreciate. Not many people understand mountain climbing.

Parking our car near Military Pass, a forested, 6,000-foot defile several miles north of the peak, we began ascending the slopes of the volcano. The terrain at first was not too pleasant, as it involved shuffling through manzanita and loose rubble. Soon, however, we were able to clamp on our skis and begin traversing the firm spring snowslopes leading into a wide basin lying beneath the north-face glaciers. We continued upward until our skis began gripping poorly on crusty snow. Here, at about 10,000 feet, with the sun sinking behind a nearby ridge, we decided it was time to set up our camp in the snow.

Using a lightweight gasoline stove, we cooked a typical mountainside dinner: split pea soup was followed by a main course consisting of minute rice, butter, and cheese and tuna. After a hot dessert, we drank several cups of tea to replace lost moisture. We were high on lonely Shasta and, having worked hard to reach camp, it was now time for sleep.

The temperature had plunged to the high 'teens by the time dawn arrived. Although the weather was clear and promising, high winds blew snow plumes off the summit area. Leaving our skis at camp, we briskly gained altitude, aiming for the spur separating the Hotlum and Bolam glaciers, where the snow was firm and crusty. All around us, great, tumbled glaciers dropped abruptly between jagged spurs of lava, and we were acutely aware of climbing a volcano.

Shasta has erupted frequently during the past 10,000 years; its last eruption took place only a few centuries ago. The lower slopes of the mountain—below the level of our high camp—consist of broad, smooth aprons of pyroclastics (ejected rock fragments) and mudflows. These mudflows, composed of water-saturated rock debris that flowed downslope as a fluid, extend as far as twenty miles from the mountain.

Shasta's main cone is so young that it still preserves a symmetry relatively unbroken by erosion. Shastina, the western cone climbed by Clarence King in 1870, forms the mountain's only major subpeak; it came into existence about 7,000 years ago following a 2,500-year period when viscous lava slowly oozed from a new vent on the main peak.

Climbing a high peak when unacclimated requires periodic rest stops, and thus we were able to absorb many lessons in elemental geology as we progressed up the cone. At a crevassed area near the 11,500-foot level on the Hotlum Glacier, we strapped crampons to our boots and roped up as a safeguard in case one of us broke through into a crevasse. As Bill and I neared the summit crags, we noticed that the howling wind was loosening ice debris into the chute we had intended to climb. This sobering sight caused us to change course and traverse sharply to the right. Later, as we rounded a shaded spur, we became exposed to a gale-force wind as well as a "river" (as Bill called it) of falling ice. Chunks the size of a fist streamed past us. The mind contemplated retreat because of the hostility of these elements, but as we gained on the summit from the northwest, the topmost landmarks came into view and renewed our hopes.

We crested the summit ridge in late morning to be greeted by a blast of wind in excess of sixty miles per hour. The shrieking had a beauty about it, but the clarity of the scene was blurred somewhat by our watering eyes. We drew the rope to half-length between us, but it was still bowed horizontally several feet off the surface. We both were knocked to the ground by the force of the moving air at least once; a diffused sun indicated that a storm was imminent.

Our summit stay was a brief, cold crouch in the lee of the highest crag. Then we made a hasty retreat, the wind having a cushioning effect on our backs. Hours later, even before we had taken off our skis, whirling clouds engulfed the entire upper mountain. The elements were a reminder that man is not always a welcome visitor in a kingdom he cannot control.

Above: **The saw-whet owl nests in forests throughout the mountainous West. By Rick Kline.**

Facing page: **Mount Shasta from Heart Lake, to the southwest. By David Muench.**

CHAPTER TWENTY-SEVEN

Mount Hood

In September of 1864, in company with three gentlemen of Vancouver, I first attempted to reach the summit of Mount Hood. On reaching an altitude about 800 feet below the summit, a dense cloud came sweeping against the north side of the mountain, and, drifting rapidly over it, instantly enveloped us in its folds. The air changed suddenly to a fierce cold. The driving snow filled the air so entirely that a cliff of rocks 300 feet high, standing not more than fifty feet from us, was invisible. To go up or to go down, was, for the time, alike impossible. One of my companions was chilled nearly to insensibility, but we struggled against the tempest for hours, unwilling to be defeated in our purpose to reach the summit.

Reverend H. K. Hines
Report to the Royal Geographic Society, 1867

THEIR exceptionally rich mountain mythology may have made it difficult for the Indians of the Northwest to feel at home among the high peaks of the Cascade Range. When storm clouds gathered over the mountains, winds shrieked with reckless fury, and volcanos erupted with fire, is it any wonder the Indians felt there was a raging war among the mountains?

The best known of the tribal myths concerns the creation of the Bridge of Gods and the Columbia River Gorge. Romantic legends were told about two brothers who were the sons of Soclai Tyee (the Great Spirit). Known as Wy'east (Mount Hood) and Klickitat, or Pah-to (Mount Adams), the brothers fought over a beautiful maiden, Loo-wit (Mount St. Helens).

During these battles the opposing forces had formed a tunnel through the base of the mountain range. The inland sea drained away and formed a natural bridge above the Columbia River. The destructive warfare continued; finally, great stones were hurled so vigorously onto the bridge that it collapsed; the fallen stones became the Cascades. The lovely Loo-wit belonged to Pah-to, the victor, but her heart was with Wy'east—so she became a sleeping beauty.

In the Pacific Northwest volcanic turmoil not only gave the Indians an inexhaustible source of legends, it has also given the land its mineral-rich soil and much of its superlative scenery. Here in the Cascades, the internal forces of the earth have long been active. About 200 million years ago a part of the floor of the Pacific Ocean known as the Gorda plate began to collide with the North American continent and slide beneath its western edge; a process geologists call subduction.

Typical of most land volcanos, which erupt along plate boundaries where oceanic plates plunge deeply under continental edges, Mount Hood and the other Cascade volcanos are the product of the subduction of the Gorda plate. Lying offshore beneath the Pacific Ocean, this small oceanic plate is partially melted into pockets of magma as it creeps under the North American plate at an annual rate of one inch; the melted rock may later rise to the surface. Vulcanism parallel to the subduction zone, but about 100 miles inland, has long created episodic activity in the high Cascades of Oregon.

During Miocene time, some 16 to 10 million years ago, basalt floods covered most of Oregon east of the Cascades. Enormous outpourings of lava accumulated to build the Columbia River Plateau to

Above: Weathered whitebark
pines at timberline on Mount
Hood. By Russell Lamb.

Page 190: The Eliot Glacier
tumbles down the north face
of Mount Hood; the Cooper
Spur forms the left skyline.
By Ed Cooper.

a thickness of more than one mile in places. Sporadic eruptions along the Cascade Range have occurred throughout the past 60 million years and still do, as evidenced by the recent eruption of Mount St. Helens.

The Cascades of Oregon are composed of Tertiary volcanic rocks surmounted by volcanic cones of later age. Mount Hood's cone was built on the eroded root of an older volcano. Three major eruptive periods produced dacite domes, pyroclastic flows, and mudflows—but virtually no pumice. The earliest flows filled the north-sloping valleys; later, the bedrock ridges were eroded and the lava today caps ridges, a curious topographic reversal. This fact suggests that enormous amounts of rock have been eroded since Mount Hood's birth.

On the smooth south and southwest slopes of Mount Hood a fan of pyroclastic material and mudflows formed about 200-300 years ago, during the last major emissions of lava from the mountain. The walls of Zigzag Canyon, southwest of the peak, display evidence of this huge fan. Another geological curiosity is Crater Rock, a prominent formation high on the south flank of Hood. This landmark is a remnant of a young dacite dome that erupted about 250 years ago; this dome apparently originated inside a crater that had been blown out of the upper southwest slope.

Soon after major volcanic activity ceased, glaciers began dissecting Mount Hood's cone, reducing its height by nearly 1,000 feet. The last major advance of Hood's glaciers probably reached maximum downvalley extent 18,000 years ago. From that time until about 11,000 years ago these valley glaciers generally retreated. During the last ten millenia these icefields have varied greatly in extent; today, the mountain has eleven glaciers, the biggest of which is but two miles long.

Although Mount Hood is by no means the highest or most glaciated of the numerous volcanos of the Pacific Northwest, its soaring shape early on attracted the notice of white men. In October, 1792, Captain George Vancouver, of Britain's Royal Navy, estimated its height at 25,000 feet and thought it might well be the world's highest peak. Vancouver saw the mountain from near the mouth of the Columbia River during his historic voyage down the coast of North America. He directed Lieutenant William R. Broughton to assemble a crew and row up the river to investigate. "A very distant high snowy mountain," the lieutenant later reported, "now appeared rising beautifully conspicuous in the midst of an extensive tract of low, or moderately elevated, land." Broughton honored the "lofty summit" with the name of Lord Samuel Hood, the Admiralty member who had signed the original naval instructions for the voyage.

Meriwether Lewis and William Clark spotted the volcano in the autumn of 1805 as they neared the end of their great trek across America; they noted that the local Indians called the peak "falls mountain," a probable reference to the numerous cascades in its vicinity. Not long after these explorers saw the peak, the volcano was renamed Mount Adams, but this name was shortly transferred to a higher peak north of the Columbia River. By the 1830s the symmetrical volcano south of the river was known to all as Mount Hood.

Early settlers and other explorers were generally overimpressed with the height of Mount Hood, perhaps because it rises so loftily only twenty-four miles south of the Columbia, without the interference of forepeaks. A paper read at the Royal Geographic Society in 1867 by Reverend H. K. Hines told of his ascent of Mount Hood. In reporting this adventurous feat, the *Alpine Journal* stated: "It will be seen he believes it to be higher than any other in Europe or North America." Following an ascent in 1866 the Reverend Mr. Atkinson calculated the mountain to be 17,430 feet high, not too far from the figure of 18,361 feet given by publisher Thomas Dryer a few years earlier. Professor Josiah Whitney's survey came far closer to the mark; it found Hood to be 11,700 feet, close to the present-day calculation of 11,235 feet.

The chain of mountains in which Mount Hood lies was called the "Western Mountains" by Lewis and Clark, but this name was not destined to last long. David Douglas, the notable early botanist of the American West, applied the term "Cascade Mountains" to the range during his travels in the region in the mid-1820s. This name seems eminently suited for the system of volcanos and other peaks which extend about 650 miles from California's Lassen Peak to beyond the Canadian border.

On the Wilkes government map of 1841 the term Cascade Range emphasizes the peaks both north and south of the Columbia River. John C. Frémont, that peripatetic explorer of the West, apparently concurred: he felt that the Sacramento, Klamath, and Columbia rivers all emerged in cascades from the heart of the range and that the Columbia itself "gives the idea of cascades to the whole range; and hence the name of the Cascade Range...."

Many immigrants observed Mount Hood at close range between the years 1841 and 1875, for the famous Oregon Trail ran along the south bank of the

Columbia River. Control over the Oregon Territory, which included all of the Pacific Northwest, was contested for many years by the British and the Americans. A treaty signed in 1846 established the present boundary between Canada and the United States, and settlers flocked west along numerous tracks, one of which was the Oregon Trail.

These early immigrants made no serious efforts to scale Mount Hood, perhaps concurring with David Douglas, who had written that Hood's "appearance presented barriers that could not be surmounted by any person. . . ." The first documented attempt to reach the top of the prominent volcano was made by Joel Palmer; in 1845 he attained a point above timberline, turning back when his two companions lost interest.

In 1854 Thomas Dryer—the man who claimed the peak was more than 18,000 feet high—published an account of his climb in his newspaper, the *Weekly Oregonian*. Although he claimed to have reached the summit with a companion, historians of the mountain, writing in the early years of this century, believed that Dryer reached only the top of Steel Cliff, a prominent landmark high on the volcano's southeast ridge. Dryer later scornfully rebutted the story of the Reverend T. A. Wood, H. L. Pittock, Wilbur Cornell, and Lyman Chittenden, who claimed the first true ascent on July 11, 1857. Little is known about this party's ascent, but it is regarded today as authentic.

Soon Mount Hood became a popular ascent; around the turn of the century mass ascents came into vogue. The well-known Oregon climbing and hiking club, the Mazamas, was actually organized atop Hood; 193 mountaineers stood on the windswept summit on that historic day in 1894. Because of its relative ease, the south-side route—the route used by the early parties—became the route of choice. The chief problem of this ascent lies not far above Crater Rock, where a moderately steep slope offers several variations. Early mountaineering parties vastly overestimated the angle of this slope; one newspaper stated it was seventy-five degrees. Later measurements were to prove the slope was a bit less than thirty-four degrees.

The normal route is not really difficult, but it can prove frustrating and even dangerous in poor weather. Certainly weather and snow conditions are a major factor in personal experiences. One climber gave a picture of his summit stay in these words: "I have been cold in Alaska when the thermometer registered 70 below zero, but never was there such biting, overpowering cold as on that mountain-top, nor a wind so piercing and persistent." Beatrice Young, who in 1913 wrote an account in *Mazama*, commented: "Several parties went to the mountain and came back with all sorts of tales about it, some saying it was easy as pie, no trick at all, etc., while others declared it was simply awful, the most nerve-trying experience within memory of man."

There have been numerous accidents on Mount Hood, a statistic not surprising, for it is said to be the most often climbed snowclad peak in the nation. A relatively accessible objective, it is routinely attempted by inexperienced persons, but sudden weather changes and a lack of physical fitness have resulted in tragedies. In 1956 a party of 18 youths, tied together on a 240-foot rope, were led up the peak by a single guide. All went well on the ascent, but on the way down one tired climber slipped on the snow-slope above Crater Rock. The entire party fell, bouncing off rocks, some 200 feet. One climber was killed; thirteen others had to be carried in litters down the mountain. It was the largest rescue operation ever undertaken in the Cascades.

Another accident, a recent one, was even more tragic. In June, 1981, four climbers were killed in a similar uncontrollable slide on the Cooper Spur, the second most popular route on Mount Hood.

These incidents, sad though they are, make up only a small segment of the peak's history. Thousands of mountaineers have safely made it up and down Oregon's highest peak, and thirteen routes, all with their own interesting stories, have been worked out. Most of these routes had been climbed by the mid-1930s, but one remained virgin much longer. In the 1936 *Mazama*, well-known Hood climber Everett Darr described a ridge on the mountain's west side as "one of the few rock masses on Mount Hood that have defied all attempts to scale it." Various climbing parties had scrutinized this serrated rock crest, known as the Yocum Ridge, but all had found the crumbling rock too dangerous to trust.

In my experience with such loose-rock problems in the Cascades I found that the right combination of winter conditions can render possible an otherwise unsafe route. In April, 1959, the Austrian climber Leo Scheiblehner and I decided to attempt the Yocum Ridge, envisioning a first winter ascent. At the time we did not realize that the ridge had never been climbed in its entirety, winter or summer.

Climbers ascending the upper portion of Mount Hood's normal route. By John V.A.F. Neal.

On the drive to Timberline Lodge—the famous resort at the 6,000-foot level on the peak's south flank—we were elated to see that the mountain was in splendid condition following a long dry spell. As we ski toured with climbing skins to Illumination Saddle, the firm surface suggested that we had the opportunity to be successful. We pitched a small tent near the 9,000-foot level, cooked dinner on our gasoline stove, then slept until first light.

Crampons made the traverse of the Reid Glacier very straightforward. As we strode along, the ice towers of the Yocum Ridge, silhouetted against the west face, hinted of steep and challenging ice work. A sixty-degree slope of firm ice rose to the lowest towers of the ridgecrest; our ski-mountaineering boots were ideal for front-pointing with crampons. Leo led the way to the spectacular, wintry crest, vocally exuding confidence in the superb conditions. "We make it," he shouted in a strong, reassuring accent. I felt equally confident, though I silently wondered how we would connect a route through and over the thin rock towers of the ridge, now sheathed with ice and feathers of rime.

The answer was startlingly clear once I reached Leo's position: we would have to climb directly along the narrow, fearsome edge, carefully belaying each other and trusting to luck that towers would not block the route. Every kick of the crampons took us farther up the ridge, and the thought of retreat became distasteful. Ice pitons would not hold in the wild white feathers, and our aluminum pickets rotated insecurely after placement. We had to put all our trust in our ice axes, crampons, and good balance.

After one traverse to avoid the point of an ice pinnacle I stemmed a chimney for about sixty feet, the rope behind me swinging free on the overhanging ice wall. It was no place to err. We continued slowly and carefully, relying on our skills and our faith in each other. The late-morning sun finally struck the ice towers, but the overwhelming beauty of the wintry scene was temporarily lost on us: we could savor the enjoyment later. Our progress took us along the ridgecrest nearly the whole distance, but at one great overhanging tower it was necessary to make a difficult traverse to the right. Above, we had to crampon vertically, swinging the ice axe well above the head in order to anchor the pick firmly. Fortunately, the sun had no adverse effect on surface conditions, and the west wind kept the surface granules frozen solidly in place.

While belaying Leo up a menacing wall that looked like an endless mushroom leading into the blue sky, I reflected on the combination of events that was making the Yocum Ridge climb into a splendid adventure: a skilled partner, the long daylight of April, the glorious weather, and the firm ice surface. Not often have I enjoyed all these things on a single climb.

Many hours later I felt a great happiness as the slope began to round off. In a few more rope lengths we saw that the success we had strived for was certain: the ridge continued smoothly toward the summit, and the crazily shaped towers of ice were behind us. Soon we would make the easy descent to Crater Rock, and from there, point our skis homeward on the long, gradual south slope.

Mount St. Helens

There was not a cloud visible in the sky at the time I commenced my sketch, and not a breath of air was perceptible; suddenly a stream of white smoke shot up from the crater of the mountain and hovered a short time over its summit; it then settled down like a cap.

Paul Kane
Wanderings of an Artist Among the Indians of North America, 1925

A T 8:32 on the morning of May 18, 1980, an earthquake of magnitude 5.1 on the Richter scale shook Mount St. Helens. Within fifteen seconds the mountain's slumping north slope had collapsed and become an avalanche of gigantic blocks of ice and rock. The collapse—like the uncovering of a steam boiler—released the pressure that had been building up within the volcano; dissolved gas burst from volatile magma and superheated water quickly flashed into steam. An explosion hurled a dense, hot mixture of steam, other gases, and rock debris laterally through the breach in the north slope. Rocks that contained pockets of confined, pressurized gas were blown into dust. Further fracturing of the summit crater permitted material to be vented straight up. A mixture of rock fragments and volcanic gases—a pyroclastic flow— as hot as 900 degrees Fahrenheit poured down the north slope at 150-200 miles per hour, overtaking the avalanche debris. Comparisons to the human potential for destruction are inevitable: it has been estimated that the explosion released energy at a rate equivalent to 500 of the type of atomic bomb that was dropped on Hiroshima.

The force of the eruption threw ash twelve miles into the southern Washington sky for most of the day, while superheated mud continued to race down the north slope into the valley of the Toutle River. Eventually a semicircular crater more than two miles in diameter and 2,100 feet deep formed. Roughly one cubic mile of material had been ejected and the mountain's elevation lowered from 9,677 feet to 8,364 feet.

The events of May 18 were not unexpected. Specialized scientific equipment such as seismographs and heat-monitoring devices had been placed on the mountain, photographers were ready to capture the eruption, and a pair of geologists were above St. Helens in a small plane when the initial tremor and avalanche occurred.

On March 20 a seismograph on St. Helens had recorded an earthquake of magnitude 4. With increasing frequency tremors occurred that were centered at shallow depths below the mountain's north flank. On March 27 wisps of steam escaped and a new crater formed on the snow-covered summit. Large east-west oriented cracks developed in the snow. On March 29 blue flames were visible at night.

Small eruptions during the following weeks threw steam and ash a few miles into the air. The ash blackened the mountain's upper slopes and the widening crater. Meanwhile, a bulge was forming under the Forsyth Glacier high on the north slope; its continuing growth suggested that magma was being forced up close to the surface. Swelling by as much as five feet per day, the bulge was 450 feet high when the volcano exploded. The growth of the bulge was accompanied by the expansion of the network of cracks in the snow and rupturing of the glacier. Sci-

entists expected the bulge to trigger either an avalanche or an eruption, though, of course, they could not predict that the event would happen on May 18 or occur with the violence that it in fact did. In particular, it was the *lateral* force of the blast that took observers by surprise and was responsible for much of the loss of life that occurred.

Indians knew of St. Helens' past eruptions and were inspired to both fear and reverence. According to Klickitat legend, Loo-wit—the "Lady of Fire"—was a fair maiden who was transformed into the mountain we call St. Helens. A nineteenth-century geologist, Samuel Emmons, reported he could find no Indians to approach the volcano with him, that they regarded it as an evil spirit who would lure them to destruction.

St. Helens has been the most active volcano in the forty-eight contiguous states over the past 4,500 years, during that period having undergone at least twenty episodes of eruptions. The eruptions of 1980 were the first in the lower forty-eight states since Lassen Peak in California exploded several times between 1914 and 1917. An eruption of St. Helens around 1900 B.C. is believed to have been more violent than the recent explosion. Eruptions in about 1500 A.D. sent mudflows forty miles down the valley of the Lewis River. Spirit Lake, nestled below the mountain's north slope, was created by mudflows damming the headwaters of the Toutle River's north fork.

St. Helens is a young mountain, a volcano made up of alternating strata of lava and rock fragments—a type of volcano which, sealing off internal pressure most effectively, is potentially most explosive. Much of the visible cone apparently formed within the past thousand years, for ice-age glaciers did not gouge cirques as they did on Mounts Hood and Rainier. St. Helens' eleven modern glaciers have barely dented the surface, and streams on the lower slopes have produced only minor erosion. Professor William D. Lyman commented in 1883 that St. Helens "is wrapped as smoothly in her mantle of snow as a garden lawn."

Before the recent eruptions, St. Helens was last active between 1831 and 1857. Samuel Parker, a missionary, reported an eruption in 1831; geologist James D. Dana noted activity in 1841. Explosions in 1842 were mentioned by John C. Frémont. A settler named Peter H. Burnett, in a letter dated December 28, 1844, reported that "this mountain is now a burning volcano. It commenced about a year ago. . . . Ashes fell at the Dalles to the depth of one half an inch." Lieutenant Thomas W. Symons of the Corps of Engineers wrote that "dense masses of smoke rose up in immense columns, and wreathed the whole crest of the peak in somber and massive clouds."

The activity of Mount St. Helens and other volcanos of the Cascade Range is related to the movement of the Gorda plate, which is trapped between the main Pacific plate and the North American plate. As the Pacific plate moves north, this small oceanic plate is forced northwestward toward the coast of Washington and Oregon. As it submerges beneath the continent, the heat and pressure generated by the subduction creates pockets of magma. When this magma works its way to the surface, a volcano is rekindled, as Lassen was in 1914 and St. Helens was in 1980.

St. Helens' recent violence has made people forget that the mountain was once a serene snow cone of classic symmetry, an American counterpart of Japan's Fujiyama. British navigator George Vancouver, exploring the coast and its inlets, wrote in his log for April 10, 1792, that "the clearness of the atmosphere enabled us to see the high round snowy mountain, noticed when in the southern parts of the Admiralty inlet, to the southward of mount Rainier. . . . This I have distinguished by the name of Mount St. Helens, in honor of his Brittanic Majesty's ambassador at the court of Madrid."

Lewis and Clark, descending the Columbia River in 1805, had read Vancouver's description of the region and were on the lookout for his mountain. They first mistook Mount Adams, a sister volcano to the east, for St. Helens, but on November 4 identified the correct peak, which Lewis described as "emensely high and covered with snow, rising in a kind of cone." The explorers suspected it of being the highest peak in America. Nine years later fur trader Alexander Henry also saw St. Helens from the Columbia and admired it as "an immense cone enveloped in snow," which "presented a conspicuous and romantic prospect."

Even Hall J. Kelley found cause to be eloquent in portraying the volcano. Kelley, a humorless Bostonian who believed himself chosen by God to lead a migration to Oregon, arrived in 1834 and did what he could to promote Oregon as "the paradise on earth." Kelley described St. Helens as the "most remarkable of all the mountains in Western America" and declared that its summit reached a "stupendous height." "Its hoary head," he wrote, "is lifted into

The May 18, 1980 eruption of Mount St. Helens, from a farm north of Vancouver, Washington. By Alan Kearney.

regions of perpetual frost, above the sport of whirl-winds, or the darts of vengeful lightnings." In an effort to name the Cascades the "Presidential Range," Kelley designated the volcano as "Mount Washington" on an 1839 map of Oregon, but his renaming did not succeed.

Thomas Dryer, publisher of the *Weekly Oregonian*, described climbing St. Helens on August 27, 1853. His claim to have climbed Mount Hood the following year was later proved false, so doubt was cast on his St. Helens climb. But his description of the crater and the view from the summit is believable, and he is credited with the first ascent.

I have had the fortune of climbing St. Helens twice. Both ascents were made in the 1940s, the more memorable being done on skis. On a perfect spring morning Paul Gilbreath, my brother Helmy, and I zigzagged up the long north slope. The edges of our skis bit firmly into the surface of the glistening corn snow. We made a fast ascent and spent little time on the summit, for the prospects of a downhill run of more than 5,000 feet intrigued us. Much of the slope was greater than thirty degrees—steep for skiing—but the firm, granular surface held the old wooden hickories so well that our long, sweeping turns seemed effortless. A long glide, a twist of the body, an unweighting, and a shift of weight to the downhill ski: we felt as graceful as ballet dancers. Gilbreath, who once won the famous Silver Skis race on Mount Rainier, was a hard man to keep up with. Too soon we reached the soft snow below timberline and stopped to rest our tired knees. Then we slogged through the trees toward Spirit Lake at the mountain's north base.

The May 18, 1980, avalanche that triggered the eruption of St. Helens dumped half a cubic mile of pulverized rock and glacial ice into Spirit Lake and the North Fork of the Toutle River. Fumaroles boiled at the edge of the devastated lake, and a superheated mudflow raced down the river valley. The steaming mudflow turned a lush forest into an unearthly wasteland, destroying everything in its path before it stopped—seventeen miles from the mountain. A forest of 200-foot-high Douglas firs had been flattened as though the trees were toothpicks. The blast of hot air accompanying the flow did as much damage as rushing debris; the needles of trees on the periphery of the mudflow were so scorched by hot winds that the trees would not recover. Areas up to twelve miles distant were completely devastated, and sear zones extended to fifteen miles. All told, 60,000 acres of Douglas-fir forest were destroyed—including, ironically, logging areas that had outraged conservationists. Trees that survived the fifty-mile-per-hour mudflow in the lower valley were caked with a gray cement.

The churning mud took with it not only logs, but also cars and bridge sections; it overturned hundred-ton logging trucks and obliterated some 300 homes. Also destroyed were about 200 square miles of wildlife habitat, 150 miles of trout streams, and 26 lakes. The Washington State Game Department estimated that, including birds, a million and a half animals had been killed, the most important in terms of game being more than 5,000 elk.

Eight hundred thousand tons of ash—a hundred

Above: The smoking crater of Mount St. Helens, October 18, 1980. By Gary Braasch.

Facing page: Mount St. Helens and Spirit Lake in a tranquil mood before the 1980 eruption. By Bob and Ira Spring.

The view from devastated Spirit Lake; the smoke-enshrouded crater lies five miles to the south. By Gary Braasch.

tons per acre—settled on the city of Yakima, eighty miles to the northeast, and turned the sky dark as night. Drifts up to three feet thick closed roads in eastern Washington. Soot fell as far away as Maine and Alabama.

Sixty-one people perished as a result of St. Helens' eruption. Geologists had warned of the danger of the Forsyth Glacier avalanching and, in the event of an eruption, mudflows racing down the valleys, but the public had adopted a carnival atmosphere. Onlookers enjoyed the risk and ran sheriffs' roadblocks. The news media persisted in locating people who boasted of their lack of concern with the time bomb looming above them; the attention gave them temporary stature as folk heroes. Some were among the dead, or among the hundreds evacuated by helicopter.

Smaller ash explosions occurred on May 25, June 12, July 22, August 7, and from October 16 to 18. Volcanic activity at St. Helens could continue for years. Lassen Peak erupted 392 times between 1914 and 1917.

St. Helens has become a scientific laboratory, with experts from various fields monitoring the vol-

cano's activities. A lava dome—a solid cap on top of a column of magma—is especially puzzling. The formation of the lava dome should, according to the prevailing theory, indicate the end of the volcano's explosive stage. Yet, though a dome formed after the June 12 blast, it was reduced six weeks later.

The environs of St. Helens are beginning to recover. Plant life above the ground was destroyed, but the soil was not sterilized. Even by the end of the summer of 1980 many plants were sprouting in the devastated landscape. Fireweed is especially well adapted to sprout from surviving roots and push through the ash crust. Areas that were covered by snow at the time of the eruption were somewhat protected and have recovered rapidly.

Conifers did not reappear immediately, because of a lack of nitrogen in volcanic ash. The first seeds to reforest the devastated area produced alder, for a specialized nodule on alder roots is able to extract nitrogen from the air and convert it to a soluble compound that can be used by plants. The leaf litter from alders begins to enrich the soil with nitrogen. Alders are not a long-lived species—mature alders die within fifty years—but the decaying wood will continue to return nitrogen to the soil. Hemlocks will appear in the underbrush, then become the dominant tree; eventually they are replaced by lodgepole pine and Pacific silver fir. In areas that were subject to blowdown and ashfall, a stable conifer forest may be expected within 100 years; in more devastated zones this type of foliage may develop in 200 years.

Science has been gaining the expertise needed to predict such natural disasters as the St. Helens eruptions. Dwight Crandell and Donal Mullineaux wrote the following, after a fifteen-year study of volcanos in the Pacific Northwest, for the U.S. Geological Survey:

> In the future Mount St. Helens probably will erupt violently and intermittently just as it has in the recent geologic past, and these future eruptions will affect human life and health, property, agriculture and general economic welfare over a broad area. . . . The volcano's behavior pattern suggests that the current quiet interval will not last as long as 1,000 years; instead an eruption is more likely to occur within the next 100 years, and perhaps even before the end of this century.

The report was issued in 1978, two years before the recent eruptions.

Mankind must acquire the wisdom to heed the warnings of science. "Nature is not subject to government regulations and property boundaries," wrote Professor Leonard Palmer. Noting that the floor of the Toutle River valley had been formed by older mudflows, Palmer commented, "We build many of our own disasters by usurping the territory better reserved and respected as areas of the natural process."

Mount Rainier

The view [from the top of Rainier] was inexpressibly grand and comprehensive, although the whole landscape, below an altitude of five thousand feet, was swallowed up in a sea of vapor, leaving the higher mountains standing out like islands. . . . An occasional gust of wind would tear open the veil for a few moments, exposing to momentary view the precipitous canyons and crags for thousands of feet down the mountain's sides. We seemed to be floating in a dark blue ocean, having no connection with the earth below, and the mountain appeared to rest gently upon its encompassing clouds.

George B. Bayley
Overland Monthly, September, 1886

INDIANS of the Puget Sound region called it *Tahoma*, "the mountain that was God." Unfortunately, this name of prehistory did not survive, and today the highest volcano in the Lower 48 is known as Mount Rainier. The 14,410-foot peak captured the imagination of both Indians and early explorers, for its glaciated bulk is so stupendous that sometimes it is difficult to believe that it belongs to this world. At times during calm summer weather the mountain appears as a great rounded iceberg floating on a sea of clouds; in this textbook example of air inversion, the volcano remains clear while its foothills are draped in fog.

Unaware of the Indian's name for the mountain—or variants such as Tacoma and Takhoma—famed navigator George Vancouver followed the European tradition of honoring men from the homeland. In 1792 he described a "round snowy moun-

tain" on which he bestowed the name of his friend, Rear Admiral Peter Rainier. This name often met with challenge in the following years, for some people preferred the Indian's name for the peak. The Northern Pacific Railroad, for instance, showed it as Tacoma on their maps and other publications. As the town of Tacoma became a rival of nearby Seattle in the last decades of the nineteenth century, pressure was further exerted on the authorities to change the name back to its original form. The matter was finally resolved in 1924 by the United States Board on Geographic Names: it was to be Mount Rainier.

The mountain's snowclad majesty and its relative accessibility from Puget Sound lured early explorers, some of whom undoubtedly remarked on the glaciers that are Rainier's outstanding feature. Exposed to the full force of the storm systems which move in from the Pacific Ocean, Mount Rainier receives an annual snowfall of more than forty-five feet. By springtime more than fifteen feet of new snow still blankets the glaciers. The consolidation of this snow and its recrystallization into thirty-five square miles of glacier ice has resulted in an incomparable network of twenty-six named glaciers, the most on any single massif in the nation. One of these glaciers, the Emmons, ranks as the largest valley glacier in the lower forty-eight states.

Of all the peak's glaciers, the steep, fast-moving Nisqually Glacier is the most interesting and the most studied. This narrow glacier, nearly five miles in length, lies on the south flank of the volcano and is conspicuous from Paradise Inn, the popular tourist complex at the 5,500-foot level. The upper half of this glacier has a mean slope of thirty degrees and is badly crevassed; the lower portion is a narrow, temperate valley glacier whose bed is complex, producing a complicated flow pattern. The southerly exposure and low terminus elevation (4,000 feet) causes heavy ablation—melting and evaporation on the glacier's surface—during the summer months; as a result, the glacier's surface is lowered.

Recent studies on the Nisqually have suggested that the seasonal variations in the velocity of a glacier are correlated with the amount of liquid water temporarily stored within the glacier; this stored water may be released catastrophically. The hydraulic pressure of impounded meltwater may cause floods of debris-filled and turbulent water. A great outburst flood in October, 1955, carried six-foot boulders down the valley and destroyed the highway bridge below the Nisqually Glacier. A destructive mudflow in the Kautz Creek valley in October, 1947, broke up the lower glacier and caused heavy damage to forests and highways. Outburst floods in the valley of Tahoma Creek have been similarly destructive.

Mount Rainier is almost completely covered by glaciers that flow radially from the summit icecap. Ice sheets covered the Rainier region at least five times during the Pleistocene Epoch. During the last major glaciation, between 50,000 and 15,000 years ago, valley glaciers reached lengths of fifteen to forty miles. Moraines are visible proof that glaciers expanded once again about 3,000 to 2,500 years ago, and they were larger during the period from 1600 to 1900 than they are at present. Mount Rainier's glaciers have repeatedly scoured the valleys, leaving well-formed moraines to mark their past advances.

The numerous glaciers of Rainier are so impressive that one can easily forget that the mountain is a volcano. The peak formed on an upland surface when great extrusions of a fine-grained rock called andesite poured forth from a centrally located vent. Explosive pyroclastic eruptions and lava from the vent slowly built, in prehistoric Pleistocene time, a great cone that may have been more than 16,000 feet in height. But in later great explosions, and with an inward collapse of the summit, the highest cone vanished partly in huge mudflows. As early traveler Theodore Winthrop observed in his eloquent book, *The Canoe and the Saddle*, "The dome that swelled up passionately had crusted over and then fallen in upon itself, not vigorous enough with internal life to bear up in smooth proportion."

Volcanically, Mount Rainier was quiescent when Dr. William Tolmie, a botanist and physician of the Hudson's Bay Company, approached the mountain in 1833, the first white man to do so. His report indicates that he actually considered climbing the peak: "Mount Rainier is at all times a very striking object from the prairies about Nisqually.... The ascent of these mountains has never been effected, but it was my intention to attempt it, if my dates permitted." With Indian guides, Tolmie climbed a minor peak near Mowich Lake, not far from Rainier's northwestern flank, but as far as we know came no closer to Rainier itself.

Lieutenant August Valentine Kautz, a German-born adventurer with a passion for exploration, fell under the spell of Mount Rainier while stationed at Fort Steilacoom, near Tacoma, in the mid-1850s. Kautz, who ultimately rose to the rank of brigadier general following service in the Civil War, described his fascination with the mountain in an article written many years later:

> My quarters fronted Mt. Rainier, which is about sixty miles nearly east of Fort Steilicoom in an air line.... It is a grand and inspiring view, and I had expressed so often my determination to make the ascent, without doing it, that my fellow-officers finally became incredulous.... My resolution, however, took shape and form about the first of July. Nearly all the officers had been very free to volunteer to go with me as long as they felt certain I was not going; but when I was ready to go, I should have been compelled to go alone but for the doctor, who was on a visit to the post.

Kautz, having studied an account of the ascent of Mont Blanc, fashioned four iron-tipped alpenstocks, the first ever seen in North America. Ice creepers were made by driving nails through an extra boot sole, then sewing this sole onto the boots. With these cleverly designed pieces of equipment finished, Kautz finally felt it was time to depart. In early July, 1857, he set forth from Fort Steilacoom with Dr. Robert Orr Craig and two volunteers, Nicholas Dogue and William Carrol, both enlisted men.

Expecting to make fast time through the low-

Facing page: **A foggy August morning in the subalpine meadows of Mount Rainier National Park; lupine and paintbrush in the foreground. By John I. Hendrickson.**

Page 204: **The south flank of Mount Rainier looms above the evergreen forest. The Kautz (left) and Nisqually (right) glaciers are clearly seen. By Russell Lamb.**

land belt of virgin forest, the men soon found they had severely underestimated the rough terrain and consequent travel problems. Having taken only a six-day supply of food, the men must have felt extremely discouraged by the slow pace. The path was so poor that the horses soon had to be left behind; fortunately, the expedition's Indian guide, Wapowety, knew a route that led through the leafy underbrush and big firs to the upper Nisqually River. The doctor, not accustomed to this sort of labor, became fatigued, and, in order to continue, Wapowety carried his pack in addition to his own gear. On the seventh day the Kautz party was finally able to contemplate an ascent of the great volcano, having placed a camp near timberline.

Not accustomed to judging distances at altitude—a problem that still plagues present-day mountaineers—Kautz erred in leaving camp late for the more than 9,000-foot climb to Rainier's summit. The group quickly discovered that distances were deceptive on the snowfields and glaciers, and that lack of previous acclimation greatly slowed their pace. Soft snow and routefinding problems delayed them also, yet by afternoon it seemed the summit was now nearby. The altitude, however, was beginning to be felt, and by late afternoon only Dogue still kept up with Kautz. High on the mountain they reached a difficult section, probably an icefall. Kautz made this report in the May, 1875 issue of *Overland Monthly*:

It proved to be the crest of the mountain, where the comparatively smooth surface was broken up, and inaccessible pinnacles of ice and deep crevasses interrupted our progress. It was not only difficult to go ahead, but exceedingly dangerous; a false step, or the loss of a foot-hold, would have been certain destruction. Dogue was evidently alarmed, for every time that I was unable to proceed, and turned back to find another passage, he would say, "I guess, Lieutenant, we petter go pack."

Finally we reached what may be called the top, for although there were points higher yet, the mountain spread out comparatively flat, and it was much easier to get along.

The soldier was now exhausted and could go no further, so Kautz went on alone for a while before realizing the ascent was hopeless. The late hour and fierce, cold wind created a hazardous situation; without blankets Kautz would be in danger of freezing to death. He reluctantly began the long descent back to timberline.

Kautz's gallant effort ended high on the mountain, probably above the 13,000-foot level; the attempt might well have been successful if the party had carried more food, allowed for more time to acclimate, and had established a higher camp. As it was, the state of provisions barred a second attempt, and the party began the journey back. Not until the fourteenth day did the haggard and sunburned group return to Fort Steilacoom. Their clothes were in such a state of disarray that they passed for Indians for some time. "We were received," Kautz wrote, "by the officers with a shout at our ludicrous appearance. They were all sitting under the oak-trees in front of quarters, discussing what had probably become of us, and proposing means for our rescue, when we came up."

Kautz's near-success was the most enterprising American mountaineering expedition up to that time. While the ascent was not as demanding as previous climbs in the Alps, the entire adventure, with its difficult and unknown approach, ranks as a truly audacious achievement. Kautz cracked the aura of Mount Rainier, established a route, and deserved the honor of the first ascent. The route which he pioneered—now called the Kautz Glacier Route—may not have been completed until 1920.

The first successful climb of Mount Rainier was made in 1870 by Hazard Stevens and Philemon Van Trump. This pair chose a route farther to the east than Kautz's and succeeded for two reasons: they established a camp at about 6,000 feet—considerably higher than Kautz's—and they persevered when nightfall caught them high on the mountain. Stevens, then Surveyor-General of Washington Territory, and Van Trump had the advantage of support from James Longmire, a nearby rancher, and pack horses which transported supplies to near the mountain. There the men were able to procure the services of Sluiskin, a Yakima Indian who took them as far as timberline.

On August 16 the two mountaineers reconnoitered the route to 10,000 feet, a wise decision. But the next day, in their overconfidence, they left behind coats and blankets; at the summit they were spared from freezing when they discovered a steam cave which existed in the crater.

Many climbers visited Mount Rainier in the next few decades, establishing other routes on the various flanks of the ice-clad volcano. By the turn of

Climbers ascend the heavily crevassed Ingraham Glacier en route to the summit of Mount Rainier. By David Hiser.

Mountain goat with two kids in a field of spring flowers. The goats are ubiquitous in the mountains of the Pacific Northwest. By David C. Fritts.

the century the most popular route still followed the line established by Stevens and Van Trump: the Gibraltar Route, named for the huge rock formation high on the peak's southeast flank. A mass ascent of this route took place in 1905 when members of three clubs—Sierra, Mazama, and Appalachian—participated in a joint climb. This group found the rockfall-prone cliffs of Gibraltar easier than expected; the only dangerous passage lay not far above, where an icy face gave a modicum of trouble. Sixty-two persons climbed to the summit on that long-ago day. Willoughby Rodman, who wrote of the 1905 outing's bivouac at 10,000 feet in the May, 1906 issue of *Out West*, evoked the splendor of nightfall high on the mountain: "Owing to our elevation, twilight lingered with us long after the lower lands were shrouded in shadows. Indeed, it seemed that the night never became entirely dark. The light seemed to be not of sun or moon, but an ethereal radiance which softened the outlines of crag and peak, and gave the snow-fields a peculiar bluish tint."

There are numerous climbing achievements

that stand out in the history of Mount Rainier, but none are more eventful than those of the year 1936, when two classic-looking ridges on the precipitous north side of the volcano—Ptarmigan and Liberty ridges—were climbed by adventurous and capable teams. Both of these alpine routes are still desirable today. Later, the forcing of routes up the Willis Wall, the great northern façade of rock cliff overhung with ice, had an air of danger, technical difficulty, and contrivance.

One hundred years after the significant near-ascent by Kautz, I became one of five climbers to challenge the steep, unclimbed Mowich Face, a broad triangle of snow and ice that rises 5,000 feet in one bold sweep between the Ptarmigan and Sunset ridges. This wall has several ice cliffs which cling to the face and on its northern portion is a crowning icecap.

Donald Claunch, John Rupley, Tom Hornbein, Herb Staley, and I hiked five hours to St. Andrews Park on June 22, 1957, then ascended to an 8,200-foot-high camp at the top of Colonnade Ridge. A late start and little sleep the previous night barely allowed us to reach this camp before the stars attained their full brilliance.

Whipping gusts of wind at dawn presaged a cloudy day. We left camp at five o'clock in worsening weather; there was no time for inertia, for our safety lay in speed. Above the bergschrund the snow was soft, but higher on the wall it became hard and icy. When the angle topped forty-five degrees, we had to cut some steps: this was in the days before the advent of rigid crampons. Occasionally we substituted ice-screw protection for courage, but sometimes the objective dangers demanded unbelayed climbing, which added tension to our adventure.

I had begun this climb tired from a Friday night in the city, an unwise practice before undertaking such a major route. So, while Claunch and Rupley accepted leadership of the lower slopes, I carried on with minimum strength. The sun glowed behind a veil of clouds, but its pale fire was dimming minute by minute.

Higher on the wall my energy level rose, and I took my share of the leads on the steep upper portion where our route merged with the upper Sunset Ridge. The continuation to Liberty Cap—the volcano's northern summit—was simple, but near-whiteout conditions prevailed. Our plan to descend via the Tahoma Glacier was stymied by the lack of visibility, so we instead descended the Mowich Face, an adventure as thrilling as the ascent. It took the alertness of five persons to spot the crampon marks made on the way up; they were rapidly vanishing.

In a recent year more than 4,000 persons reached the summit of Mount Rainier, a testimonial to the prestige of the ascent. One of the objectives of the Park Service is to disperse and separate hiking and climbing parties. By issuing a limited number of permits, the rangers insure that hundreds of hikers will not converge simultaneously upon a scenic parkland—or that hordes of climbers will not strike out for the summit along the same route. It has been questioned whether land managers should attempt to insure a quality wilderness experience, and there is certainly great variety in the search for both privacy and companionship among the users themselves. In many cases, however well intentioned each individual turns out to be, the sheer force of numbers will annoy others and may leave scars on the terrain.

An experience on Mount Rainier is no longer guaranteed to be a Shangri-la. The meadows and snowfields on a pleasant summer day are likely to be dotted by the colorful clothing of humanity, and only in poor weather does the mountain seem like a lost, forbidden symbol.

CHAPTER THIRTY
Mount Shuksan

On that day we had our best view of great old crag-turreted Shuksan. But the gigantic crawling glaciers scarred with seracs and mighty crevasses which lay between the dark frowning cleavers, and the slender sheer pinnacle girt with swirling clouds held out little encouragement. It seemed invulnerable.

Laurie R. Frazeur
The Mountaineer, 1916

MOUNT SHUKSAN, sometimes called "The Showpiece of the Cascades," is one of the most celebrated tourist attractions in the state of Washington, a mountain that has captured the imagination of both sightseers and mountaineers alike. This bastion of steep ice and rock, whose Indian name means "steep and rugged," can be seen in its full splendor from Mount Baker Lodge and the highway at Austin Pass. The spectacular backdrop provided by Shuksan resulted in the choice of this locale in 1934 for the filming of *The Call of the Wild.* Rising 7,700 feet in just three miles from the North Fork of the Nooksack River, Mount Shuksan's magnificence is crowned with tiers of glacier ice and steep snow plaques.

Not much more than 100 years ago, white men were not even aware of this mountain's existence. Although Captain George Vancouver saw and named the higher and closer Mount Baker in 1792, its great mass hid the lower peak. Henry Custer, with the International Boundary Survey in 1859, was probably the first explorer to penetrate the North Fork valley, and he referred to the mountain and its Indian name, "Tsuskan." Custer was impressed by the peak's "immense rocky perpendicular wall," but Edmund T. Coleman, during the first ascent of Mount Baker nine years later, failed to single out Shuksan.

Prospectors followed Indian trails into the Nooksack region, and by 1892 the State Trail had been built to Milepost 20 on Ruth Creek, immediately north of Shuksan. What the gold-seekers thought of this replica of the Swiss Alps is not preserved in the historical record, but Banning Austin and R. M. Lyle, who on a road survey explored Austin Pass, then ventured on to the head of the North Fork, spoke of "impassable cliffs." The year 1896 saw a small gold rush to Ruth Creek, with the camps of Excelsior, Hill City (Shuksan), and Gold City springing up to house some 1,500 miners. The late years of the nineteenth century were the heyday of mining in the Shuksan region. Hardy men forged a route over Mamie Pass to the Lone Jack, the mine which yielded the richest ore. These prospectors were interested in geology only as it related to ore lodes, not to the shape of the magnificent peaks that surrounded them. The ice-clad towers of the North Cascades were simply impediments to travel and prospecting.

The landforms of the North Cascades have been produced by the interaction of Pacific winds, ice, and geologic forces. Its mantle of thick forests has made the geology of this region hard to decipher, but the rocks of the region show evidence of a long, complex geologic history dating back as far as 2 billion years. From about 300 million to 100 million years ago, the present site of the Cascades was covered by a sea in which sedimentary and volcanic rocks accumulated.

With deposition occurring near the continental margin, pressure and heat caused the rocks at depth to metamorphose, thus forming the rocks known today as the Shuksan Metamorphic Suite. These rocks can be found in a fault slice on the western flank of the range.

The greenschist and phyllite which form this suite are unlike any other rock in the region, one indication that this rock unit was thrust in from another location. The upper portion of the greenschist may represent a segment of sea-floor basalt that has been metamorphosed in a subduction zone, some fifteen miles below the earth's surface, along the border between two colliding plates—similar to what is happening to the rocks of the Gorda plate now being forced beneath the western edge of North America.

The Cascade Range, as we know it, follows the trend of an uparching which began about 6 million years ago and probably continues today. During this relatively recent uplift, the North Cascades were raised higher than other sections of the Cascades and were more eroded, exposing their resistant core rocks.

Mount Shuksan, with its 9,127-foot height and considerable bulk, provides an ideal surface for present-day glaciers to maintain themselves in a postglacial climate. Shuksan's seven glaciers are among the most visible of the 756 glaciers catalogued in the North Cascades, which in volume comprise about one-half of all the glaciers in the United States south of Alaska. During the glacial ages thick ice occupied the Nooksack's North Fork valley, flanking Shuksan in a great white flow, and its erosive power created the deep U-shaped profile seen today.

Similar erosion on Mount Shuksan is continuing today, but this destruction is a consequence of the action of slope (hanging) glaciers, such as the Nooksack, Price, Hanging, and Curtis glaciers. Debris encased in the lower ice level rides on top of bedrock surfaces, and as the ice flows forward and melts along the sides and front, the debris is freed. End and lateral moraines, visible at numerous localities beyond Shuksan's glaciers, are debris ridges that mark the former position of the glacier; they form only when the ice front or margin remains in position for some time. At depth, ice moves by a combination of the glacier sliding on a water-lubricated base and complex internal flow mechanisms. The crevasses on Shuksan's steep glaciers are formed by differential flow, for ice in its upper layers is the most brittle.

The nature of the rock and the results of ice-carving partly determine the form of the North Cascade landscape. The deposits of rock, silt, and gravel left by glaciers during their periods of recession and stability provide scenic diversity. One of the scenic highlights of the region is the varied vegetation. The pattern of this vegetation seen along the Nooksack valley reflects the legacy of past events, as well as present-day climatic and soil characteristics.

The nature of the forest and vegetation within each principal life zone varies locally according to the extent of avalanching and bedrock outcrops, the slope exposure to the sun, the length of the snow-free period, and the texture, depth, and stability of the soil. For instance, the immense Douglas fir tends to

Above: **The hoary marmot is a frequently seen resident of the Cascades; its range extends north through Canada into Alaska. By Stephen J. Krasemann/DRK Photo.**

Page 212: **Mount Shuksan from the northwest, in the subalpine forest near Heather Meadows. By Art Wolfe.**

Climbers ascend the edge of the Easton Glacier, high on Mount Baker. By John V. A. F. Neal.

thrive on deep valley soils, while the hardy Alaska cedar is usually seen growing on bedrock cliffs with thin soil cover.

The forests of the North Cascades are a sanctuary, sometimes sparkling and glorious, always luxuriant. The Douglas fir—a tree that towers as high as 250 feet—is the undisputed king of this evergreen land. Its height may result both from an unusually diverse set of genes and from its adaptability. This species, which ranges from Mexico to British Columbia, grows only on moist, well-drained terrain. Its original range extended much farther north than now, but as ice-age glaciers crept southward, the tree was forced in that direction. The fir arrived in the Mount Shuksan region about a million years ago and became eminently suited to the new post–ice-age climate. The tree's heavy bark guards against fires and its strong wood gives it long life: specimens have survived 1,325 years.

For me there has always been some inexplicable sense of communion with the exquisite green undergrowth and canopy of fir, hemlock, and cedar. In the broad, deep valleys that penetrate to the very base of the icy peaks, the soaring conifers provide a sense of mystery, for they cloak much of the sky and often all the vista. Great fallen trees give a vitality to others: often a young tree takes root on another's carcass. Trees become covered with moss as they die and are succeeded everywhere by new evergreen shoots. Throughout this dense forest small animals such as squirrels scamper across the logs and up the great trunks. In the mossy carpet are many frogs whose bulbous and jocular eyes seem to focus on hikers forcing a passage through the understory.

The dense forest and rugged terrain of the North Cascades are the chief reasons why Mount Shuksan was not climbed until some of the more accessible peaks had been visited. The mountain's first ascent took place during the Mazamas' outing of 1906, when Asahel Curtis and W. Montelius Price carried out a bold plan. All reports this pair had heard about the mountain told of perpendicular crags, hanging glaciers, and avalanches—a discouraging climbing prospect indeed. The two men first attempted to reach the upper glaciers of the mountain via Shuksan Arm, a westward-extending subalpine ridge. But this extensive approach disheartened them, so they worked south into the valley of Shuksan Creek, hoping to succeed on the more moderate rock slopes of the southwest flank. Upward they progressed, at one point scrambling along a narrow shelf beneath a 200-foot waterfall. At nightfall the two climbers built a protective shelter of rocks, but their bivouac was made without blankets. Curtis later recalled the evening: "Dimly outlined against the sky above all this appeared the great mass of Baker like the Japanese drawings of Fuji-yama. The first of the stars had come out by the time we had gathered enough wood for the night's fire and had eaten supper, so with shoes under our heads we fell asleep."

In the morning the men followed a rock ridge rising between snowfields to gain the broad glacial plateau of the south slope—now called the Sulphide Glacier. They logically trod up this gentle icefield to the base of the unmistakable, dark-toned summit pinnacle. (This formation was described by John D. Scott in 1930 as composed of "slabs, one atop the other, all slanting downward toward the climber.") Here Curtis and Price found few holds on the smooth, downsloping rock and had to resort to such tactics as lifting each other to successive ledges and breaking rock crevices with the back of a hatchet. For some reason they dragged along their alpenstocks.

Although some mountaineers of the day felt that a man named Joe Morovits had climbed Shuksan in 1897, Curtis asserted that "there was no trace of a previous ascent; no rocks had been disturbed." He had also commented that before the outing they "determined to make the ascent if possible, even at the expense of the main climb on Mount Baker, and made every effort to learn of a previous ascent, but were unable to find record of any."

During the next two decades the Curtis-Price route was repeated only a few times. But in 1927 Clarence A. Fisher discovered a system of easy chimneys on the upper Shuksan Arm. These slots led to the easy glaciers above, and Fisher's route—shorter and more direct than the original one—became the standard route up the mountain.

Shuksan has an intimate side never seen by tourists or even by the casual climber: the eastern cirques, where two great glaciers—the Price and the Nooksack—topple in shining cascades from the summit ice table. Rising above the head of the North Fork of the Nooksack River are cliffs threaded with waterfalls from the melting glaciers. Enclosing rock slabs sweep around the glaciers in a lofty semicircle to culminate in the jagged turret of the summit pinnacle.

Here is exciting alpine terrain on a scale suited to the individual adventure, in a true and rigorous wilderness setting. My first trip to the forbidding northeast façade of Mount Shuksan took place in September, 1945. Bill Granston, Jack Schwabland, and I had the audacity to attempt an alpine traverse of the mountain, our plan being to climb the unknown Price Glacier and descend the normal route. We left our car shortly after midnight. Using headlamps, we crossed the Nooksack River, then groped our way up brushy gullies. At dawn we reached the 5,000-foot level on the heather-covered ridge above Price Lake. Ruddy reflections cast by the first phase of sunrise greeted our eyes, with a long horizon of orange and yellow tinge on the nearby Chilliwack peaks.

The mosaic of ice gullies on the fluted glacier walls above the lake had an indigo-blue color. As the sun illuminated the ice curtains, we could see a series of benches in a ruinous icefall—a fanciful picture. Our route took us across towers of ice, tilted ramps, and occasional frail snowbridges that linked this steep fairyland of ice architecture. At the 7,000-foot level we climbed across fractured benches in a zigzag pattern. Higher, a great bergschrund forced us onto the rock wall flanking the final ice chute. This was a welcome change, despite a veneer of fresh snow. In seven roped leads we climbed to the 8,250-foot col at the head of the Price Glacier, where we could exit safely to the gentle summit glacier field.

My next venture to this remote façade of Mount Shuksan was with Clifford Schmidtke in July, 1946, for the purpose of scaling the great rock shaft of Nooksack Tower, the 8,268-foot spearhead rising between the Price and Nooksack glaciers. This time we had the good sense not to travel in pitch darkness; we spent the first night on the gravel bars of the North Fork.

At dawn we were off again, climbing to the sloping ridge above Price Lake. Here we encountered several acres of heather meadows that formed a

A deer pauses on a steep meadow in the North Cascades; the Dana Glacier spills over cliffs in the background. By Bob and Ira Spring.

nourishing bed for multitudes of bees, mosquitoes, and other insects. We strode through this growth, each step bringing us more closely in tune with this small, fragile world.

To those persons who don't explore, the private realities of the meadows remain unperceived. The insects cared little that intruders came through a domain clearly not theirs, but our visibility and tramping noises startled marmots, who uttered shrill, piercing whistles to warn all mammals of our presence. The marmot and cony (also a member of the *Rodentia* family) live perennially in such meadows. Perhaps it is the combination of open terrain and height above the valley which triggers in humans the physical sensations that characterize true empathy. We find these feelings for a larger wilderness when our visions of boundless terrain are localized by the microscopic floral clumps.

Price Glacier, whose edge we climbed, has been observed to have increased its volume between 1946 and 1954, burying earlier exposed bedrock. The ice segment we climbed below Nooksack Tower later almost filled its cirque.

After cramponing some 800 feet up a steep couloir above a bergschrund, we were greeted by a clattering of stonefall. We were pleased to get out of this dangerous funnel and reach a protected position on the tower's sheer wall. Rock slabs towered skyward. But the climbing became classic, and we felt inclined to use only one piton for protection in the next 1,200 feet. Shuksan's great eastern satellite was climbed with an intrepid spirit that day.

The next year Bob Craig and I returned to Shuksan to climb the north buttress. We chatted with tourists at Mount Baker Lodge, built in 1926 during the early popularity of skiing—the days of woolen leg wraps and heavy hickory skis. Our route took us to treeline on White Salmon Ridge, where we bivouacked in sleeping bag covers. In the morning the late-summer snow crust was so frozen atop ice that our crampons left no marks. The physical movements were pure ecstasy. The vista of wild ice and rock was superb, a scene never known by those who would not venture beyond sight of the lodge.

Mount Waddington

We stood on Icefall Point, and Mount Waddington, the "Mountain of Mystery," cast her irresistible spell over us. On our first view, from many miles down the Franklin Glacier, the mountain had seemed a far away goal. All day it had been out of sight as we trudged up the deep trough of the glacier. Now, as we climbed to the top of this thousand-foot headland and looked across the upper Franklin Glacier, the whole scene was dominated by the imminent presence of the mountain. We now knew the grip which great peaks have on the souls of climbers.

Bestor Robinson
Sierra Club Bulletin, February, 1936

To mountaineers fortunate enough to glimpse its savage form, Mount Waddington presents an intimidating spectacle. Its great rock walls are adorned with chaotic hanging glaciers, and its fanglike summit tower, generally plastered with rime icing, seems more typical of a great spear in the Karakoram Himalaya than of a 13,177-foot peak hidden deep in the Coast Mountains of British Columbia. Situated in remote splendor beyond the head of Knight Inlet, one of the long fjords of the island waterway, and not visible from any inhabited locality, Waddington has stirred the imagination of mountaineers since 1928, when Donald Munday described the summit structure as "almost a nightmare in its grim inaccessibility, in its terrific upthrust, in its baffling rock structure." Anyone who has seen the mountain will agree that it produces a lasting sense of the greatness and sublimity of nature's works. Waddington imparts a feeling of primitive isolation and dignity that is becoming harder to find as the limits of our once-boundless frontier have been attained.

Mount Waddington is still nearly as remote as it was in 1863, when Alfred Waddington built some forty bridges along the turbulent Homathko River, inland from Bute Inlet, during an effort to construct a toll road to the Cariboo goldfields. His resourceful venture ended in disaster when frenzied Chilcotin Indians killed twelve of his men while they were camped on a sandbar in April, 1864, a massacre which led to the "Chilcotin War" punitive expedition. Waddington, nearly bankrupted by this catastrophe, abandoned his plan.

Waddington was aware of the rough nature of the high mountains between the coastal waterways and the interior plateau, but he was not interested in the alpine aspects of geography. There had been reports of great peaks in the Coast Mountains since the mid-nineteenth century, but as of the early 1920s their location and height were still conjectural. Maps of this time showed three peaks near Chilko Lake as being higher than 10,000 feet, but this was simply an educated guess. In 1922, surveyor Robert Bishop sighted and triangulated Mount Waddington from the interior, but in the files of bureaucracy the importance of the dominating mountain was lost.

At a time when the Rocky Mountains and the Interior Ranges had been thoroughly explored, the intriguing Coast Mountains remained mysterious. The hostile terrain, including deep, rocky river canyons and vast icefields, made both surveyors and mountaineers apprehensive about exploration.

As late as 1925, Canadian mapmakers were not fully aware of the existence of the great mountain

Above: The summit tower of Mount Waddington, seen from the northwest peak. The north face lies in shadow to the left, the northwest ridge drops toward the camera, and the upper part of the southwest face is profiled on the right. By Don Serl.

Page 218: Clouds enshroud the ice-clad mass of Mount Waddington, highest peak in the Coast Mountains of British Columbia. By Barry Hagen.

Facing page: Leading a rock pitch in the chimney on the summit tower of Mount Waddington. By Doug Herchmer.

twenty-four miles from tidewater; they still considered Mount Robson to be the highest peak in provincial Canada. But Don and Phyllis Munday of Vancouver had an abiding curiosity about a high, gleaming peak they had scrutinized with binoculars from a summit on Vancouver Island. At the time no climbers had penetrated the unmapped inland mountains, and the Mundays' description of the intriguing peak conjured the title "Mystery Mountain." It was left for the Mundays to assess the importance of Mount Waddington—as it became known officially—and to direct their energies toward its exploration and ascent.

The prospective adventure cast its spell on the Mundays, who were among the most resourceful of Canadian mountaineers. In all, they made eleven forays into the Coast Mountains, the first, in 1925, taking them as far as the Homathko River. On their second venture, in 1926, the Mundays reached the glaciers of the Waddington area after battling their way up the Homathko River valley. Dense tangles of underbrush impeded travel, but the worst hazards the pair encountered were narrow gorges and log jams; hand lines were sometimes used to cross flooded tributaries. By the end of two weeks they had traveled a mere thirty miles and gained only a few hundred vertical feet! On June 23 they saw for the first time the great bulk of the mystery mountain, its summit crowned by an ice-feathered tower. A cloak of glaciers—some 400 square miles in extent—surrounded the peak; it was a truly alpine landscape. The party advanced to a col on the mountain's southeast ridge before turning back; they had, however, far outrun the mapmakers.

In the summer of 1927 the Mundays spent nearly a month in the region, this time making the entry via Knight Inlet to the north. They managed to make a serious attempt on the mountain, but, failing to find a suitable route, directed their attention to the lower northwest peak. There the Mundays made some progress, but the weather turned foul and the pair retreated.

The following year the indomitable couple succeeded in reaching the summit of the northwest peak, taking fifteen hours to climb from their high camp to the snow-crowned point. There they reflected on the grim inaccessibility of the higher rock summit, only several hundred yards distant. It was covered, Munday wrote, "with plumes of huge, crumbling ice-feathers." After the Mundays returned home the *Illustrated London News* carried an article entitled "Unclimbable Mt. Mystery."

The notoriety of Waddington was firmly established when a climber named Alec Dalgleish was

killed during an attempt on the peak in 1934; his rope broke over a sharp edge after he had slipped. The same summer an adventurous trio from Winnipeg, Campbell Secord, and the brothers Roger and Ferris Neave, found their way through very difficult terrain from the interior: at one point they spent two days building a bridge across a torrential stream. On the north face of Waddington the climbers had to chip ice off rock with ice axes, for the entire upper mountain was "permanently encased in ice." During inclement weather their ropes and gloves froze; if anyone had fallen, they all likely would have gone down. Nevertheless, the trio climbed to within 800 feet of the summit, proving that the mountain was not invincible.

One has to admire the collective courage of these early expeditions. The quality of their efforts left no doubt that this mountain could bring forth the best from climbers: courage, strength, and teamwork. But all the early parties had been handicapped by weather, approach problems, and limitations in their rock climbing skills.

By the mid-1930s Mount Waddington had become a focal point for American and Canadian mountaineers. Munday's description of the final summit tower—an "incredible nightmarish thing"—

proved irresistible to Sierra Club rock specialists who had been successful in climbing sheer cliffs in Yosemite Valley. A group of Californians led by Bestor Robinson attempted Waddington's south face in 1935, but managed to climb only the northwest peak. Camping too low, their efforts on the main objective failed, perhaps because they were awed by the alpine nature of the problems: they had missed the obvious lines of weakness and favored the spiny rock ribs. In 1936 some members of the same California group joined a Canadian team for another attempt. This time the unwieldy party of nine climbed to about 12,500 feet on the south face, a creditable performance. But the real and psychological barriers of stonefall, threatening weather, couloir ice, a reluctance to bivouac, and the presence of a rival party led by the seasoned alpinist Fritz Wiessner, proved insurmountable. These climbers learned that it would take more than technical ability to conquer Waddington.

Meanwhile, Wiessner and Bill House, who had agreed to let the larger group make the first summit bid, studied the technical problems and chose a route up the snow-and-ice couloir leading to the notch between the main and northwest summits. Their first attempt was blocked by steep rock at the head of the couloir, but they persisted, and on July 21 took a more central route. The last 1,000 feet of the south face, which Wiessner termed "sheer forbidding-looking rocks," required hours of difficult climbing. Wiessner led the steep and often ice-covered rock pitches in rope-soled shoes, at one time standing on House's shoulders in order to reach higher holds. A chimney proved to be the key to success and the summit was won with a spirited struggle. The victory was due not only to the ability of the two men and their experience on both steep ice and rock, but also in their willingness to commit themselves totally to the effort. Wiessner's experience in the Alps made him well acquainted with the technical and psychological problems of serious alpine routes.

The North Cascades of Washington State offer similar alpine challenges, and after trips in the early 1940s to the Picket Range and Mount Shuksan, my brother Helmy and I felt reasonably confident on such terrain. Unexpected problems on big walls and difficult approaches had honed our self-reliance. Keyed with youthful vigor (Helmy was sixteen and I was nineteen) and uninhibited by tradition, we prepared ourselves physically and mentally for the ascent of Mount Waddington in the summer of 1942.

After making the delightful two-day steamer voyage from Vancouver to the cannery at Knight Inlet, Helmy and I, accompanied by another climber, Erick Larson, followed a plan recommended to us by the Mundays. A fisherman deposited us on the shores of the Franklin River. An approach inland from tidewater, with a glacier only seven miles distant, was a new experience for us.

The rumor of nearby grizzly bears and the sight of gigantic footprints made us alert for noises in the underbrush. We promptly hung our reserve food supplies from fir limbs high above the ground, then began relaying heavy loads along the meager valley trail: the sooner we left bear country the better. Hiking was difficult, for alder branches and logs slowed progress, and the ever-present devil's club had to be pushed aside carefully. Larson had to put up not only with the rough going, but with our arrogance and enthusiasm as well; he decided he would head back for home. This turnabout was a logistical blow, for we had counted on three for safety. We pondered the added risk for a party of two, then resolutely continued. Our involvement and isolation was total, our doubts were gone. The loads were now heavier, for a basic amount of expedition gear had to be carried regardless of the number in the party. While toiling under heavy loads, we had little good to say about Larson.

On Franklin Glacier we soon felt the strong glacier wind, which slides down close to the surface, beneath the upvalley wind, blowing day and night in summer with approximately constant strength. This wind is produced by the temperature differential between the glacier and the warmer surrounding terrain. Each time we packed a load up from the valley, we enjoyed the wind's refreshing effect as we exited from the forest.

By August 5 we had moved a week's food from the Franklin Glacier through the Dais Glacier icefall to a camp beneath the south face of our objective. We were determined not to repeat the mistake of the Sierra Club parties, who had placed their final camps too low. Our next task was to hang a fixed rope for a more direct start on the morning of our attempt. This tactic would save time, a most important factor in getting above the rockfall zone of the great couloir during the cold morning hours. Once the sun's rays warmed the rime-ice features and frozen rocks of the upper face, a barrage of stonefall would begin, funneling at high speed into the parallel couloirs of the lower face. Wiessner and House had been willing to risk dangerous rockfall, and this was an important factor in their success. Only by climbing the natural lines of ascent, the great snow-and-ice couloirs, can a party rapidly get high on the south face: it was our goal to begin at dawn and reach the summit on our first day.

The weather had settled, and it was apparent that a high-pressure ridge had set in on the Coast Mountains. Despite the promise of fine weather Helmy and I slept poorly the night before our attempt. Nevertheless, we were on our way by four o'clock on August 7, a time when the couloir ice would be relatively free from rockfall. Belays were necessary in the couloirs of the lower face, yet because it was imperative to move fast and steadily, we climbed together for a time. On such a great face it is important that momentum continue, and that indecision not be allowed to pervade one's attitude.

We were climbing in tricouni-nailed boots, but we also carried tennis shoes for the expected steep rock work. In the late afternoon I donned my tennis shoes and slipped on specially fitted felt pullovers. On the mixed sections of the upper face I led the rock pitches; Helmy, still wearing his boots, led the ice. This technique proved successful, and soon we reached a point only 500 feet below the summit.

Perhaps it was intuition, perhaps it was the thud of ominous rockfall in the chimney climbed by Wiessner and House, but we decided to depart from the first-ascent route and tackle the smooth rock face leading directly to the summit. Looking upward, we saw that the exposed windward edges of the

The glacier-draped northwest
face of Brother Peak in the
Niut Range, east of Mount
Waddington. By Fred Beckey.

ridgecrest were encrusted with fragile tufts of ice. This was my first experience with rime, which here grew from tiny white feathers into massive formations. The rock acts as a nuclei for condensation when supercooled water droplets are carried by the wind in fog or clouds. These "frost-feather" growths depend mainly on wind speed and instantaneous freezing, not on snow precipitation. On warming, the rime may break off in chunks and endanger the climber.

The character of the rock began to change: climbing became steeper and more demanding, more difficult to protect with our soft-steel pitons. We followed what seemed the line of least resistance. There were difficult moves, one wet lieback standing out: my pullovers made this and other icy spots possible. Strenuous climbing continued, then in great spirits we followed a steep crack leading to the summit ridge. At 8:30 we stood triumphantly on the tiny highest point.

The purpling sky canopied an incredible array of mountains, a scene we recognized from photographs in the *Canadian Alpine Journal.* We left our names in Wiessner's metallic register, then descended a short distance to a ledge large enough to bivouac in our light tent sack.

Despite the discomfort and chill, I sensed why we were here and had accepted the challenge of Waddington. This was pure joy and intriguing effort. As Gaston Rébuffat wrote, "In this modern age, very little remains that is real. Night has been banished, so have the cold, the wind, and the stars. They have all been neutralised. Where is the rhythm of life?"

The descent was a slow epic of rappels, enlivened by the hazard of rockfall. Eventually we decided to wait for the evening freeze. On the lower portion of the face, perched on a protruding rock rib, we felt safe from the stony missiles. Much later in the evening we moved down the open couloir, back into the firing line. Despite the freeze, a barrage whizzed past us; in the dusk we could not determine how to dance away from it, and Helmy was struck in the knee. Concern for the injury prompted us to retreat to the rock, where we waited until the next night before finishing the descent. It had been a daring and rewarding adventure.

Devils Thumb

The Katete debouches through a thick screen of swamp. A wide valley funnels back to mountains and saddles which encircle the end. The Iskut, the largest tributary on the Stikine, is next, even more barricaded behind islands and sloughs. It's a classic straight corridor through a vast steep valley of virgin trees, each as straight as if it had been plumbed. The Stikine weaves, like the highway it is. As we approach the mountains before us, they slowly open a gap, which closes again after we pass. We feel our way over the snags, often nuzzling so closely against an island that we can hear the songbirds over the noise.

Edward Hoagland
*Notes from the Century Before: A Journal from
British Columbia,* 1969

A LTHOUGH I have never lived in Alaska, I have always felt a proprietary zeal about its rugged, fascinating mountains, particularly the more remote ranges, the ones few people knew about. While attending the University of Washington in Seattle I became keen to venture beyond the familiar Cascade Range and seek alpine rewards in the "Panhandle" of southeastern Alaska, choosing the great summits and icefields near the Stikine River for the site of my first northland expedition.

The Coast Mountains in the "Panhandle" present a formidable, intriguing, and altogether confusing panorama. So complex is the topography that much of the region's early history of exploration and political determination reads like a compendium of geographers' errors. The Boundary Ranges of the Coast Mountains begin at the shores of the Portland Canal—just north of Prince Rupert, British Columbia—and extend onward to about the Fifty-Ninth Parallel. The ranges' consistently jagged form is due to the resistance of hard rocks to stream and glacial erosion. The peaks are part of a composite granitic batholith nearly 1,000 miles long, one of the world's greatest plutonic masses, an intrusion accompanied by great crustal compression and followed by glacial sculpting.

The mountain ranges of this portion of Alaska and Canada are an aggregate of massifs that act as a climatic barrier between the sea and interior. On the maritime flank the peaks drop precipitously into Pacific waters, creating a labyrinth of fjords or drowned glacier valleys that twist into a giant jigsaw puzzle of islands, some of which are hundreds of miles in length.

The present Alaska-Canada boundary results largely from the 1827 map of A. J. de Krusenstern, a Russian navigator. His map showed the frontier of Russian Alaska following the coastal sinuosities at a distance of ten marine leagues inland. Captain George Vancouver adopted the general features of this map, and subsequent mapmakers and diplomats came to regard the supposed single mountain chain as a natural boundary. Later explorations sent to clarify political claims found no concise mountain chain, only a sea of mountains. Not until after 1900 did the two governments dispatch field parties to determine the exact boundary points. This was a difficult and lengthy procedure, for the rugged mountains of this land were still totally unexplored. William P. Blake, a geologist who in 1863 had examined the glaciers that fed into the Stikine River, noted

the belief of the coastal Tlingit Indians that spirits dwelled among the heights; he found it impossible to find anyone to accompany him on his ventures from a boat.

The most compelling peaks in the vast glaciated region between the Stikine River and the island archipelago of the coast are Devils Thumb (9,077 feet) and Kates Needle (10,002 feet). Devils Thumb is one of the boundary peaks; the much-debated line passes directly over its summit. In a report, one of the government boundary surveyors modestly referred to Devils Thumb as "a high sugarloaf peak." But photographs taken by surveyors disclosed a granitic bastion rising as a sheer pillar amid its chaotic rock and ice surroundings; one flank actually soared 6,000 feet above an ice passage leading to the fjordlike Thomas Bay.

Above: **The snow- and ice-plastered south face of Devils Thumb. The upper part of the Cats Ears is visible on the left; the upper east ridge, route of the first ascent, lies on the right. By George Bracksieck.**

Facing page: **A white-tailed ptarmigan in winter plumage nestles in the snow for insulation. By David C. Fritts.**

Pages 226-227: **Aerial view of Devils Thumb. The southwest face is in the center, Cats Ears pinnacle lies to the left, and the east ridge is to the right. By Paul Starr.**

If there had been any mountaineering done in this mysterious region, I could find nothing in the annals of literature except for a 1937 attempt on Kates Needle by Fritz Wiessner and Bestor Robinson. Poor weather had frustrated their effort. My correspondence with Wiessner about this remarkable region early in 1946 resulted in mutual enthusiasm for an attempt that summer on both Kates Needle and Devils Thumb. He agreed that they would be superb challenges and that the difficult approach and terrain would add to the prize of conquest. His approach route of 1937, the Stikine River, was the most logical one, for a flat-bottomed freight-and-passenger boat plied the river as far as Telegraph Creek, a famed route of the Cassiar and Klondike gold seekers. About fifty miles up the Stikine, the Flood Glacier drained the eastern flank of the vast icefields of the Pacific Divide. Topographic maps of Boundary Survey vintage and more recent photography indicated that we should be able to find a possible entry to our objectives from this inland approach.

I had shipped most of our food ahead by boat, so when I met Wiessner and his friend Donald Brown at Wrangell on July 9, all was ready for our departure. As we carried our loads of climbing equipment and three weeks' worth of food to the dock, the crew and other passengers studied us with curiosity. Soon after the boat turned out of the bay, heading for the cleft in the coastal mountains which identified the entrance of the Stikine, pilot Al Ritchie asked us where our guns were. "We don't have any," we replied. He thereupon told us a story about a dairy farmer who had just been killed by a grizzly. "Don't worry about the grizzlies," Ritchie remarked, "they will hunt you!"

Once landed on the gravel beach opposite the Flood Glacier, we began packing loads through a difficult understory jungle of devil's club, slide alder, and fallen logs. At one point, plagued by mosquitoes, we had to swim a deep stream channel while ferrying loads across by means of a "tyrolean traverse." By July 14 we had transported all our equipment and food onto the moraine of the seventeen-mile-long Flood Glacier.

Wiessner had injured his knee falling off a slippery log in the underbrush, and after several days of packing loads up the glacier it was evident that his condition was worsening. He tested the knee on a snowslope, but it did not feel right. After packing loads to a small alp at a bend in the glacier, thirteen miles from the river, we reluctantly called off the expedition. However, I decided to leave much of the gear and some food at the alp; I had the rest of the summer free and was virtually certain I could obtain the company of Bob Craig and Cliff Schmidtke, with whom I had already made plans to climb in Canada's Coast Mountains in August. I was confident my enthusiasm would coax them into changing destination plans and come instead to the Stikine.

Upon our return to Wrangell I telegraphed Craig and soon received a message that they would leave Seattle by the next boat. Meanwhile, I spent a week with a survey party.

After my two new companions arrived, we repeated the boat trip up the river, finding a cache I had left hanging from a big tree near the gravel bar still in good condition. But when we went through the food we discovered that a cloth sack of beans, which I had brought along from an earlier expedition, was no longer full of beans—it contained only husks and maggots!

Now more fearful than ever of grizzlies, we periodically blew police whistles to forewarn them of our presence and hoped that our reading of Emerson's "Self Reliance" would prime our confidence. The long trek up the glacier went well, but upon reaching the site of the alp cache we made a dismaying discovery. An account by Craig describes our consternation: "Goats had pushed aside the large rocks and gnawed into some of our most vital items. Completely vanished were five pounds of imported cheese, three pounds of salami, two pounds of butter, three pounds of sugar, and the burglars even went so far as to chew a Klim can into fine bits. Having no firearms at hand, Schmidtke proposed starting avalanches on the Billys as they grazed on the nearby spur."

Fortunately, the goats had not consumed everything; we could get by. Our first effort was to pack loads to the edge of the 6,000-foot ice plateau—some 3,000 feet above our camp—via a spur which Bob had named "Pilferage Ridge." Although this portage was

for a cache to supply Devils Thumb, it put us in a good position to study the great ice-clad slopes of Kates Needle, our first objective. Partway up the ridge, displaying extraordinary accuracy, Cliff killed three of a flock of ptarmigans with rocks. We later regretted this impetuous act (even though we ate the birds), but we all took part in the stonings, perhaps in revenge for the attack on our provisions by goats.

During the following days we made the first ascent of the region's highest summit, Kates Needle. This proved to be a beautiful climb up corniced ridges and fluted ice walls. There was little time for exhilaration on the summit, for clouds were enveloping much of the landscape.

Following a period of storms and rest days, we began moving supplies toward our chief goal, Devils Thumb. Approaching this rock fang, I gazed in amazement at its spectacular outline. It was easy to see in this great spire, which resembled a truncated Matterhorn, that anathema of mountaineers: personal failure. Still, I could taste a certain pleasure in the prospects to come. The long trek to our position and discovering the route to the objective had crystallized my love for Alaskan mountain adventure.

We completed the ski trek across the divide with heavy packs, using the rope among the dangerous crevasses of the ice plateau. Near the pass separating Devils Thumb and the plateau, at about the 6,000-foot level, we pegged our tent in a wind-scoured hollow adjacent to a rock wall. Binoculars helped us study our proposed routes on the south face and east ridge. We all agreed the ascent would test our capacities to the utmost.

Dawn on August 17 brought no sunrise, just a reddish tint to the overcast that had floated in during the night. There was a warm wind when we left the tent to explore the peak's lower flanks. We laid out a route up the glacier to a large bergschrund on the southeast flank, then climbed with great care up a crusted firn slope. Higher, we cut steps with our ice axes along the base of a rock wall, then ascended steep but firm rock to the tip of a buttress at 8,000 feet. Swirling mists soon shrouded the forbidding upper south face; it was clearly time to retreat. The gloom increased and an icy downpour soaked us on the descent, but we had the knowledge that we had been closer to the summit than humans ever had.

The following morning we arose late, expecting the worst, but found skies clearing. We made plans to start up again immediately, packing equipment and food for a possible benightment. Totally self-supporting, we would have to remain calm and collected on this somewhat impetuous adventure, dozens of miles from civilization.

Our route led up precipitous snow-and-rock slopes on the south face to a point just below a notch in the east ridge. But the summit lay at the extreme west corner of the face; the extra distance would increase the difficulty of attaining it. We climbed three rope lengths of wet rock on the ridge in tennis shoes. Then we confronted the crucial next problem: a sheer pinnacle, encrusted in places with verglas and nearly devoid of piton cracks, which I led with the aid of slings and a considerable jolt of adrenalin. On the next pitch an ice piton helped Cliff over a bulge as he climbed a V-shaped crack leading to the ridge behind the pinnacle. I was happy to change into my boots, for my feet were nearly frozen. Darkness was at hand, so we began to search for a bivouac spot. Finally, we dug a cavity in a snowpatch, taking our time, for the exercise warmed us.

As we shivered, the weather worsened. When light finally appeared, we climbed to a narrow snow crest where we could see the summit. Not for long, however, for snow began to fall. Aware of the consequences of being caught on the exposed ridge in a storm, we reluctantly made a retreat.

By noon the next day a storm had grown into a howling torrent: a sixty-mile-an-hour gale swept rain through the tent. We emptied fourteen gallons of water out the door with a "bucket brigade" before devising a system of drainage canals. The fury continued three more days; later we learned that the Stikine River had risen three feet during this storm. Rain had eaten away most of our tent support, and we were sleeping on a tiny pedestal. A new crevasse opened four feet from our tent door and Bob almost stepped through. Our hopes for success were fading as time and food ran short; indeed, much of our conversation had to do with plans for a new assault the following year. Finally we had to repitch our tent in a snowstorm.

During all this discomfort our spirits never flagged. We wondered why we were so persistent. Why did we not give up with this weather? In a sense we climbed to give ourselves a truer picture of aspiration. By now we had come to terms with Devils Thumb. We were living with the mountain, beginning to learn its moods, learning where the wind blew, where avalanches tended to slide. We were far from ready to quit.

On August 24 we awoke to glorious sunshine; the Thumb glistened in powdered whiteness. We climbed quickly to the steep ice slope, but, as expected, found conditions unreasonably hazardous. The hot sun melted much snow off the rocks, however, and we laid plans for one final attempt: we had become intense and dedicated.

A crystal-clear sky greeted our 3:00 A.M. start, and as we retraced the difficult route, our optimism soared. The weather was marvelous and our progress fast. At noon we reached the previous high mark, helped by several short pieces of rope we had left at the crucial difficulties. Above, we were elated to see a promising route. We worked along the ridge, straddling several narrow blocks, and reached a recess at the foot of an imposing step. From a piton belay I traversed left and up, over a rim on tiny clawlike holds. Success was now certain, and we traversed quickly over to the true summit.

This was an airy perch. The ice-plastered north face plummeted 5,000 feet, almost vertically, to an arm of the Baird Glacier. The atmosphere was so clear that Mounts Fairweather and Crillon, 230 miles to the northwest, were visible. Now, many years after the summit was reached, I still feel a glow of happiness in our success. At the time it was the ultimate satisfaction of my climbing career.

We built a cairn on a ledge beneath the summit block and left the customary notes in a metal can. During the descent, the rappel from the pinnacle was spectacular; one kept fifteen to twenty feet out from the wall for nearly a hundred feet. The remainder of the descent proved uneventful, but we took great care and reached camp before nightfall.

Skis were a blessing the next day as we crossed the ice plateau. Almost totally exhausted, we reached the Stikine River at two in the morning, having covered twenty miles of glacier, moraine, and forest jungle—the latter in total darkness. We fell asleep after building a roaring bonfire, knowing that Al Ritchie on his boat would see the smoke when he came around a bend. Just before the boat arrived, Bob and Cliff went for a swim downstream. Later, as we chugged by this bathing spot, a female grizzly with two cubs reared up at us, a symbol of the fierce northland. Perhaps the boat had rescued us just in time!

CHAPTER THIRTY-THREE

Mount St. Elias

What a glorious sight awaited me! The heavens were without a cloud, and the sun shone with dazzling splendor on the white peaks around. . . . On the steep cliffs the snow hung in folds like drapery, tier above tier, while the angular peaks above stood out like crystals against the sky. St. Elias was one vast pyramid of alabaster.

Israel C. Russell
National Geographic, May 29, 1891

V ITUS BERING, a Dane in the employ of Russia, made three voyages across the North Pacific from Siberia. In 1728, Bering sailed into the strait that separates Asia from North America and has since been given his name, but he did not see the Alaskan mainland. During Bering's third voyage, though, the log of his ship, the *St. Peter,* records that on July 16, 1741, "high, snow-covered mountains" were sighted. A few days after this sighting—which was the European discovery of Alaska—the *St. Peter* anchored off a cape that the navigator named St. Elias for the patron saint of the day. The highest peak also became known as St. Elias, and after it was sighted again in 1778 by James Cook of England, a chart published as a consequence of this voyage carried the mountain's name. The mountains were seen again in 1786 by the French navigator J. F. G. de La Pérouse; he mentions "Bering's Mount Saint Elias, the summit of which appeared above the clouds."

The mountains sighted by Bering, Cook, and La Pérouse constitute the highest coastal range on earth. Mount St. Elias, only thirty-five miles from the ocean and twenty miles from the tidewater of Icy Bay, rises 18,008 feet above sea level; it is the fourth-highest summit in North America. But the prestige of this alpine titan derives as much from its elegant form as from its height and bulk. Inland from St. Elias, which lies on the border between Alaska and Canada's Yukon Territory, lies Canada's highest peak and North America's second highest, the massive 19,850-foot Mount Logan. The St. Elias Mountains are the largest uplift in North America, exceeding the Alaska Range in everything but the elevation of the highest peak (Mount McKinley in the Alaska Range holds that honor). The St. Elias Mountains are considered one of the Icefield Ranges, a group that includes the Fairweather Range to the south.

The part of the Cordillera that lies in western Canada and southern Alaska is a belt some 500 miles wide. It has undergone repeated episodes of mountain building for much of the earth's history. The St. Elias Mountains in particular rise abruptly from sea level to great heights and apparently are among the earth's youngest landforms. The complex process resulting in this recent uplift has involved the addition of marine sediments to the continent, followed by crustal compression and thrust faulting.

A vivid description of the St. Elias Mountains was given by H. S. Bostock in a monograph published by the Canadian government:

St. Elias Mountains appear as a broad swelling on the horizon out of which giant peaks project like islands of ice and snow. When haze and smoke shroud the lower levels, these peaks, high in the crystal clear atmosphere above, are sometimes still to be seen, a line of magnificent icebergs floating on the denser air. . . . Above a

An aerial view of Mount St. Elias and the vast Malaspina Glacier. By William Boehm.

sea of lesser peaks and wide ice-fields the great peaks stand solitary or in compact, isolated groups. Besides their colossal size, this individual aloofness adds much to the impressiveness of their vast, wild, and icy beauty, and contrasts them sharply with the jumbled rivalry of summits around many of the main peaks of the Coast, Rocky, and Mackenzie Mountains, and other mountains of the Canadian Cordillera.

Bostock goes on to describe the glaciation on the peaks:

Another outstanding feature is the mantle of snow and ice that even in summer cloaks a great part of them. It spreads unbroken over their gentler summit areas, smoothing the contours of their upper slopes and concealing bedrock. As the slopes steepen downward, it overhangs the edges of precipices in great cliffs of ice from which it cascades in mighty avalanches thousands of feet to the broad fields of snow and ice below, where it feeds the glaciers that lead away between the peaks. Almost the only exposures of rock in all the vast expanse of white and blue around the great peaks are in their precipices. Below these dazzling monarchs a sea of lesser peaks, mighty themselves in other company, form a jagged and rocky platform.

The St. Elias Mountains are covered by the largest system of glacial ice in North America. This vast domain of ice extends 250 miles from Glacier Bay, which is southeast of Mount St. Elias, northwest to the Copper River. The largest of the glaciers on the coastal side of the Icefield Ranges flow to the Pacific, but in the northern part of the Gulf of Alaska a coastal plain separates the mountains from the sea. Here are located two enormous piedmont glaciers: the Bering, to the west of Mount St. Elias, and the Malaspina, a smooth sheet of ice larger than Rhode Island that extends for forty miles along the south base of St. Elias and twenty-eight miles beyond. The Malaspina is fed by several glaciers falling from the flanks of St. Elias and neighboring peaks, in particular by the Seward Glacier north and east of St. Elias and the Agassiz Glacier to the southeast.

With such extensive ice cover, geologists have not been able to study the underlying rocks in detail, but there is much scientific curiosity about these glaciers. Of particular interest is the tendency of certain glaciers in the region to undergo occasional surges—periods of rapid movement somewhat analogous to flood waves in a stream. These changes in velocity are not entirely understood, but their effects on the glaciers' flow patterns are revealed by spectacularly contorted moraines.

Visitors to the St. Elias region, from the early explorers to today's mountaineers, have noted another dominant feature of the region: it has some of the worst weather in the world. The range is characterized by intense storms sweeping in from the Gulf of Alaska, the type of storms that can bury tents in snow. Summer precipitation results from the moist air of a pressure system called the "Aleutian Low" migrating east from the North Pacific. Israel Russell wrote in an account of his 1891 St. Elias expedition about the weather pattern: "Usually the first sign of the coming change when the weather is clear is a small cloud-banner on the summit of Mount St. Elias. This signal is a warning that can be seen for 150 miles at sea. Soon other peaks repeat the alarm, like bale-fires in times of invasion, and Mount Augusta and Cook and far-away Fairweather fling out their beacons to show that a storm is approaching." High lenticular clouds develop on the lee side of the St. Elias Mountains, often as many as six to ten layers thick, standing in profile like arched stacks of pancakes. Lenticular clouds indicate steep pressure gradients and violent winds. Strong gusts pouring down the interior flank of the range produce downdrafts hazardous to aircraft.

The wind, the snow, and the cold are enough to remind a man what a frail creature he is, but he must contend with sun as well. The thin air at high elevations acts but weakly as a filter for solar radiation. Scientists determined that eighty per cent of the incoming radiation reached a research station high on Mount Logan, while Kluane Lake in the low country just to the east received only fifty percent. But the stronger radiation up high does little to warm the land. Some ninety per cent of the incoming rays are reflected by the snow, creating a serious sunburn hazard for the traveler in high, snowy mountains, who is subjected to strong radiation not only from above but also from the surface below.

Toward the end of the nineteenth century, St. Elias was believed to be North America's highest summit and attracted several expeditions intent upon climbing it. The first, in 1886, was organized by Frederick Schwatka, an adventurer with Arctic experience, and sponsored by the New York Times. Awed by heavily crevassed glaciers they encountered, the small group reached an elevation of only 7,200 feet, and Heywood Seton-Karr, the only member with alpine experience, pronounced the mountain "utterly inaccessible from the south."

Two years later an expedition led by Englishman Harold Topham used canoes to reach Icy Bay from the settlement of Yakutat on the larger inlet named Yakutat Bay. The sixteen climbers hired Indians as porters; the Indians did splendidly, despite never having been on glaciers and despite a fear of bears. Topham reported startling "a very big black bear, which made off at a great pace across the glacier toward St. Elias, jumping the crevasses in grand style." The expedition supplemented its supply of dried salmon with wild strawberries, geese, and marmots taken en route, but the immensity of the mountain defeated the climbers, who by their own estimate reached 11,460 feet—apparently on a southwestern satellite of St. Elias called Haydon Peak.

In 1890 Professor Israel Russell visited the St. Elias region on a scientific expedition, during which he explored and studied geology and glaciers. This six-week-long expedition might also have achieved the first ascent of Mount St. Elias but for the onslaught of late August snowstorms. Three feet of snow fell at Russell's high camp, and his party was forced to turn back. "The white snow surface could not be distinguished from the vapor-filled air," wrote Russell. "There was no earth and no sky; we seemed to be suspended in a white, translucent medium which surrounded us like a shroud."

The next year Russell returned for further studies and another attempt on St. Elias. Although the expedition began in disaster when six men were lost in the surf at Icy Bay, the survivors continued to the Malaspina Glacier. A toboggan was hewed from a large spruce for hauling supplies; four men pulled it, two walked abreast, and one guided the sled and lifted it over crevasses from behind. For safety, the men were tied together with a hemp rope; each carried a seven-foot-long hickory alpenstock and a short ice hatchet.

As on his first attempt, Russell and his party ascended the Agassiz Glacier, then the Newton Glacier, which occupies a bowl under the east face of St. Elias and which the professor had named the year before. Crevasses were a constant hazard. At one point Russell heard an exclamation from one of his men and looked back. "I saw that he had disappeared, leaving only a hole in the snow to indicate the direction of his departure. Returning quickly, I looked down the hole, but saw only the walls of a blue crevasse; a curve in the opening had carried my companion out of sight." Fortunately, the companion had landed uninjured and could be rescued.

The expedition reached a col on St. Elias' northeast ridge and ascended the ridge to 14,500 feet. But the weather, which pinned Russell and a companion

in a large cotton tent (where they slept between canvas sheets, under wool blankets and feather quilts), finally defeated them once again.

Despite Russell's intrepid and resourceful efforts, he had failed to climb St. Elias, but he had found a feasible route. In 1897, Prince Luigi Amedeo of Savoy, Duke of the Abruzzi, arrived in Yakutat with a party of nine Europeans, including the famed alpine photographer Vittorio Sella, and several Indians and Americans to help carry loads on the approach. The duke was only twenty-four, but he had gained leadership and organizing ability through his military training, and he would one day lead successful expeditions to the Caucasus, Ruwenzori, and Karakoram.

The struggles involved in hauling sleds twenty-one miles across the Malaspina Glacier were described by the expedition's chronicler, Filippo di Filippi:

> Dragging sledges is tiring work; for although the snow is in fairly good condition, they sink too deep into it. Accordingly, the men are often obliged to lift the prows in order to get them over the heaps of caked snow in front. Four men are harnessed two by two to each sledge.

Ascending eight miles up the Newton Glacier required thirteen days. "We had to contend almost constantly," wrote de Filippi, "with persistent and dense snow-falls, which lasted entire days, enveloping us in a blinding cloud that made our surroundings strangely vague. It was heavy walking through the powdery snow, in which we often sank to our hips, while we had to grope our way patiently among the great blocks of ice."

At the 12,280-foot col in the northeast ridge, now named Russell Col, the Italians rested in tents, optimistic because three days of good weather had solidified the snow surface. The night was clear and still, with Venus shining serenely over the subsidiary summit on the northeast ridge, Mount Newton.

Sinking but a few inches into the firm snow, de Filippi recalled, "we ascended rapidly. . . . As the light grew stronger the peaks around us shone like silver." The combination of altitude and exertion made "legs seem weary as lead," but at 11:45 A.M., the guides who had been leading stepped aside so the duke could be the first to plant his boot on the summit.

The second ascent of Mount St. Elias was not accomplished until forty-nine years later, in 1946. By 1981, only thirteen ascents of the great ice pyramid had been successful. Because of its size and its weather, St. Elias is not an easy ascent. There have

Above: Climbers resting on the corniced west ridge of Mount Foresta during the first ascent of this neighboring peak of Mount St. Elias. By Rick Nolting.

Facing page: Moraine at the toe of the Donjek Glacier, Kluane National Park. By Pat Morrow.

been accidents from avalanches. In 1971, a Canadian party experienced seven feet of snow during one five-day storm.

Expeditions must prepare for the unexpected in the barren glacial wilderness of the St. Elias Mountains. Sufficient food, fuel, clothing, and proper shelter are necessary for survival. So are logistics and the wisdom and judgment developed only with experience. Logistic failure frustrated my 1975 expedition to St. Elias. Nine of us hoped to complete a route on the mountain's west flank, but problems with aircraft—used by most expeditions today, either for glacier landings or airdrops—left four of our party and most of our food stranded for eleven days on a river bar far from the mountain. Despite our failure to climb St. Elias, its beauty, its perils, and the brilliant sunshine of its heights were not lost on us as we packed loads to various high camps. Once a great roar broke the alpine silence, and we saw a gigantic avalanche pouring down a slope high above us, reminding us that, despite its allure, St. Elias can be dangerous and requires skillful routefinding judgment.

I have also made successful expeditions to the St. Elias Mountains. Early in May, 1966, Don Liska, Eric Bjornstad, Jim Stuart, Art Davidson, Herb Staley, and I made the first ascent of Mount Seattle, a massive ice peak rising to 10,185 feet just ten miles from the tidewater of Disenchantment Bay, an arm of Yakutat Bay. Our first bit of excitement was a boat trip past the calving front of the immense Hubbard Glacier and the ice-filled tide pouring into Russell Fjord. The expedition was a complete success; storms were interspersed with spells of good weather, and we encountered no avalanches. Making the entire climb from sea level to summit had the appeal of an earlier time, when mountaineers were not reliant on aircraft. The height of the frontal peaks, like Mount Seattle, is insignificant when compared to the highest summits in the Icefield Ranges but they are alpine wilderness all the way from the ocean.

On my most recent expedition to this superb region, in 1979, Rick Nolting, John Rupley, Craig Tillery, and I ascended 11,300-foot Mount Foresta. Less than twelve miles from Disenchantment Bay, this triple-summited ice massif remained unscaled while climbers focused on St. Elias, Logan, and the other giants. But we found ample reward in discovering a complex route to this little-known mountain. The small scale of the topographic map made identification of the highest of the three peaks impossible; it remained for us to locate the true summit. Poor weather barely permitted us to make the climb, which combined the hazard of collapsing seracs with a committing traverse and a long, easy, but corniced ridge. I fell into a hidden crevasse, a cold and frightening experience that made all the more rewarding the summit view. We could see, 11,000 feet below, a chaos of mammoth glaciers and the sunlit blue of the Pacific. Magnificent days are not common in these mountains, but when they occur, they are jewels in the realm of physical and aesthetic experience.

The Burwash uplands in Kluane National Park, St. Elias Mountains. By Pat Morrow.

237

CHAPTER THIRTY-FOUR

Mount Deborah

In a glance that lasted a few moments,
the expedition seemed to end. . . .
What I saw . . . was a serpentine wisp of snow,
like the curl of a ribbon on edge. . . . I could see
the double cornice—the whole of the little bridge
was undercut incredibly on both sides, so that it
looked as if a strong wind might topple it. It was
only ten feet below me and thirty feet long. The
last ten feet of it were impossibly thin. Next, I
saw the face of the mountain beyond. The
crumbly brown rock towered, flat and crackless,
a few degrees less than vertical. A thin, splotchy
coating of ice overlay most of the rock. Where the
rock overhung, great icicles grew. A few vertical
columns of plastered snow, like frozen snakes,
stuck to the coating of the ice. And above,
blocking out half the sky, was that terrible black
cliff, the six-hundred-foot wall that we had once
blithely . . . allowed three days to climb. . . .
I had never seen a mountain sight so numbing,
so haunted with impossibility and danger.

David Roberts
Deborah: A Wilderness Narrative, 1970

MOUNTAINEERS generally agree that curiosity lies at the root of the climbing impulse. The mountain "may be there"—to paraphrase George Leigh Mallory's famous explanation—but at the heart of the reason is the compelling explorative urge. The key to any adventure is the uncertainty involved and the unpredictability of events to follow; in a sense, mountaineers are frustrated explorers who gain a certain joy from the alpine struggle.

Mountain exploration reaches its zenith in pure pioneering. On Mount Deborah, in 1954, Heinrich Harrer, Henry Meybohm, and I experienced the unknown in a way that can seldom be duplicated. Mount Deborah is a remarkable-looking peak situated about 125 miles east of Mount McKinley. The showpiece of this part of the Alaska Range, Deborah rises to a height of 12,339 feet. White men must have seen the peak for the past 150 years, yet it is only within recent time that anyone has had a compelling interest to investigate it at close range. What David Roberts wrote about Mount Huntington, describing a quality common to only a few mountains in the world, equally applies to Deborah: "A sense of arrested grace, perhaps; a sculptured frailty too savage for any sculptor's hand; a kinship with the air around it that makes it seem always in motion—but these are only metaphors, unable to capture the essence of the mountain." How true it is, this ephemeral nature of substance, whatever sort of rock or ice its cloak is. We know that time will wear a mountain down to an unrecognizable form; we know that the mountain is doomed not to outlive the earth. Deborah will be monumental during only a tick in the geologic time frame.

During the past few decades, the introduction of ski-equipped aircraft revolutionized mountaineering approaches in the northland. When we planned for Deborah, the long overland approach could thus be avoided, but the aircraft presented its own problems. The tyranny of a prearranged pickup date imposes an artificial constraint on the commitment to an ascent.

Whenever I travel by air into the heart of a mountain range, I always study the map and memorize features—I want to know the way back to civilization if something untoward happens. For instance, what if the pilot has an accident? What if a war began? Sometimes pilots send an assistant who does not know the area well for pickup; on one appointment near Juneau our group was nearly missed because a new pilot thought we were waiting at the opposite end of a lake. More than once the pickup date has been stored in someone's memory, not in a log book or office wall chart. In the Chigmit Mountains we once packed camp and waited a day and a night because the pilot's wife had entered the pickup date on the wrong calendar square. Not for no reason do most climbers get the jitters near the end of an expedition!

Dependence on aircraft and radio has tended to diminish the wilderness quality of expeditions. With today's radio communication the mountain-to-civilization transition can be nearly instantaneous. It is quite possible to be picked up from a remote Alaskan glacier after a radio call and arrive at an airport in the "Lower 48" the same day. Flying *into* the mountains, of course, provides a similar shock. On the morning of June 17, 1954, Harrer, Meybohm, and I stood alongside the airstrip at McKinley Park Station, perspiring from heat and anxiety, and swatting vicious mosquitoes. Then suddenly I was airborne with pilot Don Sheldon; I would be dropped off alone with most of the equipment, while Sheldon returned for the others. The engine vibrations kept us from chatting, but Sheldon obviously shared my excitement at skimming over barren tundra and passing so close to snow-covered ridges that the snow texture could be identified. Although he was not a mountaineer, Sheldon had an obvious lust for adventure; he would soon become Alaska's most famous bush pilot.

Below us, the Alaska Range looked like a scene from the ice ages; great glaciers swept around ice-clad monoliths. We flew past the glistening white peaks toward a level landing spot at the head of the Yanert Glacier, which drops from the western flank of Deborah. Sheldon chose a smooth, uncrevassed area some two miles below the first great icefall at the head of the cirque, circled twice, then glided to a landing so smooth that I was unaware of when snow, not air, was beneath the skis of the Super Cub.

After the plane took off I felt the loneliness of the glacial wilderness; it would be hours before my companions would arrive. I did not dare walk about in the silent landscape because of the threat of hidden crevasses, so I mused about my solitary position and our whole involvement with Deborah. We could not afford the slightest miscalculation or accident,

for we did not plan a check-up flight before our agreed pickup date. There was no radio, no rescue opportunity in our plan.

The logistics demanded that we move quickly while the weather remained fair. I was intimidated by the crevassed glacier on Deborah's southwest face and the avalanche potential, and I was relieved when Sheldon brought in Harrer and Meybohm. The reality of being underway was reassuring, as was our three weeks' stockpile of food.

At the lower altitudes, we knew, the soft snow would force us to wallow in glacial slush, making us feel like plodders. The short nights prevented a hard crust from forming; accordingly we resolved to climb during the darkest and coldest hours, when the snow would at least be somewhat firm. We pitched a base-camp tent and rested until evening, for it was imperative to wait for the first difficult section—a long couloir—to solidify. We could see deep channels down which loose snow had poured, and even as we watched, a great screen of snow whirled down the couloir. Aside from avalanches, there could be other problems: we could become trapped by heavy snowfall high on the mountain; or a spell of rainy weather could lubricate the steep slopes, making retreat desperate. Still, we remained optimistic and realistic.

The beginning of our climb took place in evening shadows; it would be a long, continuous effort to climb with heavy packs from our base at 5,500 feet to a point above the first of three icefalls, but there was no place to camp on the way. Our eyes constantly scanned upward for signs of avalanches breaking away. The slope seemed steeper than the forty-five degrees we had estimated, yet ice axes gave us security, and crampons bit firmly into the crusty surface. At the point where we planned to traverse to a hanging glacier, we found that the route bore downward. Here we were forced to climb the steep wall of a lateral rock ridge, where pitons were placed for protection. Our heavy packs made the climbing cumbersome, and often I could not lead with the load. At one particularly difficult and loose area we rigged a "tyrolean traverse"—a pulley system by which we hauled the packs one by one across a chasm.

In the darkening night we strained to read the shadows. Perhaps it was blind luck, but ledges and cracks appeared where we needed them, and finally we gained the glacier. Sometime early that morning, slumping with fatigue, we set up camp at a flat spot surrounded by crevasses. We brewed up a quick meal, then slept the sleep of men who had worked very hard. Our plan was to rest most of the day, then,

Above: The southwest
escarpment of Mount Deborah
rises high above the white
spruce of the boreal forest. By
Galen Rowell.

Page 238: A climber on the
narrow northwest ridge of
Mount Deborah. By Rick
Nolting.

in late afternoon, climb through the second icefall to a final camp. Later that day, as we worked our way through an intricate system of crevasses, the sun shone with startling intensity, making every detail stand out. Above us rose the serrated south ridge, by which we hoped to gain the remote, untrodden summit. In the early evening, following a three-hour effort, we pitched the tent, knowing that a good night's rest would give us the strength necessary for the final dash to the top.

It was only a few days until the summer solstice, and the almost continuous daylight had a peculiar effect. It meant that we would not have to endure a forced bivouac, but there was also the danger that the near-eternal light could seduce us into over extending ourselves. We came close to doing so on June 19.

Climbing through the third icefall at dawn, we wound our way past a strange labyrinth of crevasses and ice bridges before ascending a steep slope leading up to the south ridge. As we reached this ridge, we emerged suddenly into the bright morning sunlight to see a fearsome sight. Above us, the ridge was composed of fragile snow cornices leaning out over an appalling dropoff. We would have to traverse these tottering "diving boards" for half a mile in order to gain the summit. The prospects of a toppling cornice had to be faced, for even experienced climbers and snow scientists cannot predict the stability of great cornices.

The details of the day have faded now, but I remember much repetitious climbing. Most of the time we were balanced on our toes, kicking steps and thrusting our ice axes into the snow above us. The cornices seemed infinite, and the angle was so steep that we could move only one at a time, with the other two belaying the rope in case of that feared fall.

On the final ridge the traversing ended and we climbed sharply upward. My companions took turns with me as we wrestled through pillars of snow and ice. Once we had to tunnel through a formation that resembled a gigantic white mushroom, using our hands, knees, and pick of the axe to gain height. Sometime after daylight ebbed, perhaps about midnight, the radiant light still enhanced the vista. Without really being aware of it, we found the difficulties easing. Slowly, savoring each step, we tramped up to the summit, almost reluctant to kick steps where no human foot had ever been. With the quiet excitement that comes with certain victory, we stepped onto the uppermost point of Deborah.

The wind was elsewhere in the world during this supreme moment of our lives. For fifteen minutes we gazed around us, watching the arctic sun flirting with the horizon, casting an orange-red glow onto myriad unknown peaks and tundra. We experienced the same feeling that David Roberts described as he stood atop Mount Huntington: "All the world we could see lay motionless in the muted splendor of sunrise. Nothing stirred, only we lived. . . ."

Exhilarated by our success, we also dreaded the long, exacting, and somewhat unsafe descent. Fortunately, as we retreated down the ridge, our steps showed us where to place our feet, and the chill kept the surface crisp. By the time we had moved twenty-four consecutive hours, our bodies began to feel the effects of self-denial, particularly the thirst and fatigue. Our minds were dulled with tiredness, but somehow we kept sufficiently alert to execute balanced moves and other tasks. At some vague hour in the morning we at last collapsed in our tent. We had succeeded in climbing and descending the south ridge, and soon we could descend to base camp and safety.

After our climb the tracks soon disappeared, so the mountain still retains a wilderness aspect for other climbers. The sense of exploration can still be felt. Other parties on Deborah have found—and will continue to find—the risks and delights of the struggle, even if the aura of uncertainty is somewhat diminished.

Male red fox pup, Alaska Range. By William Boehm/ West Stock.

CHAPTER THIRTY-FIVE

Mount McKinley

Are there, any other place on Earth, such mountains as those stupendous piles that culminate the Alaska Range? Not that they are the highest in the world, for the great peaks of the Himalayas overtop them by thousands of feet. But the Himalayan snow line is sixteen or eighteen thousand feet above sea level, while Mt. McKinley on some sides, at least, can be said to have no snow line. The whole region from its base, for miles upon miles, is loaded down with a fathomless burden of perpetual ice and snow, save where the walls are too steep for anything to cling.

Claude E. Rusk
The Pacific Monthly, January, 1911

IN HIS BOOK *To the Top of the Continent,* Dr. Frederick A. Cook claimed the first ascent of the highest summit in North America, Mount McKinley, on September 16, 1906. The text—and a prior article in *Harper's Monthly Magazine*—stated that Cook and Edward Barrill climbed ice, cornices, and glowing séracs to a final campsite at 18,400 feet, reaching it "with not enough energy left to talk or eat." The summit was supposedly reached at ten o'clock the following morning. However, Cook's accounts seemed very confusing to many pioneers of the McKinley region, and numerous persons doubted the facts as presented.

Cook, a founder of the American Alpine Club and a former president of the prestigious Explorers Club, was indisputably an accomplished explorer. He had taken part in several polar expeditions, including one to Greenland with Robert Peary in 1891–92. Three years before his claim of success on McKinley, Cook and Robert Dunn had made a serious bid to climb the northwest side of the peak. On this trip they had climbed to perhaps 11,000 feet on a buttress of McKinley's North Peak, the lower of the mountain's two summits. Dunn wrote a story of this trip in *Outing,* in which he praised Cook: "Doctor is in the lead. It was my turn to cut steps in the ice-slope but he did not seem inclined to give me the ice-axe. . . . I admired him mightily."

After claiming the main summit of McKinley, Cook mounted an expedition to the North Pole. Returning to civilization in 1909, he claimed to have reached his goal the preceding year. Peary, meanwhile, *had* reached the Pole, and immediately upon his return disputed Cook's story. This controversy naturally cast a new light upon Cook's purported climb of McKinley.

Claude E. Rusk, leader of a Mazama expedition to McKinley in 1910, scoffed at Cook's claim, knowing from firsthand experience that it would be impossible for two men to travel from the mouth of the Tokositna River—thirty-five miles away and 19,000 feet lower—to the top of McKinley in a mere nine days, the figure given by Cook. "The man does not live who can perform such a feat," Rusk wrote later. "Dr. Cook had many admirers who would have rejoiced to see his claims vindicated. . . . But it could not be."

Mountaineers Belmore Browne and Herschel Parker, both of whom had explored McKinley's southern ramparts with Cook in 1906, were equally skeptical about Cook's claim. In 1910, using Cook's photographs as a guide, they located and climbed Cook's "summit," a minor outcrop nearly twenty

Above: Mount McKinley, some thirty miles to the south, dominates the view from Wonder Lake; cottongrass lines the foreground shore. By Craig Blacklock.

Facing page: Climber on the west ridge of Mount Hunter, Alaska Range. By Jack Duggan.

244

miles from McKinley and 15,000 feet lower. Cook maintained throughout his long life—which included a five-year stint in prison for mail fraud—that both his McKinley and polar claims were valid, but neither is taken seriously today. As Rusk wrote, "had he been content to rest his laurels upon the things he had actually accomplished . . . his fame would have been secure."

An equally puzzling—but short-lived—controversy concerning the first ascent of Mount McKinley arose in 1910 when Tom Lloyd, leader of the Fairbanks Sourdough expedition, announced that his party had succeeded in reaching the top. Alaskans were divided in opinion about whether or not Lloyd had climbed the mountain. "I wouldn't believe him under oath," one man said. "He can't travel ten miles a day on level ground." Belmore Browne's 1912 party, which nearly scaled the mountain, felt that the Sourdoughs had not made the top; they saw no sign of the spruce pole the Sourdoughs had said they planted atop the peak. Browne, Parker, and a companion made a gallant effort in climbing the northeast, or Karstens, ridge to within 150 vertical feet of the top. Browne called their last day "cruel and heartbreaking." There is little doubt that Browne's party would have been first to the highest point in North America but for the intervention of a severe blizzard on their final dash. A diet restricted largely to pemmican reduced their effective food supply, so the men could not wait for better weather.

The south summit was finally reached in the summer of 1913 by Hudson Stuck, Walter Harper, Harry Karstens, and Robert Tatum. This party, which used the same route as its predecessors, cleared up the Sourdough mystery, for they spotted the fourteen-foot-high spruce pole atop the lower North Peak. The Sourdoughs had not climbed McKinley, but two of them *had* reached the 19,470-foot subsidiary summit without using any specialized equipment—a noble achievement indeed.

These early climbers needed to know all manner of wilderness skills, for the technical difficulties of the mountain could not even be attempted until the vexing problems of the lower regions were managed. The pioneers had to traverse hundreds of miles of swampy muskegs and forests, making dangerous river crossings, and finally, once on the mountain, endure miserable, frigid weather while negotiating crevassed glaciers and narrow snow ridges. The boldness of these early epics was equal to that of the finest subarctic overland voyages. Frederick Cook, for all the scorn later heaped on him, circumnavigated the peak in 1903, an accomplishment not duplicated until a skiing circuit was made in 1978.

Nearly twenty years went by before anyone reclimbed Mount McKinley, and it was not until 1942 that the third ascent was made. In that year Boston mountaineer Bradford Washburn accompanied an Army expedition to the mountain in order to test cold-weather garments and boots. Five years later Washburn returned to the mountain, this time climbing both the north and south summits. Part of the focus of this expedition—supported by both the Army and the Air Force—was a cosmic ray research program. In 1951 Washburn again led a party to the summit, but this time via a route other than the standard one up Karstens Ridge. Landing by ski-equipped plane on a glacier southwest of the mountain, the Washburn party climbed the west buttress, a route destined to be repeated hundreds of times in the ensuing decades. Over the years, Washburn's su-

perb photographs and maps have greatly contributed to an understanding of McKinley.

As with other Alaskan expeditions, the ski-equipped airplane revolutionized climbing on Mount McKinley. Climbers could save themselves the arduous approach march to the mountain, instead landing on glaciers at its very base. This tactic also meant that fewer heavy loads needed to be carried. It was not long, therefore, until almost every ridge and face of the mountain was climbed.

One of the finest of these new climbs took place in 1961, when an Italian party led by the noted mountaineer Riccardo Cassin boldly climbed a long, steep ridge of the left margin of the enormous south face. Experienced as they were in other lands, the Italians seriously misjudged the harsh Alaskan conditions, regarding their climb as simply a scaled-up Alpine problem. The party's narrow escape from vicious storms and serious frostbite (three men were hospitalized with minor frostbite) emphasizes the crucial importance of preparation for such an arctic mountain; a party must be equipped to wait out severe storms and not depend on rescue in case of the unexpected. Washburn has warned that McKinley has a "climate around its summit which may well present the most severe year-round average of any non-Polar spot on earth."

A relatively new trend of ascending the mountain rapidly has gained favor over the standard expeditionary style, but greatly increased the danger of climbers succumbing to pulmonary edema and related physiological problems. Repeated tragedies and near escapes in the past two decades are partly a consequence of inadequate knowledge about high-altitude illnesses. However, a leading authority on such afflictions, Dr. Charles Houston, has written, "what we do know for sure is that most people develop symptoms and some will die from going too rapidly above 8–10,000 feet." In 1979 two members of a Korean expedition died in a fall high on the mountain. This party had climbed the upper 6,000 feet of the peak in a single day; they were undoubtedly exhausted—and quite possibly altitude-sick—when the accident occurred on the descent. A luckier pair of climbers who barely managed to climb the peak in one day from their camp at 10,000 feet found themselves in a highly weakened state for the sake of setting a record.

My experience with Mount McKinley began and ended in 1954. Our group of five pioneered a new route to the North Peak, essentially completing the route attempted by Frederick Cook in 1903. At the base of the great northwest buttress of the mountain a ground blizzard shook our faith in the climb's prospects. A blinding combination of snow and wind stung our faces, and we kept our parka hoods tightly buckled while picking up an air drop on the Peters Glacier. This glacier resembled a frozen sea of swells, and the high winds blew loose snow pellets across the ice, giving it an ethereal glow. Higher, we were in danger from both cornices and depth hoar, the latter causing a potentially unstable snowpack. At 15,000 feet we encountered a great rock wall, and here we placed the first pitons ever used on McKinley. I recall climbing gigantic blocks of orange-toned granite with half-frozen fingers, then laboriously hauling up pack after pack.

Just after we reached the North Peak, a storm arrived. Still hoping to reach the South Peak, we waited four days in our small tent at 18,400 feet. Finally supplies ran low, and we were forced to retrace our steps down the buttress.

Although I regretted not reaching McKinley's highest point, further adventures in the Alaska Range that season more than made up for our near miss. On returning to Fairbanks, Henry Meybohm and I met the Austrian climber Heinrich Harrer, one of the men who had made the first ascent of the notorious north wall of the Eiger in 1938. Harrer was anxious to climb, and, as described in the preceding chapter, we went on to Mount Deborah. Following this superb ascent, momentum urged us to continue. Our next target was Mount Hunter, a solitary 14,578-foot monarch nine miles south of McKinley, the sight of which had captivated Meybohm and I during the earlier climb. Although not one of the highest peaks in the range, Hunter offers superb climbing. In Alaska, the steeper faces and ridges generally are at lower altitudes, a somewhat unique feature among mountains. Our ascent via the west ridge bore this out: it was difficult and complex, but ultimately victorious.

As we made our way down McKinley's slopes, however, these later climbs were far from our thoughts. Our party faced a fifty-mile walk back to civilization—the National Park Service campground at Wonder Lake—an experience closer to that of Alaska's pioneer expeditions that to the modern way of aircraft pick-ups. But we all agreed that the experience was worthwhile. After weeks of living amid rocks and ice, returning to the upland tundra was like rediscovering life. We began to see cottongrass,

Facing page: **Climbing camp on the west buttress of Mount McKinley. By Galen Rowell.**

Top: **Grizzly sow and cubs, Denali National Park. By Galen Rowell.**

Above: **Dall sheep atop a ridge, Denali National Park. By Galen Rowell.**

Facing page: **Skunk cabbage, Denali National Park. By Stephen J. Krasemann/DRK Photo.**

saxifrage, alpine arnica, anemone, and other perennial tundra plants. Wandering among the tussocks of this elevated region, we encountered willows and dwarf birches; a few times we almost stepped on rock ptarmigan that had sought the protective cover of the tundra vegetation.

We constantly scanned the horizon for Dall sheep, but they kept out of sight. The graceful movements and large, curled horns of these rare beasts make for an unforgettable sight, and we were disappointed by their elusiveness. Favored prey for the wolves that also inhabit the tundra, the sheep depend upon their agility and excellent eyesight to keep them safe from the predators.

Once, while we plodded with heavy packs along the overflow ice of a river bar, we spotted the magnificent towering antlers of the caribou, a circumpolar deer especially adapted to life in the northland. We hoped for a closer view, but these large herbivores quickly outdistanced us with their easy trot.

We were unsuccessful in seeing the two most celebrated denizens of the north country, the wolf and the grizzly bear. The wolf feeds upon small mammals such as lemmings, but it also stalks young or weakened caribou. The grizzly may occasionally kill a moose, but it is generally content to subsist on berries and the roots of tundra plants, peavine being a favorite. The bear will also dig up the turf in search of voles, and, when near a stream, will go fishing for salmon. Grizzlies often follow the exact same route many times on their tundra journeys, thus establishing shallow paths. As we traveled along these convenient trails toward Wonder Lake, we thought we might glimpse bears on their rounds, but it was not to be.

Near Wonder Lake we left behind the brown landscape of the tundra and, dropping to lower elevations, entered a world of brilliant green vegetation. Even amid this beauty, however, the terrain was rugged: on the last day we had to wade several hip-deep rivers. Once at the lake we saw why it was so named—it *was* a wondrous place indeed. In the still waters we saw the reflected image of the immense bulk of McKinley, and it seemed inconceivable that we had stood atop its north summit only ten days earlier.

Wonder Lake is the last stop on a road that winds for ninety miles through Denali National Park. Established in 1917 as Mount McKinley National Park, it was expanded to encompass nearly four-and-one-half million acres of prime Alaskan wilderness by the monumental Alaska Lands Act of 1980. At the same time, it was rechristened *Denali*— "the great one"—the name by which the Athabascan

Indians have always known Mount McKinley. (Congress has not yet changed the name of the mountain itself.)

The establishment of the park was due in considerable part to the efforts of Charles Sheldon, a naturalist who spent several years (1906–1908) studying the wildlife of the region. Sheldon was assisted in his work by Harry Karstens, an Alaskan pioneer who was one of the first ascenders of McKinley's South Peak. Karstens' colorful career began with the Klondike gold rush; later he carried mail by dogsled between Fairbanks and Valdez, and eventually became the first superintendent of McKinley National Park. Sheldon wrote of Karstens: "When I look back upon my experiences in Alaska and the Yukon, I recall no better fortune than that which befell me when Harry Karstens was engaged as an assistant packer. He is a tall, stalwart man, well poised, frank, and strictly honorable, and peculiarly fitted by youth and experience for explorations in little-known regions; he proved a most efficient and congenial companion."

Many naturalists since Sheldon's day have found the Denali parklands a rich resource for study. One of the most renowned of these, Adolph Murie, has written eloquently of the priceless value of this land to both its wild inhabitants and its human visitors. Although the recent expansion of the park is to

be applauded, the legislated guidelines for its use are somewhat open to interpretation, and further development is a possibility. Wonder Lake, for example, was once proposed as the site of a resort hotel; this and other schemes have been resisted vigorously because of potential hazards to the fragile tundra and to wildlife. Fortunately, attitudes regarding the appropriate use of wilderness have changed since 1917, when the authors of a *National Geographic* article on the proposed park wrote:

> Prodigal as nature has been in endowing us with unrivaled scenery, we have until recent years been blind to the money value of this resource. . . . Other nations not so blessed . . . have widely advertised their natural beauties in a way to attract the tourist, so that for years Americans have spent abroad millions of dollars that might have yielded them no less pleasure if they had spent it seeing America first. . . .
>
> If the United States wishes to share in the profits of the tourist business it may readily do so, for any well-chosen expenditure made in building good roads and hotels in our national parks will return large dividends not only in dollars and cents, but in the health, enjoyment, and education of our people.

The Denali wildlands have indeed contributed immeasurably to our "health, enjoyment, and education," and we know now that their continued vitality will depend on a different kind of stewardship than that proposed by the article's authors. Enjoying this magnificent region without leaving a permanent imprint in its fragile and frosty soil is a challenge no less imposing than ascending to the top of the continent's supreme peak, and ultimately, of far greater significance.

Camp at 16,000 feet on Mount McKinley. By Galen Rowell.

250

SELECTED BIBLIOGRAPHY

Introduction

Bliss, L. C. "Tundra Grasslands, Herblands, and Shrublands and the Role of Herbivores." *Geoscience and Man* 10 (1975).

Continents Adrift and Continents Aground: Readings from Scientific American. Introduction by J. Tuzo Wilson. San Francisco: W. H. Freeman, 1976.

Coolidge, W. A. B. *The Alps in Nature and History.* London: Methuen & Co., 1908.

DeBeer, G. R. *Early Travellers in the Alps.* London: Sidgwick and Jackson, 1930.

Dietz, R. S. "Geosynclines, Mountains and Continent-Building." *Scientific American,* March, 1972.

Douglas, David. *Journal Kept by David Douglas During His Travels in North America, 1823–1827.* London: Royal Horticultural Society, 1914.

Freshfield, D. W. "On Mountains and Mankind." *Alpine Journal* 22 (November, 1904).

Hamilton, Warren. "Plate Tectonics and Man." *U. S. Geological Survey, Annual Report.* Washington, D. C.: Government Printing Office, 1976.

Meier, M. F. "Glaciers and Climate." In *The Quaternary of the United States.* Edited by H. E. Wright and D. G. Frey. Princeton: Princeton University Press, 1965.

Price, Larry W. *Mountains & Man.* Berkeley, Los Angeles, and London: University of California Press, 1981.

Price, Raymond A. and Douglas, R. J. W., editors. *Variations in Tectonic Styles, Special Paper 11.* Toronto: Geological Association of Canada. 1972.

Stephen, Leslie, *The Playground of Europe.* London: Longmans, Green and Co., 1871.

Stern, Colin William; Carroll, Robert L.; and Clark, Thomas H. *The Geological Evolution of North America,* 3rd ed. New York: Wiley Publishing Co., 1979.

Mount Katahdin

Eckstrom, Fannie Hardy. "The Katahdin Legends." *Appalachia* 16 (December, 1924).

Higginson, Thomas W. "Going to Mount Katahdin." *Appalachia* 16 (June, 1925).

Hurd, Marjorie. "New Rock Routes at Katahdin." *Appalachia* 17 (June, 1928).

Tarr, Ralph S. "Glaciation of Mt. Ktaadn, Maine." *Bulletin of the Geological Society of America* 11 (1900).

Thoreau, Henry David. *The Maine Woods.* New York: Thomas Y. Crowell, 1909.

Winthrop, Theodore. *Life in the Open Air.* New York: John W. Lovell Co., 1862.

Mount Washington

Atkinson, Brooks and Olson, W. Kent. *New England's White Mountains.* Boston: Appalachian Mountain Club, 1978.

Burt, F. Allen. *The Story of Mount Washington.* Hanover, N. H.: Dartmouth Publications, 1960.

Handbook of Mount Washington Environment. Natick, Mass.: U. S. Army, Quartermaster General, 1953.

Kilbourne, Frederick W. *Chronicles of the White Mountains.* Boston and New York: Houghton Mifflin Co., 1916.

King, Thomas Starr. *The White Hills: Their Legends, Landscape, and Poetry.* Boston: Crosby, Nichols, and Co., 1860.

Packard, Winthrop. *White Mountain Trails.* Boston: Small, Maynard and Co., 1912.

Washburn, Bradford. *Bradford on Mt. Washington.* New York and London: G. P. Putnam's Sons, 1928.

Weygandt, Cornelius. *The White Hills.* Boston: Henry Holt and Co., 1934.

Mount Marcy

Adirondack Life. Keene, N. Y. Numerous issues.

Carson, Russell M. L. *Peaks and People of the Adirondacks.* Glens Falls, N. Y.: Adirondack Mountain Club, 1973.

Hudowalski, Grace L., ed. *The Adirondack High Peaks and the Forty-Sixers.* Albany: Grace L. Hudowalski, 1971.

Jamison, Paul F. *The Adirondack Reader.* New York: The Macmillan Co., 1964.

Keller, Jane Eblen. *Adirondack Wilderness.* Syracuse: Syracuse University Press, 1980.

LaBastille, Ann. "My Backyard, the Adirondacks." *National Geographic Magazine,* May, 1975.

Lindstrom, John D. "Mount Marcy." *Summit,* July-August, 1963.

Van Diver, Bradford B. *Rocks and Routes of the North Country.* Geneva, N. Y.: W. F. Humphrey Press, 1976.

Clingmans Dome

Broome, Harvey. *Out Under the Sky of the Great Smokies.* Knoxville: The Greenbrier Press, 1975.

Doolittle, Jerome. *The Southern Appalachians.* New York: Time-Life Books, 1975.

Frome, Michael. *Strangers in High Places—The Story of the Great Smoky Mountains.* New York: Doubleday and Co., 1966.

Kephart, Horace. *Our Southern Highlanders.* New York: The Macmillan Co., 1913.

King, Philip B. "Geology of the Great Smoky Mountains National Park, Tennessee and North Carolina." *Geological*

Survey Professional Paper 587. Washington, D.C.: Government Printing Office, 1968.

Porter, Eliot. Appalachian Wilderness: The Great Smoky Mountains. New York: E. P. Dutton and Co., 1970.

Smith, Clyde H. Appalachian Mountains. Portland, Ore.: Graphic Arts Publishing Co., 1980.

Young, Gordon. "Great Smokies National Park." National Geographic Magazine, October, 1968.

Pico de Orizaba

Bonney, Orrin. "The First Mountain Ascent in North America." American Alpine Journal 4 (1941).

Chamberlin, Rollin T. "The Ascent of Orizaba." American Alpine Journal 1 (1930).

Fantin, Mario. "Mexican Trilogy, 1963." Alpine Journal 70 (May, 1965).

McDowell, Bart. "The Aztecs." National Geographic Magazine, December, 1980.

McRuer, Duane. "Mazamas Mexican Meanderings." Mazama 58 (1976).

Molina, Professor Augusto F. "Tenochtitlan's Glory." National Geographic Magazine, December, 1980.

Poindexter, R.W. Jr. "Four Mexican Volcanoes." Sierra Club Bulletin 8, no. 2 (1911).

Wagner, Henry R. "Ascents of Popocatepetl by the Conquistadores." Sierra Club Bulletin 25, no. 1 (1940).

Harney Peak

Blacklock, Craig and Link, Mike. Black Hills/Badlands: The Web of the West. Bloomington, Minn.: Voyageur Press, 1980.

Dodge, Richard Irving. The Black Hills. 1876. Reprint. Minneapolis: Ross and Haines, 1965.

Grinnell, George Bird. The Cheyenne Indians, 2 vols. New Haven: Yale University Press, 1923.

Jackson, Donald. Custer's Gold: The United States Cavalry Expedition of 1874. New Haven: Yale University Press, 1966.

Parker, Watson. Gold in the Black Hills. Norman: University of Oklahoma Press, 1966.

Pikes Peak

Barry, R. G. "A Climatological Transect Along the East Slope of the Front Range, Colorado." Arctic and Alpine Research 5, no. 2 (1973).

Fetler, John. The Pikes Peak People. Caldwell, Idaho: The Caxton Printers, Ltd., 1966.

Hart, John J. Fourteen Thousand Feet. Denver: Colorado Mountain Club, 1925.

Jackson, Donald, ed. The Journals of Zebulon Montgomery Pike, vol. 2. Norman: University of Oklahoma Press, 1966.

James, Edwin. Account of an Expedition from Pittsburgh to the Rocky Mountains, vol 2. 1823. Reprint. Ann Arbor: University Microfilms, 1966.

Longs Peak

Covington, Mike. "Diamond Commentary." Mountain 40 (November, 1974).

Eberhart, Perry and Schmuck, Philip. The Fourteeners: Colorado's Great Mountains. Chicago: The Swallow Press, Inc., 1970.

Farquhar, Francis P. "Naming America's Mountains—The Colorado Rockies." American Alpine Journal 12 (1961).

Fricke, Walter W. Jr. A Climber's Guide to the Rocky Mountain National Park. Boulder: John Paddock, 1971.

Godfrey, Bob and Chelton, Dudley. Climb! Boulder: Alpine House Publishing, 1977.

Nesbit, Paul W. Longs Peak: Its Story and a Climbing Guide. Colorado Springs: Paul W. Nesbit, 1963.

Rearick, David. "The First Ascent of the Diamond, East Face of Longs Peak." American Alpine Journal 12 (1961).

Stegner, Wallace. Beyond the Hundredth Meridian. Boston: Houghton Mifflin Co., 1954.

Maroon Bells

Aspen: The 100 Year High. New York: The Living Art Co., 1980.

Bartlett, Richard. Great Surveys of the American West. Norman: University of Oklahoma Press, 1980.

Hayden, Ferdinand V. U. S. Geological and Geographical Survey of the Territories, 9th Annual Report. Washington, D. C.: Government Printing Office, 1875.

Henderson, Charles W. "Mining in Colorado." U. S. Geological Survey Professional Paper 138. Washington, D. C.: Government Printing Office, 1926.

Laing, David and Lampiris, Nicholas. Aspen High Country: The Geology. Aspen: Thunder River Press, 1980.

Muench, David and Sumner, David. Rocky Mountains. Portland, Ore.; Charles Belding, 1975.

Shoemaker, Len. Roaring Fork Valley. Silverton, Colo.: Sundance Publications, 1979.

Mount Sneffels

Benedict, J. B. "Origins of Rock Glaciers." Journal of Glaciology 12, no. 66 (1973).

Borneman, Walter R. and Lampert, Lyndon J. A Climbing Guide to Colorado's Fourteeners. Boulder: Pruett Publishing Company, 1978.

Bueler, William M. Roof of the Rockies: A History of Mountaineering in Colorado. Boulder: Pruett Publishing Company, 1974.

Crouter, George. Colorado's Highest. Silverton, Colo.: Sundance Publications, 1977.

Larsen, E.S. and Cross, Whitman. "Geology and Petrology of the San Juan Region, Southwestern Colorado." U.S. Geological Survey Professional Paper 258. Washington, D.C.: Government Printing Office, 1956.

Ormes, Robert. Guide to the Colorado Mountains. 7th ed. Colorado Springs: Robert M. Ormes, 1979.

Steven, Thomas A. and Lipman, Peter. "Calderas of the San Juan Volcanic Field, Southwestern Colorado." U.S. Geological Survey Professional Paper 958. Washington, D.C.: Government Printing Office, 1976.

Mount Moran

Fryxell, Fritiof. The Teton Peaks and Their Ascents. Grand Teton National Park, Wyo.: Crandall Studios, 1952.

Hayden, Ferdinand V. U. S. Geological and Geographical Survey of the Territories, 11th Annual Report. Washington, D. C.: Government Printing Office, 1877.

Jeffers, LeRoy. The Call of the Mountains. New York: Dodd, Mead and Co., 1922.

Morgan, Dale L. Jedediah Smith and the Opening of the West, Indianapolis and New York: The Bobbs-Merrill Co., 1953.

Norton, Boyd. The Grand Tetons. New York: Reader's Digest Press, 1977.

Ortenburger, gh. A Climber's Guide to the Teton Range. Rev. ed. San Francisco: Sierra Club, 1965.

———. "Mount Moran, 1922–1962." American Alpine Journal 13 (1963).

Roper, Steve and Steck, Allen. Fifty Classic Climbs of North America. San Francisco: Sierra Club Books, 1979.

Grand Teton

Bueler, William M. The Teton Controversy: Who First Climbed the Grand? Winona, Minn.: William M. Bueler, 1980.

Durrance, Jack. "Ascent of the North Face of the Grand Teton." Appalachia 21 (June, 1937).

Fryxell, Fritiof. "The Grand Teton by the North Face." American Alpine Journal 1 (1932).

———. *The Tetons, Interpretations of a Mountain Landscape.* Berkeley and Los Angeles: University of California Press, 1953.

Langford, Nathaniel. "The Ascent of Mount Hayden." *Scribner's Monthly* 6, no. 2 (June, 1873).

Mumey, Noley. *The Teton Mountains: Their History and Tradition.* Denver: Artcraft Press, 1945.

Owen, William O. "The Ascent of the Grand Teton." *Alpine Journal* 19 (August, 1899).

Underhill, Robert L. M. "The Grand Teton by the East Ridge." *Alpine Journal* 42 (November, 1930).

Gannett Peak

Bonney, Orrin H. and Bonney, Lorraine. *Guide to the Wyoming Mountains and Wilderness Areas.* Denver: Sage Books, 1960.

Granger, H. C.; McKay, E. J.; and Mattick, R. E. "Mineral Resources of the Glacier Primitive Area, Wyoming." *U. S. Geological Survey, Bulletin 1319F.* Washington, D. C.: Government Printing Office, 1971.

Hayden, Ferdinand V. *U. S. Geological and Geographical Survey of the Territories, 12th Annual Report, Part 1.* Washington, D.C.: Government Printing Office, 1878.

Irving, Washington. *The Adventures of Captain Bonneville, U.S.A. 1837.* Reprint. Edited by Edgeley W. Todd. Norman: University of Oklahoma Press, 1961.

Kelsey, Joe. *Climbing and Hiking in the Wind River Mountains.* San Francisco: Sierra Club Books, 1980.

Fremont Peak

Frémont, John Charles. *Report of the Exploring Expedition to the Rocky Mountains in the Year 1842, and to Oregon and North California in the Years 1843–44.* U. S. 28th Congress, 2nd Session, House Ex. Doc. 166. Washington, D. C.: Blair and Rives, 1845.

Goetzman, William H. *Army Explorations in the American West 1803–1863.* Lincoln: University of Nebraska Press, 1979.

Hayden, Ferdinand V. *U. S. Geological and Geographical Survey of the Territories, 6th Annual Report.* Washington, D. C.: Government Printing Office, 1872.

Preuss, Charles. *Exploring With Frémont.* Translated by Erwin Gudde and Elizabeth Gudde. Norman: University of Oklahoma Press, 1958.

Schubert, Frank N. *Vanguard of Expansion: Army Engineers in the Trans-Mississippi West 1819–1879.* Washington, D. C.: Office of the Chief of Engineers, 1981.

Mount Wilbur

Alt, David O. and Hyndman, Donald W. *Rock, Ice and Water: The Geology of Waterton-Glacier Park.* Missoula: Mountain Press Publishing Co., 1973.

Edwards, J. Gordon. *A Climber's Guide to Glacier National Park.* Rev. ed. Missoula: Mountain Press Publishing Co., 1976.

Hanna, Warren L. *The Grizzlies of Glacier.* Missoula: Mountain Press Publishing Co., 1977.

Ruhle, George C. *Roads and Trails of Waterton/Glacier National Parks.* Minneapolis: J. W. Forney, 1972.

Schultz, James Willard. *Blackfeet Tales of Glacier National Park.* Boston and New York: Houghton Mifflin Co., 1916.

Mount Assiniboine

Jones, Christopher A. G. "Canadian Rockies North Faces." *American Alpine Journal* 16 (1968).

Morse, Randy. *The Mountains of Canada.* Edmonton: Hurtig Publishers, 1978.

Outram, Rev. James. *In the Heart of the Canadian Rockies.* New York: The McMillan Co., 1905.

———. "The First Ascent of Mt. Assiniboine." *Alpine Journal* 21 (February, 1902).

Palmer, Howard and Thorington, J. Monroe. *A Climber's Guide to the Rocky Mountains of Canada.* New York: Knickerbocker Press, 1921.

Smythe, Frank. *Rocky Mountains.* London: Adam and Charles Black, 1948.

Wilcox, Walter D. "Early Days in the Canadian Rockies." *American Alpine Journal* 4 (1941).

Mount Robson

Claunch, Don. "Ascent of the Wishbone Arête, Mt. Robson." *American Alpine Journal* 10 (1956).

———. "The Wishbone at Last." *Canadian Alpine Journal* 39 (1956).

Coleman. A. P. *The Canadian Rockies—New and Old Trails.* New York: Charles Scribner's Sons, 1911.

Freeman, Lewis R. *On the Roof of the Rockies.* New York: Dodd, Mead and Co., 1925.

Milton, Viscount and Cheadle, Dr. W. B. *The North West Passage by Land.* London: Cassell, Petter, and Galpin, 1863.

Sherrick, Michael. "A New Route on Mount Robson." *Sierra Club Bulletin* 41, no. 10 (1956).

Smythe, Frank S. *Climbs in the Canadian Rockies.* New York: W. W. Norton and Co., Inc., 1950.

Stutfield, Hugh E. M. and Collie, J. Norman. *Climbs and Explorations in the Canadian Rockies.* London: Longmans, Green and Co., 1903.

Thorington, J. Monroe. *The Glittering Mountains of Canada.* Philadelphia: John W. Lea, 1925.

Wheeler, Arthur O. "The Alpine Club of Canada's Expedition to Jasper Park, Yellowhead Pass and Mount Robson Region, 1911." *Canadian Alpine Journal* 4 (1912).

Howser Spire

Anderson, Lloyd. "A First Ascent in the Bugaboos." *The Mountaineer* 34 (1941).

Beckey, Fred. "West Face of the South Tower of Howser Spire." *American Alpine Journal* 13 (1962).

Edwards, Ann; Morrow, Patrick; and Twomey, Arthur. *Exploring the Purcell Wilderness.* Seattle: The Mountaineers, 1979.

Kain, Conrad. *Where the Clouds Can Go.* Edited by J. Monroe Thorington. New York: American Alpine Club, 1935.

MacCarthy, Albert H. "The Howser and Bugaboo Spires, Purcell Range." *Canadian Alpine Journal* 8 (1917).

Rowell, Galen. "The Seventh Rifle." *Ascent* 1, no. 6 (1972).

Mount Sir Donald

Fay, Charles E. "Up to the Crags of Sir Donald." *Appalachia* 7, no. 2 (December, 1893).

Green, William Spotswood. *Among the Selkirk Glaciers.* London and New York: Macmillan and Co., 1890.

Longstaff, F. V. "The Story of the Swiss Guides in Canada." *Canadian Alpine Journal* 28 (1943).

Putnam, William Lowell. *A Climber's Guide to the Interior Ranges of British Columbia North.* Springfield, Mass.: American Alpine Club and Alpine Club of Canada, 1975.

Wheeler, Arthur O. *The Selkirk Range,* vols. 1 and 2. Ottawa: Government Printing Bureau, 1905.

Mount Timpanogos

Atwood, W. W. "Glaciation of the Uinta and Wasatch Mountains." *U. S. Geological Survey, Professional Paper 61.* Washington, D. C.: Government Printing Office, 1909.

Kelner, Alexis, and Hanscom, David. *Wasatch Tours: A Ski Touring Guide to the Wasatch Front.* Salt Lake City: Wasatch Publishers, 1976.

King, Clarence. *U. S. Geological Exploration of the 40th Parallel, Vol. 2.* Descriptive geology by Arnold Hague and S. F. Emmons. Washington, D. C.: Government Printing Office, 1877.

Morgan, Dale L. *Jedediah Smith and the Opening of the West.* Indianapolis: The Bobbs-Merrill Co., 1953.

Smith, Dave. *Wasatch Granite.* Salt Lake City: Wasatch Publishers, 1977.

Ship Rock

Bjornstad, Eric. "Desert Towers." *Off Belay,* February, 1981.

Blaurock, Carl. "Shiprock Again." *Trail and Timberline,* no. 237 (1938).

Brower, David. "It Couldn't Be Climbed." *Saturday Evening Post,* February 3, 1940.

Ormes, Robert. "A Piece of Bent Iron." *Saturday Evening Post,* July 22, 1939.

Robinson, Bestor. "The First Ascent of Shiprock." *Sierra Club Bulletin* 25, no. 1 (1940).

Roper, Steve and Steck, Allen. *Fifty Classic Climbs of North America.* San Francisco: Sierra Club Books, 1979.

San Francisco Peaks

Breed, Bill. "The Mountains of Fire." *Arizona Highways,* July, 1978.

Coues, Elliott. *On the Trail of a Spanish Pioneer: The Diary and Itinerary of Francisco Garces,* vols. 1 and 2. New York: Francis P. Harper, 1900.

Crampton, C. Gregory. *Land of Living Rock.* New York: Alfred A. Knopf, 1972.

Merriam, C. H. *Results of a Biological Survey of the San Francisco Mountain Region and Desert of the Little Colorado.* North American Fauna No. 3, U. S. Department of Agriculture. Washington, D. C.: Government Printing Office, 1890.

Robinson, Henry Hollister. "The San Francisco Volcanic Field, Arizona." *U. S. Geological Survey, Professional Paper 76.* Washington, D. C.: Government Printing Office, 1913.

"The San Francisco Peaks." In *Plateau,* Summer 1977. Publication of the Museum of Northern Arizona, Flagstaff, Ariz.

North Palisade

Bateman, Paul C. and Wahrhaftig, Clyde. "Geology of the Sierra Nevada." In *Geology of Northern California,* edited by E. H. Bailey. Sacramento: California Division of Mines and Geology, Bulletin 190 (1966).

Clyde, Norman. *Norman Clyde of the Sierra Nevada.* San Francisco: Scrimshaw Press, 1971.

Farquhar, Francis P. *History of the Sierra Nevada.* Berkeley, Los Angeles and London: University of California Press, 1965.

———. "Jedediah Smith and the First Crossing of the Sierra Nevada." *Sierra Club Bulletin* 28, no. 3 (1943).

LeConte, J. N. "Among the Sources of the South Fork of King's River." *Sierra Club Bulletin* 4, nos. 3 and 4 (1903).

———. "The Ascent of the North Palisades." *Sierra Club Bulletin* 5, no. 1 (1904).

Storer, Tracy I. and Usinger, Robert L. *Sierra Nevada Natural History.* Berkeley and Los Angeles: University of California Press, 1963.

Winnett, Thomas. *Sierra South.* Rev. ed. Berkeley: Wilderness Press, 1978.

Mount Whitney

Farquhar, Francis P. *History of the Sierra Nevada.* Berkeley, Los Angeles and London: University of California Press, 1965.

———. "The Story of Mount Whitney." *Sierra Club Bulletin* 14, no. 1 (1929).

———. "The Story of Mount Whitney: Part IV." *Sierra Club Bulletin* 32, no. 5 (1947).

Goetzman, William. *Exploration and Empire.* New York: Alfred A. Knopf, 1966.

King, Clarence. *Mountaineering in the Sierra Nevada.* 1872. Reprint. Lincoln: University of Nebraska Press, 1971.

Matthes, François E. "Glacial Reconnaissance of Sequoia National Park, California." *U. S. Geological Survey, Professional Paper 504A.* Washington, D. C.: Government Printing Office, 1965.

Moore, James G. *Geologic Map of the Mount Whitney Quadrangle, Inyo and Tulare Counties, California, GQ1545.* U. S. Geological Survey, 1981.

Underhill, Robert L. M. "Mount Whitney by the East Face." *Sierra Club Bulletin* 17, no. 5 (1932).

Wilkins, Thurman. *Clarence King: A Biography.* New York: The Macmillan Co., 1958.

Mount Ritter

Fultz, Francis M. "The Mt. Ritter Knapsack Trip." *Sierra Club Bulletin* 6, no. 5 (1908).

Muench, David. *Sierra Nevada.* Portland, Ore.: Graphic Arts Publishing Co., 1979.

Muir, John. *Studies in the Sierra.* Edited by William E. Colby. San Francisco: Sierra Club, 1960.

———. *The Mountains of California.* 1894. Reprint. Garden City, N. J.: Doubleday & Co., Inc., 1961.

Schumacher, Genny. *The Mammoth Lakes Sierra.* Berkeley: Wilderness Press, 1969.

Mount Shasta

Brewer, William H. *Up and Down California in 1860–1864.* Edited by Francis P. Farquhar. New Haven: Yale University Press, 1930.

Hall, Ansel F. "Mount Shasta." *Sierra Club Bulletin* 12, no. 3 (1926).

Miller, C. Dan. "Potential Hazards from Future Eruptions in the Vicinity of Mount Shasta Volcano, Northern California." *U. S. Geological Survey, Bulletin 1503.* Washington, D. C.: Government Printing Office, 1980.

Muir, John. *Steep Trails.* Boston and New York: Houghton Mifflin Co., 1918.

Roper, Steve. "Climber's Guide to Mt. Shasta." *Ascent* 1, no. 2 (1968).

Stewart, Charles L. "Early Ascents of Mount Shasta." *Sierra Club Bulletin* 19, no. 3 (1934).

Mount Hood

Crandell, Dwight R. "Recent Eruptive History of Mount Hood, Oregon, and Potential Hazards from Future Eruptions." *Geological Survey Bulletin 1492.* Washington, D. C.: Government Printing Office, 1980.

Flanagan, Latham, Jr. "Five Days on Mt. Hood." *Mazama* 52 (1970).

Grauer, Jack. *Mount Hood: A Complete History.* Portland, Ore.: Jack Grauer, 1975.

Lowe, Don and Lowe, Roberta. *Mount Hood: Portrait of a Magnificent Mountain.* Caldwell, Idaho: The Caxton Printers, Ltd., 1975.

Rollins, Philip Aston, ed. *The Discovery of the Oregon Trail.* New York and London: Charles Scribner's Sons, 1935.

Sterrett, Judith I. "The Bridge of the Gods." *The Mountaineer* 58 (1965).

Thwaites, Reuben Gold. *Original Journals of the Lewis and Clark Expedition 1804–1806,* vol. 6. New York: Dodd, Mead and Co., 1905.

Wise, William S. "The Geologic History of Mt. Hood, Oregon." *Mazama* 46 (1964).

Mount St. Helens

Beckey, Fred. *Cascade Alpine Guide: Columbia River to Stevens Pass.* Seattle: The Mountaineers, 1973.

Decker, Robert and Decker, Barbara. "The Eruption of Mount St. Helens." *Scientific American*, March, 1981.

Findley, Rowe. "Mount St. Helens: Mountain with a Death Wish." *National Geographic Magazine*, January, 1981.

Palmer, Professor Leonard and KOIN-TV Newsroom. *Mt. St. Helens: The Volcano Explodes!* Portland, Ore.: Leonard Palmer and KOIN-TV Newsroom, 1980.

Williams, Chuck. *Mount St. Helens: A Changing Landscape.* Portland, Ore.: Graphic Arts Publishing Co., 1980.

Mount Rainier

Bauer, Wolf. "The North Face of Mount Rainier." *The Mountaineer* 27 (1934).

Chase, Evelyn Hyman. *Mountain Climber: George B. Bayley, 1840–1894.* Palo Alto, Calif.: Pacific Books, 1981.

Crandell, Dwight R. "The Geologic Story of Mt. Rainier." *U. S. Geological Survey, Bulletin 1292.* Washington, D.C.: Government Printing Office, 1969.

Haines, Aubrey. *Mountain Fever: Historic Conquests of Rainier.* Portland, Ore.: Oregon Historical Society, 1962.

Kautz, A. V. "Ascent of Mount Rainier." *Overland Monthly* 14, no. 5. (May, 1875).

Kirk, Ruth. *Exploring Mount Rainier.* Seattle: University of Washington Press, 1968.

Molenaar, Dee. *The Challenge of Rainier.* Seattle: The Mountaineers, 1971.

———. "The Climbing History of Mount Rainier." *American Alpine Journal* 10 (1957).

Mount Shuksan

Beckey, Fred. *Challenge of the North Cascades.* Seattle: The Mountaineers, 1969.

Chisholm. Colin. "Shuksan Smiled on Us." *Mazama* 19 (1937).

Connelly, Dolly. "Mighty Joe Morovits." *Sports Illustrated*, January 7, 1963.

Curtis, Asahel. "Ascent of Mt. Shuksan." *Mazama* 3 (1907).

Fisher, C. A. "The Mountaineers Climb Mt. Shuksan." *The Mountaineer* 21 (1928).

Scott, John D. "Shuksan, The Formidable." *Mazama* 12 (1930).

Mount Waddington

Beckey, Helmy. "Mt. Waddington Climbed Again." *Canadian Alpine Journal* 28 (1943).

Dornan, David, ed. "An Interview with Fritz Wiessner." *Ascent* 1, no. 3 (1969).

Hagen, Barry. "Mt. Waddington." *Ascent* 1, no. 3 (1969).

Hall, Henry S. "The 1934 Attempts on Mt. Waddington." *American Alpine Journal* 2 (1935).

Munday, W. A. D. "Mt. Waddington." *Canadian Alpine Journal* 17 (1929).

———. *The Unknown Mountain.* 1948. Reprint. Seattle: The Mountaineers, 1975.

Robinson, Bestor. "Mount Waddington—1935." *Sierra Club Bulletin* 21, no. 1 (1936).

Watson, Sir Norman and King, Edward J. *Round Mystery Mountain.* New York: Longmans, Green and Co., 1935.

Wiessner, F. H. "The First Ascent of Mt. Waddington." *Canadian Alpine Journal* 24 (1936).

Devils Thumb

Beckey, Fred. "New Climbs in the Alaska Coast Range." *Alpine Journal* 56 (November, 1947).

———. "Southeast Alaska." *Ascent* 2, no. 3 (1975/76).

Craig, Robert. "West of the Stikine." *Canadian Alpine Journal* 30 (1947).

Hoagland, Edward. *Notes from the Century Before: A Journal from British Columbia.* New York: Random House, 1969.

"Stikine River." *Alaska Geographic* 6, no. 4 (1979).

Mount St. Elias

Di Filippi, Filippo. *The Ascent of Mount St. Elias.* Westminster: Archibald Constable, 1900.

Marcus, M. G., and Ragle, R. H. "Snow Accumulation in the Icefield Ranges, St. Elias Mountains, Yukon." *Arctic and Alpine Research* 2, no. 4 (1970).

Russell, Israel C. "An Expedition to Mount St. Elias, Alaska." *National Geographic Magazine*, May 29, 1891.

———. "Second Expedition to Mount St. Elias, in 1891." *U. S. Geological Survey, 13th Annual Report.* Washington, D. C.: Government Printing Office, 1893.

Schwatka, Frederick. "Mountaineering in Alaska." *New York Times*, September 20, 1886.

Sharp, Robert P. "The Latest Major Advance of Malaspina Glacier, Alaska." *Geographical Review* 48 (1958).

Theberge, John B., ed. *Kluane: Pinnacle of the Yukon.* Toronto: Doubleday Canada Ltd., 1980.

Topham, Harold. "An Expedition to Mount St. Elias, Alaska." *Alpine Journal* 14 (1889).

Wood, Walter. *A History of Mountaineering in the Saint Elias Mountains.* Banff: Alpine Club of Canada, 1967.

"Wrangell-Saint Elias: International Mountain Wilderness." *Alaska Geographic* 8, no. 1 (1981).

Mount Deborah

Beckey, Fred. "Mt. Deborah and Mt. Hunter: First Ascents." *American Alpine Journal* 9 (1955).

Farquhar, Francis P. "Naming Alaska's Mountains." *American Alpine Journal* 11 (1959).

Hyslop, Bob. "Mt. Deborah 1974." *Mazama* 56 (1974).

Okonek, Brian. "Deborah." *American Alpine Journal* 20 (1976).

Roberts, David. *Deborah: A Wilderness Narrative.* New York: The Vanguard Press, 1970.

Mount McKinley

Browne, Belmore. *The Conquest of Mount McKinley.* 1913. Reprint. Boston: Houghton Mifflin Co., 1956.

Capps, Stephen R. "A Game Country Without Rival in America: The Proposed Mt. McKinley National Park." *National Geographic Magazine*, January, 1917.

Cassin, Riccardo. "The South Face of Mount McKinley." *American Alpine Journal* 13 (1962).

Cook, Frederick A. "The Conquest of Mount McKinley." *Harper's Monthly Magazine* 114 (May, 1907).

———. *To the Top of the Continent.* London: Hodder and Stoughton, 1908.

Davidson, Art. *Minus 148°: The Winter Ascent of Mt. McKinley.* New York: W. W. Norton Co., Inc., 1969.

Dunn, Robert. *The Shameless Diary of an Explorer.* New York: Outing Publishing Co., 1907.

Moore, Terris. *Mt. McKinley: The Pioneer Climbs.* College, Alaska: University of Alaska Press, 1967.

Rusk, C. E. "On the Trail of Dr. Cook." *The Pacific Monthly*, October, 1910; November, 1910; and January, 1911.

Stuck, Hudson, *The Ascent of Denali.* New York: Charles Scribner's Sons, 1914.

Washburn, Bradford. *A Tourist Guide to Mount McKinley.* Anchorage: Northwest Publishing Co., 1971.

———. "Doctor Cook and Mount McKinley." *American Alpine Journal* 11 (1958).

The Mountains of North America

was designed by Broom & Broom Inc.,
San Francisco, California.